M000035914

The Instructor

'Tis to the Press and Pen we Mortals owe
All we believe and almost all we know.
All hail the great Preservers of those Arts
That raise our thoughts & Cultivate our hearts.

OR,

Young Man's best Companion;

CONTAINING

SPELLING, *Reading*, *Writing*, and *Arithmetic*, in an easier Way than any yet published; with Instructions to qualify any Person for Business without the Help of a Master; to write a Variety of Hands, with Copies both in Prose and Verse; Letters on Business or Friendship; Forms of Receipts, Indentures, Bonds, Bills of Sale, Wills, Leases, Releases, &c.

ALSO *Merchants Accompts*, and a short and easy method of *Shop* and *Book-keeping*; with an accurate Description of the Counties and Market-Towns in *England* and *Wales*, and their Product.

TOGETHER with the Method of measuring *Plumbers*, *Joiners*, *Carpenters*, *Sawyers*, *Bricklayers*, *Plasterers*, *Masons*, *Glaziers* and *Painters* Work, &c. The Mode of undertaking each Work, and at what Price; Rates of each Commodity and Wages of Men; a Description of *Gunter's* Line, and *Coggeshall's* Sliding Rule.

LIKEWISE Receipts for *Dying*, *Colouring*, and making of *Colours*; the *Practical Gauger* made easy; the Art of *Dialling*, and fixing *Dials*; and some general Observations for *Gardening* through every Month in the Year.

IN THIS WORK IS ALSO GIVEN

A COMPENDIUM OF THE SCIENCES

OF

GEOGRAPHY & ASTRONOMY,

CONTAINING

A brief Description of the different Parts of the Earth, and Survey of the CELESTIAL BODIES;

And some useful INTEREST-TABLES.

By *GEORGE FISHER*, Accomptant.

The Thirty-Second Edition, corrected and improved throughout.

LONDON:
PRINTED BY AND FOR
JOHN BAILEY, 116, CHANCERY-LANE.
1811.

PRICE THREE SHILLINGS AND SIXPENCE.

PREFACE.

LITTLE need be said, by way of Preface, respecting the usefulness of this Book, as its Contents are fully set forth in the Title Page; yet, as something by way of Preface is generally expected, a few remarks in regard to its utility may not be unnecessary. The first thing respects the forming the Young Mind for Business, by being made acquainted with the Mother Tongue, viz. English, which being a necessary and principal qualification is therefore the first thing to be considered in that behalf.

In the next place, to write a good, fair, free, and commendable Hand, is equally necessary in the Affairs of Life and the Occurrences of Business, and also relative to the inditing Epistles or Letters in familiar Style, on various Subjects and Occasions, with the proper Directions to subscribe or conclude Letters, according to the different Ranks of the Persons to whom they are directed.

The next necessary Acquirement, and which is amply treated of in this Book, is the excellent Science of Arithmetic, both Vulgar and Decimal: leading, by easy gradations, through its whole Course.

Next is set forth the ingenious Method of Bookkeeping after the Italian Manner, by way of Double Entry, which is very necessary to capacitate the Youth for Business. He is also informed how to draw out or make the various Accompts or Writings relating to Mercantile Affairs; as Bills of Lading, Invoices, Accompts of Sales, together with Examples of Bills of Exchange, with Notes concerning them; and Bills of Parcels of divers Kinds; with various forms of Receipts, &c. &c. and instructions relating to Business at the Water-side, as to Shipping off and Landing Goods, &c.

together

together with a Geographic Description of England *and* Wales, *each County being particularly noticed with respect to its Extent, Soil, and Product, with the Names of the several Market-Towns.*

Also easy, plain, and useful Directions for Measuring all sorts of Planes and Solids (Arithmetically and Instrumentally), such as the Works of Carpenters, Joiners, Sawyers, Bricklayers, Masons, Plasterers, Painters, Glaziers, &c. with the Prices of their different Works.

Likewise the Methods of extracting the Square and Cube Roots, and their Uses in Measuring, &c.

Also Practical Gauging of divers Kinds of Vessels, Tuns, &c. and also Didlling in various ways, with the Representation of several Sorts of Dials, and directions for beautifying and adorning them.

Next are Precedents of Law-Writings, as Bonds, Bills, Indentures, Wills, Letters of Attorney, &c. and,

Lastly, some Directions relative to the pleasant and delightful Art of Gardening, with general Observations for every Month in the Year.

In the Course of the Work is given a compendious System of Geography and Astronomy: The first is of great Utility to the trading Part of Mankind, and others who would form an adequate Idea of what they read, in History, or otherwise, relative to the Transactions in different Parts of the World; and the second is also necessary to those whose inclinations shall lead them to contemplate the Heavenly Bodies; being purposely designed to give the Youthful Reader some small Idea of that vast Number of Bodies (most of them greatly superior in Magnitude to our System), which the Almighty in his infinite Wisdom and Power has created, and exhibited to the observation and contemplation of Mankind.

TABLE

TABLE OF CONTENTS.

GEO-

ADVERTISEMENT.

ADVERTISEMENT.

THE Editor of this new Edition has carefully revised the whole, and made throughout considerable Improvements and Additions.—He trusts it will be found worthy of Public Attention, as a better or more useful Book can scarcely be put into the Hands of all those young Persons who are designed for the more active Scenes of Life; the Instructions therein contained being laid down and explained in so familiar a Manner as to render the Acquirement of Knowledge an Amusement rather than a Task.

The Patrons of Schools devoted to the Instruction of Young Persons in the inferior Ranks of Society would very much increase the Utility of their Institutions, if to each Pupil, upon leaving the School, were presented, with a Bible and other religious Books, a Work so judicious and instructive as the *" Young Man's best Companion."*

By Means of it the Youth, already instructed in reading his Mother Tongue, might, and, if of an inquisitive and active Disposition, would, gradually and effectually advance to the acquirement of every Species of Knowledge necessary to render him a respectable Member of Society.

January, 1819.

Instructions

Instructions for Youth,

TO SPELL, READ, AND WRITE,

TRUE ENGLISH.

The Use of Letters; which are Vowels and which Consonants; what Diphthongs are, their Number, and how pronounced and written.

THE design of this book being to instruct mankind, especially those who are young, in the methods of conversing and transacting business in the world; therefore those accomplishments of spelling and writing good and proper *English* claim the first notice; for let a person write ever so good a hand, yet if he be defective in spelling he will be ridiculed, and held in contempt, because his writing fair will render his orthographical faults more conspicuous.—Therefore,

First, Syllables are made of letters, words of syllables, and sentences of words, &*c.*

There are 26 letters; *viz: a, b, c, d, e, f, g, h, i, j, k, l, m, n, o, p, q, r, s, t, u, v. w, x, y, and z.* In these letters we are to observe their names, their form, and their force; their names, by which to know them; their form, whether great or small; their force, in pronunciation or utterance.

Letters are distinguished, according to their sound, into vowels and consonants: a *vowel* is a letter that sounds by itself, and these are six in number, *viz. a, e, i, o, u,* and *y* is also an *English* vowel, when it cometh after a consonant, and hath the sound of *i;* as in *by, sly; reply, syllable,* &c. but the *y* is never used in words not derived from a foreign language, otherwise than at their end. A consonant is a letter that hath no sound except it be joined with a vowel, for without one of the vowels no syllable can be made; as *b, c, d,* &c. without the aid of a vowel, cannot be sounded. Though we have 26 letters, and six of them *vowels*, yet we have 21 *consonants :* for *y,* when set before any *vowel* in the same syllable, becomes a conso-

A 4.

nant;

nant; as in *youth, yonder, beyond,* &c. *Note,* that *j* has the sound of *g,* as in *join, jingle,* &c. *W* is a vowel at the end of a word, as *law, now.*

When two vowels come together in a syllable, and are not parted in the pronunciation, but united in one sound, they are called *Diphthongs;* of these there are 13, vz. *ai, ei, oi, ui, au, eu, ou, ee,* oo, *ea, eo, oa,* and *ie;* as in *maid, faith, either, join, aul, eunuch, stout, feed, seed, food, broad, stealth, wealth, people, steeple, boat, oat, heat, beat, feat, friend, field,* &c. *Note,* In the first seven words both *vowels* are sounded; but in the other 15, one of them is scarcely heard.

There are also those that are called *Triphthongs,* where three vowels meet in one sound, as in *beauty, beau, lieu,* and *quaint:* Likewise *ay, ey, uy, aw, ew,* and *ow,* become *Dipthongs* at the end of words, but are called *improper Dipthongs:* as in *say, key, joy, saw, bow,* &c. *Note, aw, ew* and *ow,* are commonly sounded as *au, eu,* and *ou.*

Of Letters great and small, and when to be used.

Great Letters are not to be used in the middle or latter end of a word, except the whole word be so written, as in JEHOVAH LORD, or titles of books, &c. For it would be very absurd to write thus: To Mr. geoRge RoGeRs, in thaMES street; instead of, To Mr. George Rogers, in Thames-street.

Great Letters are to be written at the beginning of sentences: as *Know when to speak, and when to be silent.*

At the beginning of all proper names of places, ships, rivers, &c. as *London,* the *Lion, Thames, Severn:* Also the Christian names and surnames, of women and men must begin with great letters: as, *Samuel Sharp.*

At the beginning of the more eminent words in a sentence, as, *Faith is the Foundation of the Christian Religion;* or, if a word that we have a particular regard or deference for, as, *God, Christ, King, Queen,* &c. At the beginning of every line in poetry; and at the beginning of the names of arts, sciences, and trades; as *Writing, Arithmetic, Geometry, Music, Carpenter, Smith,* &c.

Note, The personal pronoun I, and the interjection O, must always be written in capitals; for it is ridiculous to write thus: *On Monday last i came to your house, but you was not at home; o how much it grieved me!*

The

The small letter *s* is commonly written *ſ* at the beginning and in the middle of a word, and *s* at the end; but if two of them come together in the middle of a word, they may be written thus, *ss ſs*.

Observations concerning the sound of Letters, and which are omitted in Pronunciation.

A is not sounded in *Pharaoh*, nor in *Sabaoth*, but as if written *Pharo*, or *saboth*; neither in *marriage*, but as *mar-rige*; also, *parliament* as *parliment*, and *chaplain* as *chaplin*, &c. In some proper names it is dropped in the pronunciation: as in *Aaron, Isaac, Canaan, Balaam*: which are pronounced as if written *Aron, Isac, Canan, Balam*: but we must except *Ba-al* and *Ga-al*. *A* is sounded broad, like *aw*, in words beford *ld* and *ll*; as in *bald, scald, hall, wall, fall*.

B is not sounded in *thumb, dumb, plumb, lamb, doubt, debt, subtle*, &c. but sounded as if written, *thum, dum, plum, lam, dout, det, suttle*, &c.

C is sounded hard like *K*, before *a, o* and *u*, and before *l* and *r*; as in these words, *cane, came, comb, cub, clay, crane, crab*; and soft in *cement, city*, and *tendency*. *C* loses its sound in *scene, science*, and *victuals*; likewise in *indict, indictment*; also before *k*, as *stack, rack, stick, thick, brick*. In words of *Greek* and *Hebrew* derivation, *C* is sounded like *K*, as in *sceptic, Cis, Aceldema*, &c.

Ch is sounded like *K* in many foreign words, some of which occur in the Holy Scriptures, as in *chorus, Chymist, Chrysostom, Christ*. In the word *schism*, the sound of *ch* is lost, it being sounded as if it were *sism*, and in the words *Rachel, Cherubim*, and *Archbishop*, it is sounded in the English manner. *Ch* in French words sounds like *sh*, as in *chevalier*, pronounced *shevalier*; *mareschal, marshal*; *machine, masheen*; *capuchin, capusheen*; *chaise, chaize*.

D is not sounded in *Ribband*, nor in *Wednesday*, which are pronounced *Ribbon* and *Wensday*; the termination *e*, is often shortened into *t*; as *burned, burnt*; *choked, chokt, ripped, ript*; *passed, past*; *chopps, chopt*, &c.

E is not sounded in *hearth*, &c. *E final* is that placed at the end of a word; and is seldom heard but in Monosyllables, as in *me, he, she, ye, thee*, &c. where it hath the sound of *ee*: And in Words derived from foreign Languages in which *e* has its perfect sound; as *Jesse, Jubilee*,

Jubilee, Mamre, Nineve, Candace, Cloe, Unice, Penelope, Salmone, Phebe, Epitome, Catastrophe, Gethsemane, Simile, Præmunire, &c. In all other cases *E final* serves only to lengthen the sound, and to distinguish it from other words of a different meaning, which are written without *e*, and are sounded short, as in these examples following, *viz. cane, can; hate, hat, bite, bit: fare, far; hope, hop; made, mad; scrape, scrap; stare, star; tune, tun; write, writ,* &c. In Words of more than one Syllable it strengthens the sound of the last Syllables, but does not increase the number of Syllables; as *admire, demise, blaspheme,* &c. *E* lengthens the Syllable also in some foreign words, such as *Eve, Tyre, Crete, ode, scheme. E* is seldom written after two consonants; as in *pass, turn, black.* Yet after *rs* it is used as *horse, nurse, purse.*

.. Also the words ending in *cre, gre,* and *tre,* sound the *e* before the *r*, as in these words, *acre, lucre, centre, sepulchre, mitre, lustre;* which are sounded as if written *aker, luker, center, sepulcher, miter,* and *luster. E final* also serves to soften *c* and *g*, as in *ace, place, lace, spice, truce, oblige, huge, age,* &c. If nouns in *e final* take *s* after them, with an apostrophe before it, it stands for *his*, as the *Pope's eye,* or the *eye of the Pope,* the *table's foot,* or the *foot of the table.* If without an apostrophe, it makes the plural number, as *Popes, tables.* Words derived from those written with *e final* seldom retain it, as in *writing, loving, doing,* &c. not *writeing, loveing,* or *doeing;* except in the termination *ge and ce,* before *able,* as in *changeable, peaceable,* &c.

E should not be written after a diphthong in these words; *vain, main, gain, fear, know,* &c. not *vaine, maine, gaine,* &c. *E final* is annexed, but not sounded, in those words which would otherwise end with *i, o,* or *u;* as in *die, foe, sloe, true, virtue,* &c. but there are some exceptions, as *do, so, to,* &c.

Lastly, there are some words in which the *final E* does not lengthen the sound, as *give, live, some, one, done,* &c.

F in plurals is changed into *v;* as *wife, wives; staff, staves; knife, knives.*

G is not sounded in *sign, reign, gnaw, gnat, assign, design, scignior, seraglio, phlegm,* &c. *G* is sounded soft in *gender, ginger,* and *gipsey;* but hard in *Gibeon, Giberah, Gilboa, Geth-se-mane;* and hard also in these proper names, *Gibson, Gilman,* and *Gilbert;* and likewise
in

in these common words, *gelt, geld, girt, gimp, geese, gander, gamble, gather, gild,* &c. Observe, that if *G* be hard with a long vowel, *ue* is joined and pronounced in the same syllable; as in *Plague, Prague, Hague, Rogue, League, Dialogue, Catalogue,* &c.

Gh in the End of some words, where *au* or *ou* goes before, hath the sound of *ff*, as in *tough, rough, cough, laugh,* sounded as *tuff, ruff, coff, laff*; but *buff, cuff, snuff,* and *huff*, must be so written—*Gh* is not sounded in *mighty, though, through, daughter,* and *Vaughan.*

H has place, but no sound, in *Chronicle, Christ, Ghost, John, Rhine, Schedule,* and *Schism,* &c. H is not sounded at the end of words if it be alone, but with *tc* before it, it is sounded as *snatch, watch,* &c.

I is not sounded in *adieu, juice, venison, fruit, bruise, Salisbury :* it is sounded like *ee* in *oblige, Magazine,* and *Machine,* &c. *I* is not sounded long in proper names ending in *iah*, as *Jeremiah, Hezekiah;* but short in *A-ri-el,* and *Mi-ri-am.*—*I* is sounded like *u* in *first, dirt, bird,* &c.

K is nearly allied in sound to *c*, but to know when to use one, and when the other. *Note,* that *C* has the force of *K* only before *a, o, oo,* and *u,* and these two consonants *l* and *r*; and therefore we must not write *kare* for *care, kow* for *cow, krown* for *crown :* And the use of *K* is only before *c, i,* and *u :* wherefore we must write *keep, key, knight, kill,* not *ceepe, cey, cnight,* nor *cill.* But the words *Calendar* and *Catharine* are written sometimes *Kalendar* or *Katharine. K* is written after *c* only in pure English words, such as *back, deck, sick,* &c. for the best authors have omitted it in words derived from the Greek and Latin, such as *public, music, physic,* &c.

L is not sounded in *calf, half, chalk, stalk, walk,* those words being pronounced as if written *caff, haff, chauk, stauk, wauk.* Neither is *l* sounded in *Holborn, Lincoln, salmon,* or *chaldron :* these are sounded as if written *Hoborn, Lincon, sammon, chadron ;* nor in *colonel,* where the first *l* has the sound of *r,* as *cornel.*

In the word *accompt, mp* is sounded like *un.*

N is scarcely heard in *autumn, lime-kiln, solemn, limn, hymn, column,* and *condemn.*

O is not sounded in *people, feoffe, righteous, jeopardy. O* sometimes sounds like *oo,* as in *doing, moving, proving,* &c. —*O* is sometimes sounded like *i,* as in *women,* pronounced *wimmin.* And sometimes *O* is sounded as *u,* as in *money, conduit,*

conduit, conjure, attorney, Monmouth, as if written *mun-ney, cunduit, cunjure, atturney, Munmuth,* &c. and it is sounded like *oo,* in *do, to, prove, move,* &c.

P is written, but not sounded, in *empty, presumptuous, psalm,* and *symptom,* &c.

Ph have the sound of *f,* when together in one syllable; as in *philosophy, physician, Asaph,* and *elephant;* but we must not write *filosophy, fisician,* nor *Asaf,* or *elefant.*

After *Q* always follows *u* in all words; and in some *French* and *Latin* words they have the sound of *k;* as in *risque, liquor, catholique, conquer, masquerade, chequer;* pronounced as *risk, likker, catholic,* &c. to which add *oblique, relique, antique,* &c. which are sounded as if written *oblike, relik, anteke,* &c.

S is not sounded in *island, viscount, isle, and Lisle,* which are pronounced as if written *iland, vicount, ile,* and *Lile.*

Ti before a vowel or a diphthong have the sound of *si* or *sh,* as in *patience, dictionary, oblation, nation, translation:* except when *s* goes just before it, as in these words, *question, fustian, bastion, combustion, celestial,* &c. But in some words of Hebrew and Greek, it retains its natural sound, as in *Shealtiel, Phaltiel,* and the like; and in the English derivatives *mightier, emptier, pitiable,* &c.

U is sounded like *e* in *bury, berry;* like *i* in *busy, bizzy;* *U* is sometimes written after *g* without being sounded, as in *guide, guard,* &c. It is also silent in the words *buy, built, conduit, circuit, labour, favour, honour,* &c. but it is sounded in others, as *anguish, languish, Montague,* &c.

W is not sounded in *answer, sword,* &c. neither is it heard before *r* in *wrap, wrath, wrong, wretch, wrangle, wriggle,* &c.

Wh belongs to words purely English; as *what, when, where,* and *wheel.*

X is sounded as *z* in *Xenophon, Xerxes, Xenocrates,* and *Xantippe.*

Y is either a vowel or consonant, as hinted before: A vowel in *my, by, fly, thy.* In derivative English words, having the termination *ing, y* is used in the middle of the word, as in *buying, dying, burying, marrying,* &c.

The diphthongs *ai* and *ay* have the sound of *a* in *air, fair, pair, may, stay, play:* but *a* is lost in *Calais* (a town in France) and pronounced separately in *Sinai* (a mountain in Arabia).

Ei

Ei and *ey* are sounded like *a* in *eight, streight, neighbour, heir, veil,* and *convey;* like *e* in *key;* and like *i* in *sleight.*

Oi and *oy* have a sound peculiar to themselves; as in *oil,* and *oyster.*

Au and *aw* commonly keep a proper sound, as in *augur, daw, saw,* &c. but *u* is lost in *aunt* and *gauger,* being sounded as *ant* and *gager;* they make no diphthong in *Em-ma-mus* and *Ca-per-na-um.*

Eu and *ew* have a united sound in most words, as in *eunuch, brew, new, grew,* but *eu* is no diphthong in *Zac-che-us* and *Bar-ti-me-us.*

Ou are expressed in *foul, soul, proud, loud,* and *ow* in *how, cow,* and *now;* but *ou* sounds like *oo* in *soup.*

Ee is no diphthong in *Be-er-she-ba,* and in words beginning with *re,* or *pre;* as *re-en-ter, pre-e-mi-nence;* in *Beel-ce-bub* one of the *e*'s is not sounded.

Oo is properly sounded in *cool, fool, pool, root,* and *tool;* but have the sound of *u* in *foot* and *soot:* they make no diphthong in *Co-os, co-o-pe-rate,* &c.

Ea sound like *e* in *sea, pea, ream, seam, bread, head, lead, dead, leather, feather, heaven, leaven,* and *creature;* it is no diphthong in *Ce-sa-re-a, i-de-a, re-al, be-a-ti-tude, cre a-tor;* nor in words beginning with *pre,* as *pre-am-ble,* &c.

Eo is no diphthong in *dun-ge-on, hi-de-ous, me-te-or, pi-ge-on, the-o-ry,* &c.

Oa are sounded as *o* in *goat, boat, coat;* and sounded broad as *au,* in *broad* and *groat,* but are no diphthong in *Go-a* (a city in India) or in the Hebrew word *Zo-ar,* and *Gil-bo-a.*

Ie before a single consonant sound like *ee,* as in *brief, chief,* and *thief;* but if before two consonants, sound like *e,* as in *friend, field;* but at the end of English words the *e* is not heard, as *die,* or *lie;* are no diphthong in *A-bi-e-zer, E-li-e-zer;* nor in the English words *car-ri-er, clo-thi-er;* nor in words derived from the Latin, as *client, orient, quiet,* and *sci-ence.*

Ui are sounded as *u,* in *juice, fruit,* and *suit;* but *u* is lost in *con-duit, built,* and *guise,* and is no diphthong in *je-su-it, ge-nu-ine,* and *fru-i-tion.*

Æ and *Œ* are not English diphthongs, they are used in *Æsop, Cæsar, Œdipus,* and sound like *e:* but in common words they are neglected, as in *equity, female,* and *tragedy,* though derived of *æquittus, fœmina* and *tragœdia.*

O

Of Syllables and their Division, being the Art of Spelling.

A SYLLABLE is a sound pronounced by a single impulse of the voice, as *vir-tue*, so that *virtue* being thus divided, or taken asunder, makes two syllables, viz. *vir-* and *tue;* which put together, form the word *virtue.* And many times a vowel, or a diphthong of itself makes a syllable, as in *a-bate, e-ve-ry, i-dle,* and in *au-gur, aid-er, oyst-er, oak-en.*

No syllable can be made, be there many or few consonants, without the aid of a vowel or diphthong.

The longest monosyllables we have in English are *length, strength,* and *straight;* which could not be sounded without the vowel *e* or *i.*

The Art of Spelling may be reduced to the four following general rules or heads :

1st. When a consonant comes between two vowels, in dividing the words into syllables, the consonant is joined to the latter vowel; as in *sta-ture, na-ture, de-li-ver, a-mi-ty,* &c. except compound words, which terminate in - *ed, en, est, eth, er, ing, ish,* and *ous;* as *coast-ed, gold-en, know-est, know-eth, bear-er, bar-bar-ous, fool-ish, ra-ven-ous,* and *sub-urbs.*

2dly. When two consonants come together in the middle of a word they are to be parted, if not proper to begin a word; as *num-ber, stran-ger, for-tune,* &c. not *num-ber, strang-er, fort-une.* When the same consonant is doubled in a word, the first belongs to the foregoing, and the latter to the following syllable, as in the rule above, and in these words, *Ab-ba, ac-cord, ad-der,* &c.

3dly. Consonants that begin words must not be parted in the middle; as, *a-gree, be-stow, re-frain,* not *ag-ree, bes-tow, ref-rain.*—These consonants may begin words, viz. *bl, br, cr, dr, dw, fl, fr, gh, gl, gr, kn,* &c. as *blunt, break, chaw, dry, draw, dwelt, flesh, ghost,* &c.

4thly. When two words come together, not making a diphthong, they must be divided, as in *vi-al, va-li-ant, Li-o-nel, du-el, cru-el, me-te-or,* and *La-o-di-ce-a.*

Some particular Notes.

L is doubled in words of one syllable, as *well, tell, swell, hall, wall, fall, will, hill, mill,* &c. But in words of more than one syllable the word always terminates with single *l,* as *angel, Babel, hurtful, beautiful,* and *dutiful.* Neither must *l* be doubled in *always, also, although;* not *allways, allso.*

allso, allthough, &c. but words accented on the last syllable must be excepted from the above rule, viz. *install, recall, inroll, rebell,* and *repell.*

Y must be used before the termination *ing,* as *buying, lying, carrying, paying, slaying, burying,* &c.

If you cannot write out the whole word at the end of the line, you break it off at the end of a syllable, thus, con——————————————————————————demn.

C must not be put between two consonants; as *think,* not *thinck; thank,* not *thanck;* but if a vowel goes before *c,* you must write *c* before *k,* as *brick, thick, stick,* &c.

Of *S* and *C,* some people may easily drop into error by mistaking *S* for *C,* as in the beginning of the following words, where *C* has the perfect sound of *S,* though *C* must be undoubtedly written ; viz. in

City	Citron	Cellar	Cieling	Censure
Cell	Censor	Censor	Certain	Cypress
Givet	Ceruse	Cinque	Cymbal	Circuit
Circle	Centre	Cistern	Cymon	Celestial
Cease	Cipher	Cement	Celerity	Celebrate
	Centurion	Cinnamon	Ceremony.	

These words must be written with *S* and *C,* viz.

Science	Sceptre	Scarcity	Sciatica
Schedule	Scheme	Schism	Scythian.

The following words should be written

with ti	*with* si
Contention	Confusion
Action	Occasion
Contradiction	Contusion
Attention	Oppression
Benediction	Allusion
Apparition	Ascension
Concoction	Aversion
Declaration	Aspersion
Ambition	Commission
Contrition	Comprehension
Oration	Circumcision
Oblation	Conclusion

The following words should be spelled thus :

Passion, *not* Pashon	Salisbury, *not* Salsbury
Fashion, *not* Fation	Leicester, *not* Lester
Cushion, *not* Cution	Shrewsbury, *not* Shrusbury
Gloucester, *not* Gloster	Carlisle, *not* Carlile
Worcester, *not* Worster	Westminster, *not* Westmister

Another

Another qualification in Spelling is, rightly to distinguish words of the same sound, or nearly the same sound, though widely different in their sense and signification; such as the following:

A

Abel, Cain's Brother
Able, to do a Thing
Accidents, Chances
Accidence, in Grammar
Acre, of Land
Achor, a Valley of that Name
Advice, Counsel
Advise, to counsel
Account, Esteem
Accompt, or Reckoning
Ale, a Drink
Ail, Trouble
All, every one
Awl, for Shoemakers
Allay, to give Ease
Alloy, base Metal
Altar, for Sacrifice
Alter, to change
Alehoof, an Herb
Aloof, at a Distance
Allowed, approved
Aloud, to speak so
Ant, a Pismire
Aunt, a Father's Sister
Anchor, of a Ship
Anker, a Runlet
Are, they be
Air, we breathe
Heir, to an Estate
Arrant, notorious
Errand, a Message
Arras, Hangings
Harass, to fatigue
Ascent, a going up
Assent, Agreement
Assistance, Help
Assistants, Helpers
Augur, a Soothsayer
Augre, to bore with

Are, to cut with
Acts, of Parliament

B

Bacon, Hogs Flesh
Baken, in the Oven
Beckon, to make a Sign
Beacon, a Fire on a Hill
Bail, a Security
Bale, of Goods
Bald, without Hair
Bawl'd, cried out
Ball, to play with
Bawl, to cry aloud
Barbara, a Woman's Name
Barbary, in Africa
Barberry, a Fruit
Bare, naked
Bear, a Beast, or to bear
Bays, of Bay-trees
Baize, slight woollen cloth
Base, vile
Bass, in Music
Be, they are
Bee, that makes Honey
Beer, to drink
Bier, to carry the Dead on
Bell, to ring
Bel, an Idol
Berry, a small Fruit
Bury, to inter
Blue, a Colour
Blew, as the Wind
Board, a Plank
Bored, a Hole
Boar, a male Swine
Bore, to make hollow
Boor, a country Fellow
Bold, confident
Bowled, at the Jack
Bolt, to fasten

Boult,

Boult, to sift Meal
Beau, a Fop
Bow, to bend, or the Bow
Bough, of a Tree
Boy, a Lad
Buoy, of an Anchor
Bread, to eat
Bred, brought up
Breeches, to wear
Breaches, broken Places
Bruit, a Noise
Brute, Beast
Burrow, for Rabbits
Borough, a Corporation
By, near
Buy, wih Money
Brews, he breweth
Bruise, a Hurt
Buss, a fishing Vessel
Buz, the Noise of a Fly

C

Cain, that killed his Brother
Cane, to walk with
Caen, in Normandy
Calais, in France
Chalice, a Cup
Call, by Name
Cawl, Suet
Cannon, a great Gun
Canon, a Rule
Canon, of a Cathedral
Capital, great or chief
Capitol, a Tower in Rome
Career, full Speed
Carrier, of Goods
Cellar, for Liquors
Seller, that selleth
Censer, for Incense
Censor, a Reformer
Censure, to judge
Centaury, an Herb
Century, an Hundred Years
Sentry, a Soldier on Guard
Chair, to sit on

Chare, a Job of Work
Champaigne, Wine of France
Campaigne, a wide Field or military Expedition
Choler, Rage or Anger
Collar, of the Neck
Coller, of Beef or Brawn
Cieling, of a Room
Sealing, with a Seal
Cittern, Musical Instrument
Citron, a Fruit
Clause, Part of a Sentence
Claws, of a Beast or Bird
Coat, a Garment
Cote, for Sheep
Commit, to do
Comet, a blazing Star
Condemn, to Death
Contemn, to despise
Council, of the King
Counsel, take Advice
Coarse, not fine
Course, to be run
Cou'd, or could
Cud, to chew as Beasts
Current, a running Stream
Courant, a Messenger or News-paper
Currants, Fruit
Crick, in the Neck
Creek, of the Sea or River
Cousin, a Relation
Couzen, to cheat
Cymbal, a Musical Instrument
Symbol, a Mark or Sign
Cypress a Tree
Cyprus, an Island
Cruse, for Oil
Cruise, a Voyage
Cygnet, a young Swan
Signet, a Seal

D

Dame, a Mistress

Dam.

Dam, to stop Water
Damn, to condemn
Deign, to vouchsafe
Dane, an Inhabitant of Denmark
Dear, in Price
Deer, in a Park
Deceased, dead
Diseased, sick
Decent, becoming
Descent, going down
Dissent, to disagree
Deep, low in Earth
Dieppe, a Town in France
Defer, to put off
Differ, to disagree
Derby, a City of Asia
Derby, a Town in England
Desert, Merit
Desart, Wilderness.
Dew, falling Mist
Do, to make
Doe, a Female Deer
Dough, Paste
Don, a Spanish Lord
Done, performed
Dun, a Colour
Devices, Inventions
Devizes, a Town in Wiltshire
Doer, that doeth
Door, of a House
Dragon, a Serpent
Dragoon, a Soldier
Dolor, Grief or Pain
Dollar, a Piece of Money
Demure, sober
Demur, a Pause or Doubt

E

Ear, of the Head
E'er, ever
Year, twelve Months
Yearly, every Year
Early, betimes
Earth, the Ground

Hearth, of a Chimney
Easter, the Festival
Esther, a Woman's Name
Enter, to go in
Inter, to bury
Elder, not the Younger
Elder, a Tree
Eaten, or swallowed
Eaton, a Town's Name
Eminent, famous
Emminent, over Head
Enow, in Number
Enough, in Quantity
Earn, to deserve
Yarn, Woollen Thread
Yearn, to pity
East, the Wind
Yeast, used in making Bread
Envy, or Hatred
Envoy, a Messenger
Exercise, Labour or Practice
Exorcise, to conjure
Err, to mistake
Er, Brother to Onan
Extant, in being
Extent, Distance

F

Fain, desirous
Feign, to dissemble
Fair, beautiful, or a Market
Fare, Victuals
Faint, weary
Feint, a Pretence
Fourth, in Number
Forth, to go out
Feed, to eat
Feed, rewarded
Fir, Wood
Fur, or Ha i
Felon, a Criminal
Felon, a Whitlow
File, of Steel
Foil, put to the worst
Fly, as a Bird

Fly,

Fly, an Insect
Fillip, with the Fingers
Philip, a Man's Name
Flower, of the Field
Flour, Meal
Floor, of a Room
Follow, to come after
Fallow, Ground not ploughed
Find, to find any Thing
Fined, amerced
Fiend, Devil
Flea, to take off the Skin, also an insect
Flee, to escape
Flue, of a Chimney
Flew, did fly
Fowl, a Bird
Foul, dirty
Francis, a Man's Name
Frances, a Woman's Name
Frays, Quarrels
Fraize, Pancake with Bacon
Frieze, a Sort of Cloth
Freeze, with Cold

G
Gall, of a Beast
Gaul, France
Garden, of Herbs
Guardian, an Overseer
Genteel, graceful
Gentile, Heathen
Gentle, mild
Gesture, Carriage
Jester, a merry Fellow
Groan, with Grief
Grown, greater
Guilt, of Sin
Gilt, with Gold
Greater, bigger.
Grater, for Nutmegs
Grave, for the Dead
Greave, Armour for the Leg
Gluttonous, greedy

Glutinous, sticking as Pitch
Great, large
Grate, for Coals, &c.
Greet, to salute
Graze, to eat Grass
Grays, a Town
Groat, Four-pence
Grot, a Cave
Gallies, Ships with Oars
Gallows, for Criminals

H
Hare, in the Field
Hair, of the Head
Heir, to an Estate
Harsh, severe
Hash, minced Meat
Haven, a Harbour
Heaven, a Place of Happiness
Heart, of the Body
Hart, in the Woods, or an over-grown Buck
Herd, of Cattle
Heard, did hear
Hard, not soft or difficult
Here, in this Place
Hear, with the Ears
High, lofty
Hie, away, make haste
Hoy, a small Ship
Him, that Man
Hymn, a spiritual Song
Hail, congealed Rain
Hail, to call or hail
Hall, in the House
Haul, pull
Heel, of the Foot
Heal, to cure
He'll, he will
Higher, taller
Hire, Wages
His, of Him
Hiss, as a Snake, or to deride
Hoar, a Frost

Whore,

Whore, a lewd Woman
Hole, or Hollow
Whole, entire
Hallow, to make holy
Hollow, having a cavity
Holy, pious, *Wholly*, entirely
Holly, a Tree
Home, one's House
Whom? What Man?
Holme, Holly
Hoop, for a Tub
Whoop, or ho! lo!
Hugh, a Man's Name
Hue, a Colour
Hew, with an Axe

I

I, I myself
Eye, to see with
Idle, lazy
Idol, an Image
I'll, I will
Aisle, of a Church
Isle, an Island
Oil, of Olives
Inn, for Travellers
Incite, to stir up
Insight, Knowledge
Ingenious, of quick Parts
Ingenuous, candid
Itch, a Distemper
Hitch, to catch hold

K

Ketch, a small Ship
Catch, to lay hold of
Kill, to slay
Kiln, for Lime
Kind, good-natured
Coined, made into Money
Knave, dishonest
Nave, of a Wheel
Knight, by honour
Night, darkness
Kennel, for Dogs
Channel, for Water

L

Laid, placed
Lade, to throw out Water
Lane, a narrow Street
Lain, did lie
Latin, a Language
Latten, Tin
Ladder, to ascend
Lather, made with Soap
Lettice, a Woman's Name
Lettuce, a Salad
Lease, of a House
Leash, Three
Lees, of Wine
Leese, an old Word for lose
Leaper, one who jumps
Leper, one leprous
Lessen, to make less
Lesson, to read
Least, smallest
Lest, for fear
Lethargy, Sleepiness
Liturgy, Church Service
Lier, in wait
Liar, that tells Lies
Limb, a Member
Limn, to paint
Line, Length
Loin, of Veal
Liquorish, fond of Dainties
Liquorice, a Plant, or its Root
Low, humble
Lo! behold
Lose, to suffer Loss
Loose, to let go
Lower, to let down
Lour, a Frown
Loathe, to abhor
Loth, unwilling

M

Made, finished
Maid, a young Woman
Main, Chief
Mane, of Horse

Male,

Male, the He of any Species
Mail, Armour
Manner, Custom
Manor, a Lordship
Market, to buy or sell in
Marked, noted
Marsh, low Ground
Mash, for a Horse
Martin, a Man's Name
Marten, a Bird
Mead, a Meadow
Mede, one of Media
Mean, of low Value
Mien, Carriage or Aspect
Meat, to eat
Meet, fit
Mele, to measure
Message, Business
Messuage, a House
Mews, for Hawks or Horses
Muse, to meditate
Mighty, powerful
Moiety, Half
Mile, Measure
Moil, to labour
Might, Strength
Mite, in Cheese
Moat, a Ditch
Mote, a small Particle
Moan, to lament
Mown, cut down
More, in Quantity
Moor, a Black
Mower, that moweth
Moor, barren Ground
Mortar, made of Lime
Mortar, to pound in
Mole, a little Animal
Mould, to cast in
Muscle, a Shell Fish
Muzzle, to cover the Mouth

N

Nay, denial
Neigh, as a Horse

Neither, none of the two
Nether, lower
New, not old
Knew, did know
Naught, bad
Nought, nothing
Nice, curious; also a Town
Niece, a Brother's Daughter
Not, denying
Knot, to tie
Note, Mark
Note, of one's Hand
Nose, of the Face
Knows, understands
No, Denial
Know, to understand
Neal, to harden Glass
Kneel, on the Knees
None, not one
Known, understood
News, Tidings
Noose, a Snare

O

Oar, of a Boat
Ore, crude Metal
O'er, over
Off, cast off
Of, belonging to
Our, belonging to us
Hour, of the Day
Oh! Alas!
Owe, in Debt
One, in Number
Won, at Play
Own, to acknowledge
Order, Rule
Ordure, Dung

P

Pair, a Couple
Pare, cut off
Pear, a Fruit
Pain, Anguish
Pane, of Glass
Patten, for a Woman

Patent

Patent, a Grant
Peer, a Lord
Pier, of Dover
Peter, a Man's Name
Petre, Salt
Pail, for Water
Pale, of Countenance
Pale, a Fence
Pall, for a Funeral
Paul, a Man's Name
Plait, the Hair
Plate, Metal
Place, Room
Plaice, a Fish
Parson, of the Parish
Person, any Man or Woman
Pole, for Hops
Poll, of the Head
Pool, of Water
Pore, with the Eyes, or of the Skin
Poor, necessitous
Palate, of the Mouth
Pallet, Bed
Palliate, to cover or hide
Point, a Stop
Pint, Half a Quart
Posy, a Nosegay
Poesy, Poetry
Power, might
Pour, as Water
Prey, a Booty
Pray, to beseech
Profit, Gain
Prophet, a Foreteller
Prophecy, a Foretelling
Prophecy, to foretell
Practice, Exercise
Practise, to exercise
Presence, being here
Presents, Gifts
Prince, the King's Son
Prints, Drawings
Please, to content

Pleas, Excuses or Defences
Precedent, an Example
President, Chief
Principal, Chief
Principle, the first Rule

Q

Quire, of Paper
Choir, of Singers
Queen, the King's Wife
Quean, a bad Woman

R

Rack, to torment
Wreck, of a Ship
Arrack, a strong Liquor
Rain, Water
Reign, of the King
Rein, of a Bridle
Rays, of the Sun
Raise, lift up
Raisin, a Fruit
Reason, Argument
Race, to run
Rase, to demolish
Rice, Grain
Rise, to get up
Read, the Book
Reed, growing in the Water
Relic, a Remainder
Relict, a Widow
Roe, of a Fish, or Deer
Row, the Boat
Right, not wrong
Rite, a Ceremony
Write, with a Pen
Wright, a Wheelwright
Reddish, Colour
Radish, a Root
Rest, Quiet
Wrest, to prevent
Roof, the Top of a House
Ruff, for the Neck
Rough, not smooth
Rye, Corn
Rye, a Town in Sussex

Wry,

Wry, crooked
Ring, the Bells
Wring, the Hands
Rime, a Fog or Mist
Rhyme, Verse
Rode, did ride
Road, the Highway
Rowed, did row
Room, Part of a House
Rome, the Name of a City
Roam, to wander
Rheum, a Humour
Rote, got by Heart
Wrote, did write
Wrought, did work

S

Salary, Wages
Celery, an Herb
Savour, Taste or Smell
Saviour, that saves
Satiety, Fulness
Society, Company
Sheep, a useful Animal
Ship, for the Sea
Sight, View
Cite, to summon
Site, Situation
Sail, of a Ship
Sale, of Goods
Sea, the Ocean
See, with the Eyes
Seam, in a Coat
Seem, appear
Seen, beheld
Scene, in a Play
Seas, great Waters
Seize, to lay hold of
Sease, to leave off.
Sent, did send
Scent, a Smell
Show, to make appear
Shoe, for the Foot
Sink, sink down
Sinque, five
Slight, to despise

Sleight, of Hand
Shoar, a Prop
Shore, the Sea Coast
Sewer, a common Drain
Shown, viewed
Shone, did shine
Slow, not quick
Sloe, a sour Fruit
Sew, with a Needle
Sue, at Law
Sow, Seed
So, thus
Some, a Part
Sum, of Money
Soul, or Spirit
Sole, a Fish
Soal, of a Shoe or Foot
Son, of a Father
Sun, in the Firmament
Sore, painful
Soar, aloft
Swore, did swear
Sword, a Weapon
Soared, did soar
Stare, to look earnestly at
Stair, a Step
Stile, to get over
Style, of Writing
Sound, whole, firm; also
    Noise
Swoon, to faint away
Soon, quickly
Statue, an Image
Statute, a Law
Stature, Height
Stead, in Place
Steed, a Horse
Straight, not crooked
Strait, narrow
Succour, Help
Sucker, a young Sprig
Spear, a Weapon
Sphere, a Globe

T

Then at that Time

B

Than, in comparison
Tame, genle, not wild
Thame, a Town in Oxon.
Tear, to rend
Tear, of the Eye
Tare, an Allowance in weight
Tare, Vetch
Tail, of a Beast
Tale, a Story
Tiles, for the House
Toil, to labour
Toil, a net
There, in that Place
Their, of them
Thorough, complete
Throw, a Stone
Throne, of the King
Thrown, as a Stone
Tide, a flowing Water
Tied, made fast
Time, of the Day
Thyme, an Herb
Team, of Horses
Teem, with Child
To, the Preposition
Toe, of the Foot
Tow, to be spun, to draw
Too, likewise
Two, a Couple
Told, as a Story
Tolled, as a Bell
Tour, a Journey
Tower, of a Church

V

Vacation, Leisure
Vocation, a Calling
Veil, a Covering
Vale, between two Hills
Vain, foolish
Vein, of the Body
Vane, a Weathercock
Value, Worth
Valley, a Vale

Vial, a Bottle
Viol, a Fiddle

U

Your, of you
Ewer, a Basin
Use, Practice
Use, to be wont
Ewes, Sheep

W

Wages, pay for service
Wagers, Bets
Wade, in Water
Weighed, in the Scales
Whale, a great Fish
Wail, to lament
Waist, the Middle
Waste, to spend
Wait, to stay for
Weight, Heaviness
Wear, the act of Wearing
Ware, Merchandise
Were, was
Where, what Place
Weighed, to poise
Wey, five Quarters
Whey, of Milk
Wield, a Sword
Weald, of Sussex or Kent
Wen, in the Neck
When, at what Time
Witch, that conjures
Which, who or what
Whist, Silence
Whist, a Game
Wist, knew
Wood, of Trees
Wou'd, or would

Y

Yea, yes
Ye, yourselves
Yew, a Tree
You, yourselves
Yarn, made of Wool
Yearn, to pity

Of Stops and other Marks, used in Reading and Writing.

THESE are of absolute necessity; and great regard ought to be had to them for the better understanding of what we read and write ourselves; they are likewise of use to others who shall hear us read, or see our writing.

Stops, or Pauses, considered as intervals in reading, are no more than four; though there are other marks to be taken notice of. The names of the four Stops are, a Comma, Semicolon, Colon, and Period, or Full Stop: and these bear to each other a kind of progressional proportion of time; for the Comma signifies a stop of leisurely telling one, the Semicolon two, the Colon three, and the Period four—And are made or marked thus:

Comma (,) at the foot of a word.
Semicolon (;) a point over the Comma.
Colon (:) two points.
Period (.) in single point at the foot of a word.

, Example of the Comma (,): There is not any thing in the world, perhaps, that is more talked of, and less understood, than the business of a happy life.

; Example of a Semicolon (;): The orator makes the truth plain to his hearers; he awakens them; he excites them to action; he shows them their impending danger.

: Example of the Colon (:) A sound mind is not to be shaken with popular applause: but anger is startled at every accident.

. Example of the Period (.): It is a shame, says Fabius, for a commander to excuse himself by saying, " I was not aware of it." A cruelty that was only fit for Marius to suffer, Sylla to command, and Catiline to act.

By the foregoing Examples we may easily note, that a Comma is a note of a short pause between words in the sentence; and therefore the tenor of the voice must still be kept up.—The Semicolon is a little longer, and the tone of the voice very little abated.—The Colon signifies perfect sense, though not the end of a sentence; and the voice somewhat abated.—The Period denotes perfect sense, and the end of the sentence.

? When the Question is asked, there is a crooked mark made over the period, thus? and is called a Note of Interrogation. Example, What could be happier than the state of mankind, when people lived without either avarice or envy? The true time of pause for this top is the same as with the Semicolon,

! If a sudden cry-out, or wondering be expressed, then this mark is made over the Full Stop, thus! and called a Note of Admiration or Exclamation. Example, Oh the astonishing wonders that are in the Starry Heavens!

( ) If one sentence be within another, of which it is no part, then it is placed between two Semicircles or Parentheses, made thus ( ). Example, Pompey, on the other side, who hardly ever spoke in public, without a blush, had a wonderful sweetness of nature. Again: Of authors be sure to make choice of the best, and (as I said before) stick close to them. In reading a Parenthesis, the tone must be somewhat lower, as a thing or matter that comes in by the bye, The time is equal to a Comma, and ought to be read pretty quick, lest it detain the ear too long from the sense of the more important matter.

' *Apostrophe*, is a Comma at the head of letters, signifying some letter or letters left out in poetry, as *would'st* for *wouldest*, *ne'er* for *never*, *'tis* for *it is*, *e'er* for *over*. Or to denote a Genetive Case; as my Father's House, my Uncle's Wife, &c.

' *Accent* is placed over a vowel, to denote that the stress or sound in pronunciation is on that syllable.

˘ *Breve*, or crooked mark over a vowel, signifies it must be sounded short or quick.

A *Caret* signifies something is wanting, and is placed underneath the line, just where any thing omitted should be brought in.

A *Circumflex* is of the same shape with a Caret, but is placed over some vowel, to show that the syllable is long, as *Eu-phrâ-tes*.

·· *Diæresis*, two points placed over vowels, to signify they are parted, being no diphthong, as a-ë-ri-al.

- *Hyphen* or *Note of Connection*, is a straight line, which shows that the syllables of a word are parted, and the remainder of it is at the beginning of the next line. Sometimes the hyphen is used in compound words, as heart-breaking, book-keeper. When you have not room to write the whole word at the end of a line, but are obliged to finish it at the beginning of the next, such words must be truly divided, according to the rules of spelling.

☞ *Index* is a note like a hand, pointing to something very remarkable.

* *Asterism* or *Star*, directs to some remark in the margin, or at the foot of the page. Several of them together denote something defective in that passage of the author.

† *Obelisk* is a mark like a dagger, and refers to the margin, as the *Asterism:* and in dictionaries it signifies the word to be obsolete or old, and out of use.

¶ *Paragraph* denotes a division, comprehending several sentences under one head.

§ *Section* signifies the beginning of a new head of discourse, and it is used in sub-dividing a chapter, or book, into lesser parts or proportions.

[ ] *Brackets* or *Crotchets*, generally include a word or sentence, explanatory of what went before; or words of the same sense, which may be used in their stead.

" *Quotation*, or double Comma inverted, is used at the beginning of the line, and shows what is quoted from an author to be his own words, as an excellent Poet says,

" The proper Study of Mankind is Man."

Of Abbreviations.

To be ready in these shows a Dexterity in Writing, and is very necessary for Dispatch; for by these we expeditiously express, or set down a Word, shortening it by making some initial Letter, or Letters, belonging to the Word, to express it, as in the Table following:

A. B. Bachelor of Arts

A. Bp. Archbisop

A. D. Anno Domini, Year of the Lord

A. M. Anno Mundi, Year of the World

Admrs. Administrators

A.M. Artium Magister, Master of Arts

Ana, of each a like Quantity

Adml. Admiral

Aug. August

A. R. Anno Regni, in the Year of the Reign

Ast.P. G. Astronomy Professor at Gresham College

B. A. Bachelor of Arts

B. D. Bachelor of Divinity

B. V. Blessed Virgin

Bart. Baronet

Bp. Bishop

Cant. Canticles, or Canterbury

Chap. Chapter

Cent. Centum

Chron. Chronicles

Capt. Captain

Col. Colossians

Cl. Clericus

Col. Colonel

Cor. Corinthians or Corollary

Cr Creditor

C. C C. Corpus Christi College

C. S. Custos Sigilli, Keeper of the Seal

C P. S Custos Privati Sigilli, Keeper of the Privy Seal

Dr. Doctor or Debtor

Do Ditto, or the same

Deut. Deuteronomy

Dec Deceased

D. D Doctor of Divinity

E. Earl

Earld Earldom

Ex. gr or *e. g.* Exempli gratia, for Example

Eph. Ephesians

Eccl

Eccl. Ecclesiastes
Ex. Exodus or Example
Esq. Esquire
Exon Exeter
Feb. February
F. R S Fellow of the Royal Society
Gal. Galatians
Gen. Genesis
Genmo. Generalissimo
G. R. Georgius Rex, George the King
Gen. General
Gent. Gentleman
Heb. Hebrews
i. e. id. est, that is
I. H. S. Jesu Hominum Salvator, Jesus Saviour of Men
Ib. Ibidem, in the same Place
Id. Idem, the same
Jan. January
Jer. Jeremiah
Judg. Judges
J. D. Jurium Doctor, Doctor of Laws
Jos. Joshua
Knt. Knight
l. Liber, a Book
L. Libræ, Pounds
Lieut Lieutenant
LL D. Legum Doctor, Doctor of Laws
Lam. Lamentations
Lev. Leviticus
L. C. J. Lord Chief Justice
M. One Thousand
Mat. Matthew
m Manipulus, a Handful
M. A. Master of Arts
Mons. Monsieur
Mr. Master
Mrs. Mistress
M. D. Medicinæ Doctor, Doctor of Physic
M S. Memoriæ Sacrum, Sacred to the Memory
MS. Manuscript
MSS Manuscripts
Mich. Michael, or Michaelmas
N B. Nota Bene, Note, or mark well
N. S. New Style
No. Number

Nov. November
O. S. Old Style
Oct. October
Oxon. Oxford
Pugil, a Handful
Pd. Paid
Parl. Parliament
Philo Math. Philo Mathematicus, a Lover of the Mathematics
P. M. G. Professor of Music at Gresham College
Ps. Psalm
P. S. Postscript
Penult. last save one
Q. Query
q. d. quasi dicat, as if he should say
q. l. quantum libet, as much as you please
q. s. quantum sufficit, a sufficient quantity
qr. Quarter, or a Farthing
Rev. Reverend, or Revelation
Reg. Prof. Regius Professor
Rom. Romans
Rt. Honble. Right Honourable
Rt. Worpl. Right Worshipful
St. Saint, or Street
Sect. Section
Sept. September
Serj Serjeant
Salop, Shropshire
ss. Semissis, half a Pound
S. T. P. a Professor or Doctor of Divinity
Thess. Thessalonians
V. Virgin, or Verse
Ult. Ultimus, the last
Vid. see
Viz. Videlicet, to wit, or that is to say
V. gr. Verbi Gratia, for Example
Xn Christian
Xt. Christ
Xtopher. Christopher
ye, the
yn, then
ym, them
yt, that
yr, your
&, et, and
&c. et cetera, and the rest, or and so forth.

DIRECTIONS

DIRECTIONS to BEGINNERS in WRITING.

FIRST, it is necessary to be provided with the following Implements, viz. good Pens, and Ink and Paper; likewise a flat Ruler for exactness; and a round one for Dispatch; with a Plummet or Pencil to rule lines.

How to hold the Pen.

THE Pen must be held somewhat sloping, with the Thumb and the two Fingers next to it; the Ball of the Middle-finger must be placed straight, just against the upper part of the Cut or Cradle, to keep the Pen steady; the fore finger lying straight on the Middle-finger; and the Thumb must be fixed a little higher than the end of the fore finger bending in the joint; and the Pen so placed as to be held easily without griping it. The Elbow must be drawn towards the Body, but not too close. You must support your Hand by leaning on the Table-edge, resting it half-way between your Wrist and Elbow, not suffering the Ball or fleshy part of your Hand to touch the Paper; but resting your Hand on the end of your little finger, that and your fore-finger bending inwards, and supported on the Table. So fixed, and sitting pretty upright, not leaning your Breast against the Table, proceed to the making the small *a, c, e, i, m, r, s, w* and *x*; which must be all made of equal size and height; the distance or width between the two strokes of the *n* must be the same with the distance or width in the three strokes of the *m*; the same proportion or width must be observed in the *u, w,* and *o.* The Letters with Stems, or Heads, must be of equal height; as the *b, d, f, h, l,* and *f,* and those with tails must be of equal depth, as the *f, g, p, q.* and *f.* The Capitals must bear the same proportion to one another with respect to size and height, as *A, B, C, D, E, F, G, H, and I,* &c. All upright strokes, and those leaning to the left hand, must be fine or hair strokes, and all downright strokes must be fuller or blacker. Due care must be taken, that there be an equal distance between Letter and Letter, and also between Word and Word. The Distance between Word and Word may be the space the small *m* takes up; but between Letter and Letter not quite so much. Sit not long at writing, especially at the first, lest it weary you, and you grow tired of learning. Imitate

the

the best Examples; have a constant eye to your Copy; and be not ambitious of writing fast, before you write well : Expedition will follow naturally when you have gained a habit of writing fair and free ; for it is much more commendable to be an hour in writing six Lines well, than to be able to writy sixty Lines in the same time, which perhaps will be unintelligible.   And beside by a slow and fair procedure you will learn in half the time, and therefore it is in vain in a Learner to desire to be quick before he has acquired Experience, and a Freedom of Writing by frequent practice. Never overcharge your Pen with Ink; but shake what is too much into the Inkstand again.

How to make a Pen.

THIS is gained sooner by Experience and Observation from others who can make a Pen well, than by verbal Directions.   But before you begin to cut the Quill, scrape off the superfluous Scurf with the Back of your Penknife; scrape most on the Back of the Quill, that the Slit may be the finer.   After you have scraped the Quill, cut it at the End, half through, on the back Part, and then turning up the Belly, cut the other Part, or Half, quite through, viz. about a quarter or almost half an Inch, at the end of the Quill, which will then appear forked.   Enter the Penknife a little in the back Notch, and then putting the peg of the Penknife-haft into the back notch (holding your Thumb pretty hard on the Back of the Quill, as high as you intend the slit to be) with a sudden or quick Twitch force up the slit; it must be sudden and smart, that the slit may be clearer.   Then by several cuts on each side bring the Quill into equal shape or form on both sides ; and having brought it to a fine point, place the inside of the Nib on the Nail of your Thumb, and enter the Knife at the Extremity of the Nib, and cut it through a little sloping, then with an almost downright cut of the Knife cut off the Nib.   The breadth of the Nib must be proportioned to the breadth of the Body, or downright back-strokes of the Letters, in whatever hand you write, whether small or Text.   Note, In sitting to write, place yourself directly against a fore-right Light, or else have it on your left Hand, but by no means have the Light on the right Hand, because the shadow of your Writing-hand will obstruct your Sight.

A

A B C D E F G H I J K
L M N O P Q R S T
U V W X Y Z Æ

a b c d e f g h i j k l m n o
p q r s t u v w x y z &

Note, It is necessary for all those who would qualify themselves for Business, often to imitate this Print-hand, to make clean Marks on Bales of Goods, or plain Directions on Parcels.

COPIES in Alphabetical ORDER.

A. Art is gained by great Labour and Industry.
A covetous Man is always, as he fancies, in Want.

B. Beauty is commendable in some, but it ruins others.
By Delight and some Care, we attain to write fair.

C. Contentment is preferable to Riches and Honour.
Can they be deemed wise who Counsel Despise?

D. Deride not Infirmities, nor triumph over Injuries.
Delight in Virtue's Ways, and then you'll merit Praise.

E. Every Plant and Flower displays to us God's Power.
Example oft doth rule the wise Man and the Fool.

F. Fair Words are often used to hide bad Deeds.
Few do Good with what they have gotten ill.

G. Godliness with Content is great Gain.
Great Minds and small Means ruin many Men.

H. Hasty Resolutions are seldom fortunate.
Haste makes Waste of Paper, Ink and Time.

I. Instruction and a good Education are a durable Portion.
Ignorance is the greatest Enemy to Learning.

K. Keep a close Mouth if you'd have a wise Head.
Kings as well as mean Men must die.

L. Learn to live as you would wish to die.
Learn to unlearn what you have learned amiss.

M. Modesty has more Charms than Beauty.
Make Use of Time now whilst you're in your Prime.

N. Necessity is commonly the Mother of Invention.
Next to a good Conscience prefer a good Name.

O. Opportunity neglected brings severe Repentance.
Of all Prodigality that of Time is the worst.

P. Poor Men want many Things, but covetous Men all.
Patience and Time run through the roughest Day.

Q. Quick Promisers are commonly slow Performers.
Qualify exorbitant Passions with Quietness and Patience.

R. Remember your Duty to God, your Neighbour, and
   yourself.
Repentance comes too late when all is consumed.

S. Sin and Sorrow are inseparable Companions.
Self Love is the greatest Flatterer in the World.

T. The End of Mirth is often the Beginning of Sorrow.
Time is so swift of Foot that none can overtake it.

V. Vain and transitory is all worldly Glory.
Virtue and Fortune work Wonders in the World.

W. Wisdom is more valuable than Riches.
What pleases God must be, none alters his Decree.

X. Xenophon

X. Xenophon was a great Captain as well as a Philosopher.
  Xerxes whipped the Sea for not obeying his Command.
Y. Young Men lament your mis-spent Time.
Z. Zeal mixed with Love is harmless as a Dove.
  Zealously strive with Emulation to write.

Short Lines *for* Text Hand.

Abandon whatsoever is ill—Be wise betimes.
Care destroys the Body—Do the things that are just.
Expect to receive as you give—Frequent good Company.
Give what you give cheerfully—Hold good Men in Esteem.
Imitate that which is good—Keep God's Commandments.
Learn to be wise—Make a right Use of Time.
Nothing get, nothing have—Observe Modesty.
Pleasures are very short—Pains are very long.
Quit all Revenge—Quit your Passions.
Recompense a good Turn—Repent of your Sins.
Silent gives Consent—Sin not at all.
Time is more precious than Gold—Turn from your Sins.
Use moderate Pleasure—Use no bad Company.
Vain are some Pleasures—Vice is detestable.
Wisdom is the principal Thing—Wise Men are scarce.
Xenophon, Xenocrates.
Yesterday cannot be recalled—Zeno and Zenobia.

As good Ink is essential to good Writing, I here give a Receipt or two for making some of the best Black Ink in the World, viz.

A Receipt *for making black* Ink.

To six Quarts of Rain or River-Water, put one Pound and a Half of fresh blue Galls of Aleppo, bruised pretty small; six Ounces of Copperas; also eight Ounces of clean, bright, and clear Gum Arabic. Let these stand together in a large Stone Bottle near a Fire, with a narrow Mouth, to keep it free from Dust; shake or stir it well, once every Day, and you will have excellent Ink in about a Month's Time, and the older it grows the better it will be for Use.

Ingredients for a Quart.

One Quart of soft Water, four Ounces of Galls, one Ounce of Copperas, and two Ounces of Gum, mixed and stirred as above, the Galls must be bruised.

How to make Red Ink.

Take three Pints of stale Beer (rather than Vinegar), and four Ounces of ground Brazil Wood ; simmer them together for an hour ; dissolve half an Ounce of Gum Arabic in it, then strain it through a Flannel, and bottle it up (well stopped) for Use.

To keep Ink from Freezing or turning Mouldy.

In very severe Weather Ink will be apt to freeze, which takes away all its Blackness and Beauty. To prevent which, put a Wine Glass of Brandy or other Spirit into a Quart, and it will not freeze. And to hinder its turning mouldy, put a little Salt in it.

FAMILIAR LETTERS,
ON SEVERAL OCCASIONS AND ON DIVERS SUBJECTS.

LETTERS are variously worded, and ought properly to express the desires, thoughts, &c. of the writer to the reader, by which the receiver of the letter may fully understand the wants or intentions of the sender. Of these I here give sundry examples.

A Letter from a Son to his Father.

Hon. Father,

AS I have not had a letter from you since your favour of the 8th of October last, which I answered by the next post, I take this opportunity of enquiring after your health, and that of my Sister. Pray give my love to my Sister, and be pleased to accept of my duty to yourself, who am,

Sir,

London, Dec. 6, 1809.

Your dutiful Son,
Anthony Addlehill.

The Answer.

Dear Son, *Pevensey, 28th Dec.* 1809.

I received your letter of the 6th instant, and thank you for inquiring after my health, which, I thank God, I perfectly enjoy at present, as I wish and hope you do. Your Sister sends her love to you, and with it a turkey and a chine of bacon, to which I wish you and your friends (if you invite any) a good appetite. Prayers to God for your welfare, temporal and eternal, are constantly offered up by

Your loving Father,
Andrew Addlehill.

LETTER WRITING.

From a Niece to her Aunt.

Dear Aunt,

THE trouble I have already given you puts me to the blush when I think of intruding again on your goodness; but necessity, which frequently obliges us to such actions as are contrary to our inclination, is the motive that induces me to be again troublesome. I pray you to excuse me if I once more beg your assistance, which I do not doubt but you very well know I stand greatly in need of at this time; and I shall ever have a grateful remembrance of your goodness to me; and I hope I shall be, one time or other, in a capacity of making some returns for the many obligations your goodness has conferred upon me.

London, May 9,   Your affectionate Niece,
    1811.   and very humble Servant,
       Penelope Finch.

From a Brother to his Sister.

Dear Sister,

MY great distance and long absence from you makes me very solicitous concerning your welfare: natural affection inclines me strongly to have you in remembrance, tendering your health and welfare in every respect, as dear as my own; and there is nothing at my command, but, if you request, it shall be freely yours. Notwithstanding the distance, I purpose to make you a visit very shortly, and I had done it before now, but an urgent occasion interposed, the particulars of which being too long for a letter, I shall acquaint you with when I see you. Pray give my due respects to all Friends.   I am,
      Dear Sister,
London, May 6,   Your affectionate Brother,
   1811.   Henry Hearty.

A Letter from a Youth at School to his Parents.

Honoured Father and Mother,

I AM very much obliged to you for all your favours: all I have to hope is, that the progress I make in my learning will be no disagreeable return for the same. Gratitude, duty, and a view to future advantages, all conspire to make me fully sensible how much I ought to labour for my own improvement and your satisfaction, in order to show myself upon all occasions, to be
Acton School, May 8,   Your dutiful Son,
   1811.   Daniel Diligent.
       Fo

A Letter of Recommendation.

Sir,

THE Bearer, Francis Bashful, I send to you as one whose honesty you may rely on; and my experience of his conduct and fidelity gives me a certain kind of confidence in recommending him to you; for you know, Sir, that I would not recommend any one to you of whose probity I had the least shadow of doubt or suspicion. I am, with due respect, Sir, your real Friend,

May 6, 1811. and humble Servant,

George Generous.

A Letter of Thanks.

Sir,

I Received your Favour, with the kind present which accompanied it: I have no other way of expressing my gratitude at present than by my hearty thanks; every thing you do has a peculiar excellence, and the manner of doing it is as agreeable as the action itself; but I must stop, lest I should offend that delicacy which I would commend, and which is constantly admired by,

May 10, 1811. Sir, your most obliged and humble Servant,

George Grateful.

A Letter in Manner of Petition to a Friend.

Honoured Sir,

I AM uncertain whether my late misfortunes have come to your knowledge; however I will presume on your good-nature, being assured, from many examples of your compassion, that you will think of and take pity on the distressed; therefore, as an object truly deserving compassion, I most humbly implore and petition you to consider the many losses and disappointments that I have lately met with, which have reduced me to such necessitous circumstances that I cannot possibly proceed in my affairs: you was pleased once to style me your Friend, and so I was indeed: I doubt not, Sir, but your generosity and goodness are great; and I hope, with all humility, you will be pleased to interpose your good offices between ruin and,

Sir,

Your unfortunate humble Servant,

Laurence Luckless.

It is as proper to know how to subscribe, and how to direct, as it is to write a Letter.

Super

SUPERSCRIPTIONS.

To the King's Most Excellent Majesty.
To the Queen's Most Excellent Majesty, &c.
To the Prince, *To his Royal Highness,* &c.
To the Princess, *To her Royal Highness,* &c.
To Archbishops.
. *To his Grace the Lord Archbishop of Canterbury,* or
To the Most Reverend Father in God, &c.
To Bishops.
To the Right Reverend Father in God, &c.
To Deacons, Archdeacons, &c.
To the Reverend A. B. D. D. Dean of W.
To the Inferior Clergy.
To the Rev. Mr. A. &c. *or To the Reverend Doctor,* &c.
To the great Offices of State.
To the Right Honourable A. Lord L. Lord High Chan-
cellor of Great Britain.—Lord President of the Council.—
Lord Privy Seal.— One of his Majesty's principal Secretaries
of State, &c.
To Temporal Lords.
His Grace the Duke of, &c. *The most Hon. the Marquis*
of, &c. *The Right Hon. the Earl of,* &c. *The Right Hon.*
the Lord Viscount, &c. *The Right Hon. the Lord* &c.

The eldest Sons of Dukes, Marquisses, and Earls, enjoy
by the Courtesy of *England,* the second Title belonging to
their Father: thus the eldest son of a Duke of *Bedford* is
called Marquis of *Tavistock;* the Duke of *Grafton, Earl* of
Euston; of the Earl of *Macclesfield,* Lord Viscount *Parker,*
&c. and their Daughters are called Ladies, with the Addition of their Christian and Surnames thus, Lady *Carolina*
Russel, Augusta Fitzroy, Lady *Betty Parker,* &c.

The younger Sons of Dukes are also called Lords: and
those of Marquisses and Earls, together with all the Child-
ren of Viscounts and Barons, are styled *Honourable.*

To a Baronet *Honourable;* a Knight, *Right Worshipful,*
and to an Esquire, *Worshipful.*—Every Privy Councillor,
though not a Nobleman, hath the Title of *Right Honourable.*
All Ambassadors have the Style of *Excellency,* as hath also
the Lord Lieutenant of *Ireland,* and the Captain General of
his Majesty's Forces. The Lord Mayor of *London,* during
his Mayoralty, hath the Title of *Right Honourable.* And
the Sheriffs, during that Office, have the Title of *Right Wor-*
shipful. All Mayors of Corporations have the Title of *Es-*
quires, during their office.

Fo-

For the Beginning of Letters.

To the King ; *Sire, or May it please your Majesty.*

To the Queen ; *Madam, or May it please your Majesty.*

To the Prince ; *Sir, or May it please your Royal Highness.*

To the Princess ; *Madam, or May it please your Royal Highness.*

To a Duke ; *My Lord, or May it please your Grace.*

To a Duchess ; *Madam, or May it please your Grace.*

To an Archbishop ; *May it please your Grace.*

To a Marquis ; *My Lord, or May it please your Lordship.*

To a Marchioness ; *Madam, or May it please your Ladyship.*

To an Earl, Viscount, or Baron ; *My Lord, or may it please your Lordship.*

To their Consorts ; *Madam, or May it please your Ladyship.*

To a Bishop ; *My Lord, or May it please your Lordship.*

To a Knight ; *Sir, or May it please your Worship.*

To his Lady ; *Madam, or May it please your Ladyship.*

To a Mayor, Justice of Peace, Esq. &c. *Sir, or May it please your Worship.*

To the Clergy ; *Reverend Sir ; Mr. Dean ; Mr. Archdeacon; Sir,* as Circumstances may require.

At subscribing your Name, conclude with the same Title you began with ; as, *My Lord, your Lordship's,* &c.

To either House of Parliament, and to Commissioners, Bodies corporate :

To the Right Honourable the Lords Spiritual and Temporal in Parliament assembled.

To the Honourable the Knights, Citizens and Burgesses in Parliament assembled.

To the Right Honourable the Lords Commissioners of the Treasury or Admiralty.

To the Honourable the Commissioners of his Majesty's Customs ; Revenue of the Excise, &c.

To the Worshipful the Governors of Christ's Hospital.

To the Master, Wardens, and Court of Assistants of the Worshipful Company of Stationers.

Of Secret Writing.

First, If you dip your pen in the Juice of a Lemon or of an Onion, or in your own Urine, and write on clean paper whatever you intend, it will not be discerned till you hold it to the fire, and then it will appear legible.

Another way ; when you write a letter the contents of which you intend shall not be discovered but by those you

think

think fit, first write your thoughts on one side of your Letter with black ink, as usual, and then, on the contrary side go over the said matter that you would have secret, with a clean pen dipped in Milk, and that writing cannot be read without holding it to the fire, when it will appear legible in a bluish colour.

A third Method is, to have two pieces of paper equal in size, and the uppermost cut in chequered holes or squares big enough to contain any Word of six or seven Syllables, and in those squares write your mind in regular sense; and then take off the said chequered paper, and fill up the Vacancies with words of any kind, which will render it perfect nonsense, and not capable of being read to any purpose, and transmit and send the said uppermost, or chequered paper, or another exactly of the same form, to your correspondent: whereby he shall, by laying it nicely on your said letter, read your intended sense, without being perplexed with the words of amusement, intermixed, which make it altogether unintelligible.

Or again, you may write to your friend in proper sense with common Ink, and let the lines be at so commodious a distance, that what you intend to be secret may be written between them with water, in which galls have been steeped a little time, but not long enough to tincture the water, and when dry, nothing of the writing between the said lines can be seen ; but when it is to be read, you must, with a fine hair-pencil dipped in copperas-water, go between the said lines, and so you make it legible.

Note. This way will excite no suspicion, because the Letter seems to carry proper sense in those lines that are set at a proper Distance.

Of ARITHMETIC.

AFTER Writing, the next necessary step towards qualifying a Person for Business is the understanding the noble Science of *Arithmetic*, a Knowledge so necessary in all the Parts of Life and Business, that scarcely any thing is done without it.

In my Directions for its Attainment I shall proceed with such Plainness of Method, and Familiarity of Style, as shall render it easy to be understood and conspicuous to the meanest Capacity. And first of *Notation and Numeration*.

Of

Of NOTATION and NUMERATION.

In *Notation* we must note, or observe, that all Numbers are expressed by, or composed of, these ten Figures, or Characters following, viz.

One,   *Two, Three, Four, Five,*   *Six, Seven, Eight, Nine, Cipher.*
  1   2   3   4   5   6   7   8   9   0

Nine of these are called significant figures, to distinguish them from the *Cipher*, which of itself signifies nothing : but as it is placed in whole Numbers, serves to increase the Value of the next Figure or Figures that stand before it ; as 3 is but three; but before the Cipher, thus, 30, the 3 becomes thirty, &c.— But in Decimal Fractions 0 decreases the Value of Figures behind it, for there, 3 is three-tenths of any thing ; but by placing 0 before it, thus, 03, it is decreased from 3 tenth Parts to 3 hundred Parts of any thing, &c. We are to observe, that every one, or any of the abovementioned nine Figures, or Digits, have two Values ; one certain, and another uncertain ; the certain Value is when it stands by itself; the uncertain is, when joined or placed with other figures or Ciphers : for when any one of these Figures stand alone, they signify no more than their own simple Value; as 5 is but five, 4 but four, 6 but six, and 3 no more than three, &c. And this is the certain Value of a Figure ; But when another Figure or Cipher is annexed, they then are increased in their Value ten Times ; as 5, or 5 Units or Ones, to 5 tens, or fifty ; 4 to 4 tens, or forty ; 6 to 6 tens, or sixty ; and 3 to 3 tens, or thirty ; as thus, 51, fifty-one ; 42, forty-two ; 63, sixty-three ; 34, thirty-four, &c. Again, if any of the said Figures stand in their Place towards the left hand, they signify so many Hundreds as they expressed Units or Ones ; as 500 is five Hundreds, 400 four Hundreds, 600 six Hundreds, and 300 three Hundreds, &c. If any of them possess the 4th Place towards the left hand, they are so many Thousands as they contain Units : and so any or every Figure increases by a ten-fold Proportion, from the right hand to the left, according to the Place it is found or stands in ; so that 5 may be either five or fifty ; five Hundred, or five Thousand ; in the first Place, 5 ; in the second, 50 ; in the third, 500 ; in the fourth place, 5000, &c.

The true Value of Figures in conjunction may be fully learned and understood by the following table :

The

THE NUMERATION TABLE.

12 C Thous. of M.	11 X Thous. of M.	10 Thous. of M.	9 C of Millions.	8 Tens of Millions.	7 Millions.	6 C of Thousands.	5 Tens of Thousands.	4 Thousands.	3 Hundreds.	2 Tens.	1 Units.	Thous. of Millions.	Millions.	Thousands.	Units or Ones.
1	2	3	4	5	6	7	8	9	0	1	2	123	456	789	012
	1	2	3	4	5	6	7	8	9	0	1	12	345	678	901
		1	2	3	4	5	6	7	8	9	0	1	234	567	890
			1	2	3	4	5	6	7	8	9		123	456	789
				1	2	3	4	5	6	7	8		12	345	678
					1	2	3	4	5	6	7		1	234	567
						1	2	3	4	5	6			123	456
							1	2	3	4	5			12	345
								1	2	3	4			1	234
									1	2	3				123
										1	2				12
											1				1

For the easier reading of any Number, first get the
Words at the Head of the Table by Heart; as Units,
tens, hundreds, thousands, &c. and apply them thus:
75, five units, five; and seven tens; seventy; that is,
seventy-five. Again 678; 8 Units, Eight; 7 Tens,
seventy; and 6 Hundreds, six Hundred; that is six
Hundred seventy-eight. Once more, 3456; Units, six;
5 tens, fifty; 4 Hundreds, four Hundreds; 3 thousands, three thousands; together, three thousand four
Hundred Fifty-six. The 4th Line of the Table, viz.
123456789, may be read thus: One Hundred twenty-three
Millions, four Hundred Fifty-six Thousand seven hundred
Eighty-nine. But the Manner of reading any Number may
be rendered more intelligible by Stops, thus: make a
comma after every third Figure or cipher, beginning at
the Right hand, and so on towards the Left, thereby distinguishing every third Place into Hundreds, as Hundreds
of Units, Hundreds of Thousands, Hundreds of Millions,
and Hundred Thousands of Millions, &c. And for trial
read the first Line of the table; where the last place in
Valuation is Hundred Thousand of Millions; and being
pointed

pointed into Periods, will stand thus 123,456,789,012, and is to be read thus, One Hundred, twenty-three thousand, four Hundred fifty-six Millions, Seven Hundred eighty-nine thousand, (no Hundreds) and twelve. Again; the following Number, viz. 276,245,678,921,460, is to be read thus : 276 Million of Millions, 245 Thousand of Millions, 678 Millions; 921 thousands, 460 Units or Ones, that is, two hundred and seventy-six Million of Millions, two Hundred forty-five Thousand six Hundred seventy-eight Millions, nine Hundred twenty-one Thousand four Hundred and Sixty. The foregoing *Table of Numeration* is on the right hand distinguished into such periods for the easier reading thereof, and the like is frequently done in the Public Offices, and by Men of Business.

Numbers to be read or written, viz.

96, *Ninety-six.*
242, *Two hundred forty-two.*
7924, *Seven thousand 9 hundred 24.*
54006, *Fifty-four thousand and six.*
524707, *Five hundred 24 thousand 707.*
4706240, *Four millions 706 thousand 240.*
62700472, *Sixty-two millions 700 thousand 472.*
474960204, *Four hundred 74 millions 960 thousand 204.*
4214007042, *Four thousand 214 millions 7 thousand 42.*
44214800240, *Forty-four thousand 214 millions 8 hundred*
        thousand 240.

Of Numerical Letters.

Numbers were anciently expressed by Letters : and it is necessary to understand them for reading the dates to years, in Title-pages of books, on Funeral Monuments, and in Roman History, &c.

I signifies One,
V Five,
X Ten,
L Fifty
C An Hundred,
CC Two Hundred,
D or IƆ Five Hundred,
M or CIƆ A Thousand,
IƆƆ Five Thousand,
CIƆƆ Ten Thousand,
CIƆƆƆ Fifty Thousand,

CCCCIƆƆƆƆ A Hundred Thousand,
IƆƆƆƆ Five Hundred Thousand,
CCCCCIƆƆƆƆƆ Ten Hundred Thousand or a Million,
M.DCCCXI. expresses the Date of the present Year 1811,
M being one Thousand, D. five Hundred, CCC three Hundred and X ten; together, one Thousand, eight Hundred and Ten.

When a Letter of inferior Value stands after one of superior, its Value is to be added thereto; thus VI, VII, and VIII, signify six, seven and eight; but when a Letter of inferior Value is placed before one of superior, then its Value is to be taken therefrom, thus IV, IX, XL, and XC, signify four, nine, forty, and ninety.

ADDITION,

IS the putting together two or more Numbers or Sums, so as their total Value may be discovered or known.

Herein we must always observe to set the Numbers to be added, orderly one under the other; that is, Units under Units, Tens under Tens, Hundreds under Hundreds, &c. as in the subsequent Examples.

Addition of Numbers of one Denomination.

Yards.		Gallons.			Pounds.				
T.	U.	H.	T.	U.	X of Th.	Th.	H.	T.	U.
2	4	7	5	6	5	7	9	6	2
4	2	4	3	2	3	9	7	4	4
6	8	5	7	8	6	7	2	2	2
8	6	6	9	6	7	9	6	7	4
2	4	4	2	2	5	2	4	9	2
4	2	6	7	8	7	2	3	9	d
2 8 6		3 5 6 2			3 6 9 4 8 4				

In addition of simple Numbers, whether it be *Yards, Gallons, Pounds,* or any thing else, remember to carry 1 for every 10 that you find in the Right hand Row, or Rank of figures, being Units. to the next row of Tens; and the like from the Rank of Tens to the Row of Hundreds, &c. and whatever it makes in the last Row, you must set down, amount to what it will.

The numbers above are set down in order, as before directed; that is, Units under Units, Tens under Tens, &c. as may be plainly understood, by being indicated at the Head of each Row or Rank, by U. T. H. &c. signifying Units, Tens, Hundreds, &c. Then in casting up each Example to know its Total, I begin at the Right hand, for Units Rank of the first Example, and say 2 and 4 is 6, and 6 is 12, and 8 is 20, and 2 is 22, and 4 is 26; in which Row there are two Tens, and 6 over; wherefore I set down 6 just under its own Rank, and carry 2 to the next Row, and say 2 that I carry and 4 makes 6, and 2 is 8, and 8 is 16, and 6 is 22, and 4 is 26, and 2 is 28; and this being the last Row, I set down the Amount, viz. 28; so that the total Number of Yards is found to be 286. And the amount of the next or 2d Example is found by the same Method to be 3562 Gallons. And in the third and last Example, the total Number of Pounds is found by the same way to be 369484. And so the total of any other Example of the same Kind, viz. simple Numbers

bers of one Denomination may be found. *Note*, That when any of the Ranks amount to just 10, 20, 30, 40, 50, &c. then you must set down the 0 under its proper Rank, and carry either 1, 2, 3, 4, or 5, according to the Number of Tens that you find to the next Row.

We come now to *Addition of Money.*

In *England*, or *Great Britain*, Accounts are kept in Pounds, Shillings, Pence, and Parts of a Penny; so you are to observe, that

4 *Farthings* make 1 *Penny*
12 *Pence* 1 *Shilling*
20 *Shillings* 1 *Pound.*

In adding of these together, you are with the same punctuality to mind that Pounds be set directly under Pounds, Shillings under Shillings, Pence under Pence, and Farthings under Farthings; as in the following Example.

But before you proceed, it will be necessary to have the following Tables by memory, for the readier remembrance of how many Shillings there are in a given Number of Pence, and how many Pounds are contained in a given Number of Shillings, &c.

Note, that *l* stands for Pounds, *s* for shillings, *d* for Pence, and *qr* for farthings, those being the initial Letters of *Libra*, *Solidus*, *Denarius*, and *Quadrans*, *Latin* Words of the same signification.

TABLES.

Pence.		s.	d.		s.		l.	s.
20	is	1	8		20	is	1	0
30	-	2	6		36	-	1	16
40	-	3	4		46	-	2	6
50	-	4	2		56	-	2	16
60	-	5	0		66	-	3	6
70	-	5	10		76	-	3	16
80	-	6	8		86	-	4	6
90	-	7	6		96	-	4	16
100	-	8	4		106	-	5	6
110	-	9	2		116	-	5	16
120	-	10	0		126	-	6	6

The Use of these Tables is this: whenever you are casting up any Sum of Money you begin at the right hand (as before in Sums of one Denomination) suppose at the Place of Pence, then if the Rank or Denomination of Pence amounts, from the bottom to the top, 56; your table of pence tells you, that 50d. is 4s. 2d. to which adding 6d. the

Sum

Sum Is 4s. 8d. If to 92d. the Table tells you, that 90d. is 7s. 6d. which with 2d. over, is 7s. 8d. And if to 81d. the table shows that 80d. is 6s. 8d. and 1d. more makes 6s. 9d. &c.

The *Shilling Table* serves to lead you to a quick Recollection of how many pounds are in so many Shillings ; as, admit the Rank of Shillings arises to 57s. the Table says that 50s. is 2l. 10s. and 7. over make 2l. 17s. If to 84s. the Table shows that 80s. are just 4l. and 4s. over, make 4l. 4s. If to 112s. the table shows that 100s. are 5l. and 12s. more make 5l. 12s. &c.

ADDITION OF MONEY.

Money owing.	£.	s.	d	Money received.	£.	s.	d.
To Mr. Umpleby	4	12	6	For Paper	46	10	9
Mr. Olding	7	6	9	Peas	79	16	0
Mr. Worth	4	12	0	Indigo	42	18	3
Mr. Sandle	6	17	7	Broad Cloth	66	12	4
Mr Dalton	5	6	6	Canary	90	16	0
Mr. Howit	4	12	3	Wine	84	7	6
Mr. Craig	6	0	0	Quills	24	12	0
Mr. Flewel	5	15	4	Logwood	60	10	0
	45	2	11		496	2	10

I begin with the right hand Rank, that is the Pence in the Example of Money owing, and say 4 and 3 are 7, and 6 is 13, and 7 is 20, and 9 is 29, and 6 makes 35 Pence ; now 30 Pence, according to the Table, is 2s. 6d. and 5d. more makes 2s. and 11d. I set down 11 exactly under the Rank of Pence, and say, 2 Shillings that I carry (which I do to the Rank of Shillings) and 5 is 7, and 2 is 9, for I take first only the Units Rank of Shillings) and 6 is 15, and 7 makes 22, and 2 is 24, and 6 is 30, and 2 makes 32 : and now being come to the top of the Sum, and it making 32, I come down with the Tens of Shillings, saying 32 and 10 is 42, and 10 is 52, and 10 is 62, and 10 is 72, and 10 makes 82 Shillings ; and the Table showing me that 80 Shillings is 4 Pounds, I then knew 82 Shillings is 4l. 2s. then I set down the odd 2s. just under the row of Shillings and carry 4 Pounds to the Pounds ; saying 4 that I carry and 5 is 9, and 6 is 15, and 4 is 19, and 5 is 24, and 6 is 30, and 4 is 34, and 7 is 41, and 4 makes 45 Pounds ; so that the total of those several Sums of Money due to the several Persons amounts to 45l. 2s. 11d.

In the Example of Money received, I begin at the Right-hand Rank as before, and say, 6 and 4 are 10, and 3 is 13,

and 9 makes 22, and 22 Pence being 1s. 10d. I set down
10 and carry 1s. to the Shillings; saying, 1 that I carry and
2 is 3, and 7 is 10, and 6 is 16, and 2 is 18, and 8 is 26, and
6 makes 32; then I come to the Tens, saying, 32 and 10
makes 42, &c. and find at the Bottom it comes to 102 Shillings, which makes 5l. 2s. I set down 2s. and carry 5l. to
the Pounds, saying, 5 that I carry and 4 is 9, &c. I find
that at the Top it amounts to 36, whereof I set down 6 exactly under its own Rank, viz. the Rank of Units of Pounds,
and carry 3 for the 3 Tens that are in 39, for at all Times in
the Addition of the Left-hand Denomination, whether it be
Money, Weight, or Measure; that is in the Denomination
of Pounds, Tons, or Yards, you must for every Ten carry
one to the next Row, &c. saying, 3 that I carry and 6 is 9,
and 2 is 11, and 8 is 19, &c. and I find that at the Top it
comes to 49; wherefore I set down 49 to the Left-hand of
the 6; and the Total Amount of the Money received for
those particular Goods or Wares sold is 496l. 2s. 10d.

MORE EXAMPLES FOR PRACTICE.

	£.	s.	d.	£.	s.	d.	£.	s.	d.
Mr. Money	17	12	6¼	146	12	3¼	4	10	6
Mr. Gaunt	26	10	2¼	287	10	9	0	7	9
Mr. Herne	50	0	0	46	16	6	1	0	0
Mr. James	44	12	1	100	0	0	1	1	0
Mr. King	60	14	0½	72	12	1	0	4	6
Mr. Long	29	16	6	69	16	6¼	0	10	1
Mr. Monk	16	10	0	460	12	9	4	14	4
Mr. Napper	20	0	4½	49	10	0	0	7	4
Total	265	15	9	1233	10	10¼	12	15	6

ADDITION OF AVOIRDUPOIS WEIGHT.

By this Weight are weighed all kinds of Grocery Goods or
Wares, or Goods subject to waste; as Tobacco, Sugars,
Fruit and Drugs; as also Flesh, Butter, Cheese, Alum,
Tallow, Iron, Brass, Copper, Lead, Tin, Pewter, Pitch,
Tar, Rosin, Hemp, Flax, Soap, &c.

A Table of this Weight is as follows:

4 Quarters make 1 Dram, marked	-	dr.
16 Drams 1 Ounce	-	ox.
16 Ounces 1 Pound	-	lb.
28 Pounds 1 Quarter of a Hundred Weight		qrs.
4 Quarters 1 Hundred Weight	-	Cwt.
20 Hundred Weight 1 Ton	-	T.

| 10 4 28 | 10 4 28 | 10 4 28 | 10 16 16 |
C. qrs. lb.	C. qrs. lb.	C. qrs. lb.	lb. oz. dr.
5—1—16	24—2—12	9—1—16	24—11—12
4—2—24	42—2—0	4—3—26	42—14—15
6—3—6	16—0—12	7—1—0	64—10—11
7—1—12	25—3—24	5—3—12	29—9—10
9—0—20	19—0—20	4—3—2	16—12—13
6—2—0	26—1—22	2—2—2	27—13—14
39—3—22	154—3—6	34—3—17	206—9—11

In these Examples the Manner of proceeding is the same as in the former, observing, that the Number of Units of each lesser Denomination, which make an Unit of the next greater, found by the preceding Table, is placed above each Rank of Numbers; that is to say, in the first Example, 28 the Number of Pounds contained in a quarter of a Hundred Weight, is placed over the Column of Pounds: now that Column, when added up, makes 78, which contains two 28's and 22 over, wherefore I set down 22 under the Column of Pounds, and carry 2 to the Column of Quarters, and so on.

Note. That in weighing at the Water-side, or elsewhere, they do not weigh by the Ton, though some Goods are sold by it, as Iron, Logwood, Cheese, &c. but by the Hundred, Quarters, and Pounds, which are afterwards reduced to and computed by Tons.

Addition of Troy Weight.

By this Weight are weighed Jewels, Gold, Silver, Pearls and Medicines; and the usual denominations are *Pounds, Ounces, Penny-weights,* and *Grains,* as in the following Table, viz.

24 *Grains make* 1 *Penny-weight,*
20 *Penny-weights* 1 *Ounce,* and
12 *Ounces* 1 *Pound Troy-weight.*

Examples of Troy Weight.

| 6 Ingots of Silv. wt. viz. | | | | 10 12 20 24 | | | | 12 20 24 | | |
	lb.	oz.	pw. gr	lb.	oz.	pw.	gr.	oz.	pw	gr.
1 Wt.	4	5	12 10	14	6	10	11	204	10	14
2	5	4	16 17	24	10	11	12	96	7	17
3	3	11	19 20	21	6	4	17	100	11	12
4	4	6	7 12	22	10	12	14	56	16	20
5	5	1	11 12	16	11	12	13	212	10	23
6	4	11	12 13	22	7	6	17	96	19	12
	28	6	0 12	123	4	18	12	767	17	2

C

HOW TO PROVE ADDITION.

IN all examples of *Addition*, whether of simple Numbers, that is, Numbers of one Denomination ; or in Examples compound, that is of divers Denominations, as *Pounds, Shillings, Pence, Farthings*, &c. the readiest Method of Proof is to cast the same downwards, beginning at the Top as you did the same upwards, beginning at the bottom, and if that is the same the Work is right. I might here give Examples of other kinds of *Addition*, as *Apothecaries Weight, Cloth, Liquid, Dry and Long Measure, Time*, &c. but this Method serves for any of them, having respect to the Tables that belong to those several Denominations, as follow, viz.

A Table of the Parts of Apothecaries Weight.

20 Grains 1 Scruple	Ɵ a Scruple
3 Scruples 1 Dram	ʒ a Dram
8 Drams 1 Ounce	℥ an Ounce
12 Ounces 1 Pound	℔ a Pound

By these Weights Apothecaries compound their Medicines, but they buy and sell by *Avoirdupois* Weight.

Note. Physicians make use of the following Characters :

℞ - Recipe, take   gutt. a Drop.

ana. { of each ingredient an equal quantity.

℔ - a Pound.

℥ - an Ounce.

ʒ - a Dram.

Ɵ - a Scruple.

gr. - a Grain.

Cochl. { a Spoonful, or half an Ounce of Syrups, or three Drams of distilled Waters.

P { Such a Quantity as may be taken between the Thumb and two fore Fingers.

M. - a Handful.

Cong. a Gallon.

Ss. - Half.

Q. s. a sufficient Quantity.

Q. l. as much as you please.

S. a. { According to the Rules of Art.

Cloth Measure.

4 Nails, or 9 Inches,	1 qr. of a Yard.
4 qrs. or 36 Inches,	1 Yard.
5 qrs or 45 Inches,	1 Ell Wide.
6 qrs. or 27 Inches,	1 Ell Flemish.
6 qss. or 54 Inches,	1 Ell French.

A Table of Wool Weight.

Note, 7lb. make 1 Clove ; 2 Cloves, or 14lb. 1 Stone ; 2 Stones, or 28lb. 1 Todd ; 6 Todd and ½ 1 Wey or 182lb. 2 Weys, or 364lb. 1 Sack ; and 12 Sacks 1 Last, or 4368lb. 240lb. 1 Pack of Wool.   *Note.*

Note. That 1*lb.* 2*oz.* 12*pw. Troy.* is equal to a Pound *Avoirdupois;* and a Pound *Troy* is about 13*oz.* 2 *Drams* and a half *Avoirdupois.*

		l.	*s.*	*d.*
A Pound weight *Troy* } of Silver is worth	{	3	2	2
A Pound wt. *Avoirdupois,* }	{	4	15	8

100*l.*	in Gold	weighs	1 11 ¾	Avoi. *Wt.*
	in Silver		26 04	

A Pound *Avoirdupois* is heavier than a Pound *Troy;* but an Ounce *Troy* is heavier than an Ounce *Avoirdupois:* i. e. 144*lb. Avoirdupois* are equal to 175 Pounds *Troy;* but 175 Ounces *Troy* are equal to 192 Ounces *Avoirdupois.*

A Table of Liquid Measure.

Liquid Measure is of two sorts, viz. one for *Wine, Brandy,* &c. and the other for *Beer and Ale.*

Wine, &c.

2 Pints 1 Quart,	84 Gallons 1 Puncheon,
4 Quarts 1 Gallon,	2 Hogsheads 1 Pipe or Butt,
42 Gallons 1 Tierce,	2 Pipes or Butts 1 Tun, or
63 Gallons 1 Hogshead,	252 Gallons.

Salad-Oil hath 236 Gallons to the Tun; but Oil from Greenland hath 252 Gallons to the Tun.

The Wine Gallon contains 231 Cubic or solid Inches, by which all Liquids are measured, except Beer and Ale.

Beer Measure.

2 Pints 1 Quart,	2 Kilderkins 1 Barrel, or 36
4 Quarts 1 Gallon,	Gallons,
9 Gallons 1 Firkin,	1 Barrel and half, or 54 Gal-
18 Gallons 1 Kilderkin,	lons, 1 Hogshead.

Ale Measure.

2 Pints 1 Quart,	2 Kilderkins 1 Barrel, or 32
4 Quarts 1 Gallon,	Gallons,
8 Gallons 1 Firkin of Ale,	1 Barrel and half, or 48 Gal-
2 Firkins 1 Kilderkin,	lons 1 Hogshead.

The Beer and Ale Gallon are the same, viz. 282 solid Inches, but with this Difference, *i. e.* the Barrel of Beer contains 4 Gallons more than the Barrel of Ale.

Dry Measure.

2 Pints 1 Quart,	5 Quarters 1 Wey,
2 Quarts 1 Pottle,	2 Weys 1 Last,
2 Pottles 1 Gallon,	36 Bushels of Sea Coal 1 Chal-
2 Gallons 1 Peck,	dron; and 21 Chaldron is
4 Pecks 1 Bushel Land-	accounted a Score in the
Measure,	River *Thames.*
8 Bushels 1 Quarter	

The

The Chaldron of Coals at London contains 36 heaped Winchester Bushels, and weighs about 28 and a half cwt. according to the Quality of the Coals. A Newcastle Chaldron weighs 53 cwt. and 8 chaldron, or 21 tons 4 cwt. make a keel.. A ship-load contains 80 keels, or 160 Chaldrons.

Long Measure.

3 Barley Corns 1 Inch	5 Yards and a Half 1 Pole,
4 Inches 1 Hand. Used in	Perch, or Rod,
measuring Horses.	6 Feet 1 Fathom, or 2 Yds.
12 Inches 1 Foot	40 Poles, or 220 Yds. 1 Fur.
3 Feet 1 Yard '	8 Furlongs 1 Mile, or 1760
3 Feet 9 Inches 1 Ell Eng.	Yards
5. Feet a Geometrical Pace	3 Miles 1 League.

Land Measure.

144 Square Inches make	1 Square Foot.
9 Square Feet	1 Square Yard.
30¼ Yards	1 Square Pole or Perch.
40 Perches	1 Rood or Quarter of an Acre.
160 Poles in Length, and	1 in Breadth is 1 Acre.
80 Poles in Length, and	2 in Breadth, 1 Acre.
40 Poles in Length, and	4 in Breadth, 1 Acre.
4 Poles in Length make	1 Chain, or 22 Yards.
16 Perches	1 Square Chain, and
10 Chains in Length, and	1 in Breadth, make 1 Acre.

Time.

60 Seconds 1 Minute	4 Weeks 1 Month
60 Minutes 1 Hour	13 Months, 1 Day, and 6
24 Hours 1 natural Day	Hours, 1 Solar Year.
7 Days 1 Week.	

The common Day begins with us at 12 o'clock at Night: the Astronomical Day begins at 12 o'clock at Noon.

The Solar Year is divided into 12 Calendar Months, which contains 365 Days, as in the following Verse :

Thirty days have September, April, June, *and* November, February *hath* 28 *alone, and all the rest have Thirty-one.*

Note. Leap Year, which happens every fourth Year, consists of 366 Days, on this occasion February contains 29 Days.

SUBSTRACTION.

THE next Rule in Arithmetic is *Subtraction,* which teaches to take a lesser Number out of a greater, and shows the Remainder or Difference.

Place

Place the less Number accurately under the greater, draw a line under them, and beginning at the right hand take each Figure in the lower Line from the Figure under which it stands. If the Figure in the lower Line is greater than that in the upper, then, in Numbers of one Denomination, ten must be borrowed and added to the Figure in the upper Line; take the Figure in the lower Line from the Sum, and write down the Remainder, but for every *ten* thus borrowed, *one* must be paid or added to the next Left-hand Figure in the lower Line. *Example:* Suppose Mr. *Andrews* owes to Mr. *Baker* 323*l.* of which Mr. *A—* hath paid to Mr. *B.* the sum of 146*l.* in part, what remains due to Mr. *Baker?* *Answer* 177*l.*

Here the lesser number 146 stands under the greater 323; and to find the Remainder, or Sum remaining due, I say 6 from 3 I cannot, but 6 from 13 (for I borrow 10 and add it to the Figure that stands directly over the Figure 6) and there remains 7; then 1 that I borrowed and 4 is 5, for as I borrowed 10 in the inferior Place, which is equal to *one* in the superior, so I must now pay the same; therefore I say, 5 from 2 I cannot, but 5 from 12 (borrowing 10, and adding it to the Figure 2, as above directed) and there remain 7; then 1 that I borrowed and 1 are 2, from 3, the Figure above it, and there remains 1, and so the Example is done; and by it shown that Mr. *A.* still owes Mr. *B.* 177 Pounds; for a Proof of its Truth, add 177 the Remainder, to 146, the lesser of the two given Numbers, and it will make 323, being the same with the greater Number or Sum of Money first due; and therefore it is a sure Proof of the Truth and Certainty of the Rule.

All Examples in *Subtraction* of Numbers of *one* denomination are performed as above; but, for the better Explanation, admit a great Sheep Master has in all 6904 Sheep, and takes out of them 2490 to dispose of at Market, how many does he leave behind? To know this set them down thus:

From 7904 the greater Number,
Take 2490 the less Number,

Answer 4414

Here I say 0 from 4, and there remains 4; then 9 from nothing (or 0) I cannot; but 9 from 10 (adding 1 to the 0) and there remains 1; and 1 that I borrowed and 4 make 5, and 5 from 9, and there remain 4; and lastly, 2 from 6, and there

C 3.

there remain also 4; so that 4414 are left behind; which put to the Number he takes to Market, makes the Number he had, viz. 6904, and shows the Deduction to be true, and the Answer right.

More Examples for Practice.

	Yards.	Gallons.	l.	Pounds.
From	37009	47200	479652	1479672
Take	19765	31976	292949	97694
Rem.	17244	15224	186703	1381978
Proof	37009	47200	479632	1479672

The distance of Time since any Remarkable Event may be found by subtracting the date thereof from the date of the present year.

Examples.

I.—1810
  1666 the fire of *London.*
Since 144 Years.

II.—1810
  1588 the *Spanish* Invasion.
Since 222 Years.

III.—1810
  1605 Gunpowder Treason.
Since 205 Years.

Subtraction of different Denominations

Here if the Figure or Figures, placed in the lower Line exceed those in the upper, then as many Units must be borrowed, as made a Unit, or one, of the next superior Denomination; and one must be carried to the next left hand Place in the lower Line, as before.

Of Money.

	l.	s.	d.
Due—	9	2	6
Paid—	6	16	4
Balan.	2	6	2

6d. and Mr. C. hath paid Mr. D. in part 6l. 16s. 4d. what remains due to Mr. Day? Answer, there is due to Mr. Day 2l. 6s. 2d.

Suppose Mr. Cape owes Mr. Day, 9l. 2s.

	l.	s.	d.
Sold for	242	16	3¾
Paid in Part.	174	12	6½
Answer	68	3	9¼
Proof	242	16	3¾

Again, Mr. Coy sells to Mr. Joy, Spanish Wool to the Value of 242l. 16s. 3d¾, and pays present money the sum of 174l. 12s. 6d½. What Money remains unpaid from Mr. Joy? Answer, 68l. 3s. 6d¾.

Ia

In the first of these Examples say 4*d.* from 6*d.* and there remains 2*d.* then 16*s.* from 2*s.* I cannot, but borrowing one Integer of the next Denomination, or 1 Pound which is 20*s.* I say 16 from 20 and there remains 4, and adding thereto the Number 2 it makes 6; wherefore I put down 6 in the Place of Shillings, and say, 1 that I borrowed and 6 is 7; now 7*l.* from 9*l.* and there remains 2*l.* so the Money due to Mr. *Day* is 2*l.* 6*s.* 2*d.* as in the Example.

In the second Example I say 2 Farthings or ½ from 3 Farthings, and there remains 1 or ¼, which I set down in its Place, viz. under the Farthings; then 6 from 3 I cannot, but 6 from 15, (I borrow 1*s.* or 12*d.* to make it 15*d.*) and there remains 9*d.* which I place under the Line of Pence; then 1*s.* that I borrowed and 12 is 13; 13*s.* from 16*s.* there remains 3, which I set down under its own Rank; then 4 from 2 I cannot, but 4 from 12, (borrowing 10) and there is 8; then 1 that I borrowed and 7 makes 8; 8 from 4 I cannot but 8 from 14, there remains 6; so that the Sum due is 68*l.* 3*s.* 9*d*¾. For its proof add the remainder 68*l.* 3*s.* 9*d*¾. to the lesser Sum, 174*l.* 12*s.* 6*d*½. it makes 242*l.* 16*s.* 3*d*¼. the Sum first due, and is a proof of the work being right.

More Examples for Practice.

	l.	*s.*	*d.*	*l.*	*s.*	*d.*	*l.*	*s.*	*d.*
Due	174	16	6¼	74	10	4	2471	7	0
Paid	97	12	4¾	29	12	9	1976	16	6¼
Remain	77	4	1½	44	17	7	494	10	5¾
Proof.	174	16	6¼	74	10	4	2471	7	0

	l.	*s.*	*d.*	*l.*	*s.*	*d.*	*l.*	*s.*	*d.*
1st. Due	74	0	0	274	16	6	796	0	0
Paid	46	12	10	197	19	4	279	11	7
Balance	27	7	2	76	17	2	516	8	5
Proof	74	0	0	274	16	6	796	0	0

Owing 353*l.*

Sometimes a Sum owing may be paid at several times,— then the several payments must be added together, then add their total and deduct it from the Sum first due, as in the following examples.

Paid at *different times*
{ 60
41
84
70
76 }

Paid in all 331 *deduct*
Remains due 22
Proof 353

	£	s.	d.		£	s.	d.
More due -	249	12	0	*Received*	100	10	0
Received at several times	24	12	6	*Paid to several Persons*	5	15	0
	18	14	6		16	0	0
	20	2	0		5	12	6
	16	16	6		9	10	0
	13	0	0		6	8	4
	23	12	6		23	13	2
Received in all	106	12	0	*Paid in all*	66	19	0
Remains due	143	0	0	*Cash in Hand*	33	11	0
Proof	£249	12	0		£100	10	0

Avoirdupoise Weight. (See Table, p. 54.)

	10 Tons.	20 C.	4 qrs.	28 lb.	10 C.	4 qrs.	28 lb.	10 lb.	16 oz.	16 dr.
From	44	12	1	10	246	2	12	146	2	10
Take	39	14	2	6	164	3	22	97	10	12
Remain	4	17	3	4	81	2	8	48	7	14
Proof	44	12	1	10	246	2	12	146	2	10

Troy Weight. (See Table, p. 55.)

	10 lb.	12 oz.	22 pwt.	24 gr.	10 oz.	20 pwt.	24 gr.
From	462	4	10	11	1247	10	13
Take	196	9	6	16	976	16	17
Remain	265	7	3	19	270	13	20
Proof	462	4	10	11	1247	10	13

This Method of Subtraction will serve for any Denomination whatever, having respect to the several Tables of Quantity in Addition.

MULTIPLICATION.

Multiplication is a compendious Method of performing Addition, and teaches to find what a given Number will amount to when repeated a certain number of Times.

It serves likewise to bring great Denominations into small, as Pounds into Shillings, Pence, or Farthings; and having the Length and Breadth of a plain Surface, we find its Contents in superficial or square Measure.

By *Multiplication*. having the Value of one Thing, or the Wages of one Person, we find the value of many such things, or the Wages of many such Persons.

In

In *Multiplication* we are particularly to take notice of these three terms, viz. the *multiplicand,* the *multiplier,* and the *prod ct.*

1. The *Multiplicand* (generally the greater of the two numbers) is the number to be multiplied.

2. The *Multiplier* is the number by which the former is to be multiplied.

3. The *product* is the result or answer. The *multiplier* and *multiplicand* are collectively called *factors.*

But, before we enter upon this Rule, it is necessary to have the following Table perfectly by heart.

The Multiplication Table.

1	2	3	4	5	6	7	8	9	10	11	12
2	4	6	8	10	12	14	16	18	20	22	24
3	6	9	12	15	18	21	24	27	30	33	36
4	8	12	16	20	24	28	32	36	40	44	48
5	10	15	20	25	30	35	40	45	50	55	60
6	12	18	24	30	36	42	48	54	60	66	72
7	14	21	28	35	42	49	56	63	70	77	84
8	16	24	32	40	48	56	64	72	80	88	96
9	18	27	36	45	54	63	72	81	90	99	108
10	20	30	40	50	60	70	80	90	100	110	120
11	22	33	44	55	66	77	88	99	110	121	132
12	24	36	48	60	72	84	96	108	120	132	144

This table is so plain and easy, that there is scarcely need of direction; for the product of any two figures will be found in that square, which is on a line with the one, and under the other: thus 54 the product of 6 times 9 will be found on a line wi h 6, and under 9; or in a line with 9, and under 6; so 7 times 8 is 56, and 8 times 7 is 56, &c.

and thus the table ought to be got by heart for the more dexterous readiness in multiplying.

Now for the Application.

Example 1. How many is 3 times 472? Which being set down in the margin; I say, 3 times 2 is 6, which place under 3 the multiplier; then 3 times 7 is 21, set down 1 under 7, and carry 2 for the two tens, as in *Addition of one Denomination*, then 3 times 4 is 12, and 2 carried is 14; which set down, and the product is 1416 : that is 3 times 472 make so much : which may be proved by *Addition*, by setting down 472 three times in additional order, and casting it up, which shows that this rule performs compendiously the office of addition.

```
472
  3
——
1416
——
```

Example 2. Again, how many are produced by multiplying 742 by 4?

742 *Multiplicand*
  4 *Multiplier.*
——
2968

Here I say 4 times 2 is 8, and 4 times 4 is 16; 6 and carry 1; and 4 times 7 is 28, and 1 is 29, which set down; so the whole product is 2968, as appears by the work.

More examples of one figure in the *Multiplier* are these :

Multiplic.	7420	4444	7460	90704	56789
Multiplier.	5	6	7	8	9
Product	37100	26664	52220	725632	511101

Compound Multiplication,

Is when the *multiplier* consists of two, three, or more figures or ciphers.

And here you must begin with that figure which is in the place of units of the *multiplier*, and go through the whole *multiplicand*, by multiplying each figure of it first by the said unit figure, then by the next, namely, by the figure in the place of tens of the *multiplier*; then with the the third, &c. to the last; always remembering to place the first figure of every product or line exactly and perpendicularly under the figure you multiply by; and then add the several lines or products together, which so collected give the total product required, as in the examples following, *viz.*

Example.

Example 1.

How many are 23 times 7426? First, I begin
with the unit figure 3 in the multiplier, saying, 3
times 6 is, 18; 8 (which I set directly under 3, by
which I multiply) and carry 1; then 3 times 2 is
6, and one is 7; then 3 times 4 is 12; 2 and
carry 1; then 3 times 7 is 21, and 1 is 22; and
so I have done with the first figure of the *Multi-*
plier, viz. 3. Then I go to the next, that is 2, and
twice 6 is 12; 2 and carry 1 (which 2 is placed. in a direct line under 2 the multiplying figure) then twice 2 is 4,
and 1 is 5; then twice 4 is 8; and lastly, twice 7 is 14,
which I set down; then I add the two products together,
saying 8 is 8, 2 and 7 are 9, &c. and the total is the true
product or result of the multiplication, *viz.* 170798. Again,

```
          7426
            23
        ------
         22278
         14852
        ------
        170798
```

Ex. 2. What is the product of——————527527

Multiply by　　285

It will be prolix and unnecessary to give
more verbal directions; and therefore the
learner is referred to the observations of
the example, as also to those two that follow, *viz.*

```
Multiply by    285
       --------
        2637635
        4220216
        1055054
       --------
      150345195
```

```
      527535                 275827
       15728                  19725
    ----------              ---------
     4220280                1379135
     1055070                 551654
     3692745                1930789
     2637675                2482443
      527535                 275827
    ----------             ----------
   8297070480             5440687575
```

When ciphers are intermixed with figures in the *multi-*
plier, then multiply the figures as above; and when you
come to a cipher in the *multiplier,* then set down another
cipher exactly and perpendicularly under it, then begin the
multiplicand again with the next figure to the cipher in the
multiplier, and go through it in the same line, placing the
first figure of that product next the cipher towards the left
hand, but then care must be taken that the next figure or
cipher of the next line must be set down one degree farther
towards the left hand, and not immediately under the last
figure

figure set down to the cipher; as in the following examples may be fully understood.

24893	784371	327586
402	23604	6030
48786	3137484	9827580
975720	47062260	19655160
	2353113	
9805986	1568742	1975343580
	18514293084	

When you have a cipher or ciphers in the *multiplier*, at the beginning towards the right-hand, then set it, or them, backward from the place of units towards the right hand; and when you have multiplied by the figure or figures, annex the cipher or ciphers.

As in these Examples.

4762	47962	4632
70	400	2600
333340	19184800	27792
		9264
		12043200

If you have ciphers both in the *multiplicand* and *multiplier*, then neglect the ciphers in both, and multiply by the figures, and annex the ciphers at last.

As in these Examples.

42600	42300	376400
220	42000	2400
852	846	15056
852	423	7528
9372000	507600000	903360000

When you are to multiply by 10, 100, 1000, or 10,000, it is only adding or annexing so many ciphers to the *multiplicand*, that is, either 1, 2, 3, or 4 ciphers, and the work is done. *Example.* Suppose I am to multiply 375 by the numbers above; if I multiply it by 10, then I join 0 to 375, and it makes, or the product is, 3750; if by 100, then I annex 00, and it makes 37500; if by 1000, I put to it 000, and it produces 375000; and lastly, if by 10,000 I then add 0000, and it makes 3750000, &c. And thus may any number be multiplied when the *multiplier* consists of a
unit

with with any number of ciphers, and done by inspection only, without any formal setting down the *multiplicand* with a line drawn under it, &c.

Our next business will be to show the use of *multiplication* in real life, and how to apply it on proper occasions, *viz.*

1. Suppose you want to know how many half crowns there are in 246*l.* you know that 8 half-crowns make 1*l.* wherefore set them down thus:

$$246l.$$

Multiply by   8

Answer   1968

Again, in 1968 half-crowns, how many pence?

30

59040

And this serves to show, that great denominations are brought into smaller by this rule, according to the definition, p. 54.

2. Admit that you want to know the square contents of a large table, 34 feet long, and 4 feet wide, multiply 34 the length by 4 the breadth, and the answer will be 136 square feet for the true contents of such a table. And this agrees with another definition of this rule.

3. If I know the value of a yard of broad cloth to be 12 shillings, what is the value of 220 yards of the said cloth in shillings?

220

Multiply by   12

440

220

2640 shillings, or 132 pounds.

If the wages of 1 seaman be 23 shillings a month, what is the wages of 250 seamen for the same time?

Multiply by   23

750

500

Answer,   5750 shillings, or 287*l.* 10*s.*

And these two examples accord with the other definition, or use of this rule.

I shall in the next place, say something concerning
                        multiplica

multiplication of Money, and a little of its use, and so conclude this rule.

Multiplication of Money.

Multiplication of money has a great affinity to *addition
of money;* the same method being taken in carrying from
one denomination to the next, *viz.* from farthings to pence,
from pence to shillings, and from shillings to pounds.—And
as in *Addition,* and other *Multiplications,* you begin at the
right hand, and proceed towards the left, so here you begin
at the least denomination, which is also at the right hand.

This method of accompting is the most apt and expedi-
tious of all others, for small quantities, and therefore extremely necessary in making bills of parcels, &c. and is,
beyond all contradiction, as sure and certain as any way
whatsoever.

The general Rule,

Is always to multiply the price by the quantity.

The first step is, for quantities from 2 to 12; and this is
done by one multiplier, as in the examples following:

Example 1.

	l.	*s.*	*d.*
Multiply ———————————————	7	12	6
(or 6 pieces of cloth at 7l. 12s. 6d. *per* piece) by			6
	45	15	0

Here I say 6 times 6 is 36 pence, which is just 3s. I
set down 0 in the place of pence, and carry 3s. to the place
of shillings, (exactly the same as in *Addition of Money)*
then 6 times 12 is 72, and 3 is 75s. or 3l. 15s. wherefore I
set down 15 in the place of shillings, and carry three to the
pounds; then 6 times 7 is 42, and 3 is 45l. So the whole
amount of the pieces of cloth, at 7l. 12s. 6d. *per* piece, is
45l. 15s.

Example 2.

Again, How much is 9 times 13s. 4d. or what is the
amount of 9 marks.

In this example I say, 9
times 4 is 36d. or 3s. I set **6 0 0**
down 0, and carry 3; then
9 times 13 is 117, and 3 makes 120; but 120 shillings
make just 6l. and so much is the value of 9 marks.

Example

Example 3.

Once more: What is the value of 12 gallons of wine at
5*s.* 4*d. per* gallon?

	s.	*d.*
	5	4
	12	

Here I say 12 times 4 is 48 ; 0 and
carry 4 ; then 12 times 5 is 60, and 4
is 64*s.* or 3*l.* 4*s. &c.*

3	4	0

The next degree of reckoning is of quantities exceeding
12, even to 12 times 12, or 144 ; all which, as far as
144, are found in the *Table of Multiplication,* which is a
ready help to all purposes of reckoning; and that you may
proceed with dexterity, you must be very ready in the said
table, that you may immediately see what component parts
suit the quantity proposed, or is pretty near it, and then
work accordingly.

If the quantity be 15 yards, I readily know that 3 times 5
is 15; and therefore 3 and 5, or 5 and 3, are to be my
multiplier: If the quantity were 21, then 3 and 7, or 7
and 3, would be multipliers; if 30, then 5 and 6, or 6 and
5 ; also 3 and 10, or 10 and 3; if 45, 48, 56. 66, 72, 96,
&c. were the quantities, then 5 and 9, 6 and 8, 7 and 8, 6
and 11, 6 and 12, and 8 and 12, *&c.* are to be my multipliers, and exactly hit the several quantities of which they
are component parts ; and examples of this kind have two
multiplications for their solution.

I shall now show some examples of regular quantities
that exceed 12, and are precisely answered at two multiplications, such as mentioned above, *viz.*

	s.	*d.*
What comes 15 yards of muslin to, at	3	5
per yard ?	3	

Here 3 times 5 is 15*d.* or 1*s.* and 3*d.*

3 and carry 1*s.* then 3 times 3 is 9, and 1	10	3
is 10*s.* so the first product is 10*s.* and 3*d.*	5	

which multiply by 5 saying, 5 times 3 is
15*d.* or 1*s.* and 3*d.* 3 and carry 1 ; then

	2	11	3

5 times 10 is 50, and 1 is 51*s.* or 2*l.* 11*s.*

So the amount of 15 yards, at 3*s.* 5*d. per* yard, is 2*l.* 11*s.*
3*d.* And demonstrable thus, *viz.* If 10*s.* 3*d.* be the value
of 3 times 3*s.* and 5*d.* then 5 times the value of 10*s.* 3*d.*
must of necessity be 15 times the value of 3*s.* 3*d.* because
5 times 3 is 15 : And its truth may be proved by *Addition*
and

and *Multiplication*, thus: set down 3s. 5d. three times, in Additional order, and put the three lines together, and the total of them multiply by 5, as before, and the answer will be the same. Or set down 17s. 1d. (the product of 3s. 5d. multiplied by 5) three times also, and add them together, and the total will be exactly the same with the result of multiplication: as in the following specimens of work.

(1)	(2)	(3)
s. d.	s. d.	s. d.
3—5	3—5	17—1
3—5	5	17—1
3—5		17—1
10—3	17—1	2—11—3
5		
2—11—3		

Here the first of these two proofs is worked by *addition* and *multiplication*, and the second by *multiplication and addition.* Also,

By this we see, that in all examples under this head we are to pitch on two numbers (for *multipliers*) in the table, which multiplied together make the quantity proposed; and then we are to multiply the price by one of the numbers (it matters not by which first) and then that product is to be multiplied by the other number, and the second or last product will be the answer.

Example 2.

Again, what is the value of 21 gallons of brandy ?

s. d.

at   7—9 *per Gallon*:
     7 and 3

2—14—3
     3

8— 2—9

In this example I say 3 times 7 is 63d. or 5s. 3d. I set down 3 and carry 5, then 7 times 7 is 49, and 5 is 54s. or 2l. 14s. So the first product is 2l. 14s. 3d. which I multiply by 3, and that produces the last product or answer, viz. 8l. 2s. 9d.

Now follow a few more examples of this sort, without any verbal directions, because I think those already given to be sufficient.

Example.

Example 3.
What is the value of 30 ells
Holland   s.   d.

at   3   3 7 per ell.
    5 10 and 3

    1 15 10
         3

Ans. 5   7   6

Example 4.
56 bushels of wheat,
         s.   d,

at   4   9
         7 and 8

1 13   3
         8

Ans. 13   6   0

Example 5.
46 pounds of raw silk
at 15s. 6d. per lb.
      5 and 9

3 17   6
        9

An. 34 17   6

Example 6.
72 broad pieces   s.   d.
      at 13   6 each
         12 and 0

14   2   0
        6

84 12   0

Example 7:
108 lbs. of indigo, Lahore,
at 7s. 8d.
     9 and 12

    3   9   0
         12

An. 41   8   0

Example 8.
81 lbs. of tea.
        s.   d.

at   7   9
         9

    3   9   9
        9 and 9

Ans. 31   7   9

Example 9.
96 Cwt. of Currants, at............ £2 13   6 per cwt.
                                    8 and 12

                                  21   8   0
                                      12

Answer 256 16   0.

The next step is of quantities, or numbers that are not to
be answered precisely at two multiplications: In this case,
you will have an addition of one line more, occasiond by
bring ng down the price of one to be added to the last product; or else a line more made by multiplying the price by
what is defective or wanting in the number by two multiplications, to make up the proposed quantity complete; as
                                               it

it may be of 2, 3, 4, 5, &c. as by the subsequent examples may be seen and understood.

Example 1. What is the product of 2*l*. 13*s*. 6*d*. multiplied by 39 ?

£ 2 13   6
            6 and 6
   16   1   0
               6
   ─────────
   96   6   0
    8   0   6
   ─────────
  104   6   6

Here I find that 6 multiplied by 6, makes 36; which is within 3 of the quantity proposed; wherefore I multiply by 6, and that product again by the other 6; the last product is 96*l*. 6*s*. which is the value of 36; but we want to know the value of 39; wherefore I multiply the price of one, viz. 2*l*. 13*s*. 6*d*. by 3 to make up 36 to 39, saying 3 times 6 is 18*d*. &*c*. And finding that 3 times 2*l*. 13*s*. 6*d*. is 8*l*. 0*s*. 6*d*. which added to 96*l*. 6*s*. 0*d*. the total gives the complete value of 39; for 36 and 3 make 39.

Ex. 2. What comes 79 cwt. of cheese to at 28*s. per* cwt.

l.   s.   d.
  1   8   0
              7 and 11
  ─────────
  9   16   0
             11
  ─────────
107   16   0
  2   16   0
  ─────────
110   12   0 *Ans.*

In this example I say, 7 times 0 is 0; then 7 times 8 is 56; which is 2*l*. 16*s*. set down 16, and carry 2; then 7 times 1 is 7, and 2 carried make 9. So the first product is 9*l*. 16*s*. 0*d*. which multiplied by 11, produces 107*l*. 16*s*. 0*d*. or the value of 77 cwt. then for the 2 wanting, I multiply the price by it, and that gives 2*l*. 16*s*. 0*d*. which added to 107*l*. 16*s*. 0*d*. makes the whole value of 79, viz. 110*l*. 12*s*. 0*d*. as in the work.

Ex. 3. 112 pounds of sugar at 5½ *per lb*. set down thus :

s.   d.
    5½ per pound
   10 and 10
  ─────────
  4 . 7
   10
  ─────────
  2   5   10
       5   6 the product of 5½*d*. by 12 defective.
  ─────────
  2   11   4 the Answer.   Here

Here, after I have multiplied by 10 and 10, the parts of 100, there want 12; wherefore I multiply $5\frac{1}{2}d$. by 12, and it gives 5s. 6d. for 12lb. at $5\frac{1}{2}d$. which added to 2l. 5s. 10d. the value of 100, makes 2l. 11s. 4d. the true value of 112lb. at $5\frac{1}{2}d$. per pound.

Ex. 4. 64 stone of beef at 22d. or 1s. 10d. *per* stone.

1s. 10d.

10 and 9

18	4
	9
	10

8	5	0
	7	4

8 12 4 *Answer.*

Here what is wanting after the two multiplications is 4; wherefore I multiply 1s. 10d. (the price) by 4, which produces 7s. 4d. to be added, &c.

Ex. 5. 97 cwt. $\frac{1}{2}$ *raisins,*

l.	s.	d.
at 1	5	6 *per cwt.*

9 and 10

11	9	6
		10

114	15	0
8	18	6 for the $\frac{1}{2}$ C.
	12	9

124 6 3

After I have multiplied by 9 and 10, I multiply the price, 25s. 6d. by the quantity wanting, and it produces 8l. 18s. 6d. then for the half cwt. I take half of the price, which is 12s. 9d. and then collect the three lines, the total of which is 124l. 6s. 3d. for the answer.

From the last example it may be observed, that there is no need of much solicitude about coming so very near by two multiplications, for there 7 is wanting to make up the true quantity; nay, if the two multiplications be short by 10 or 11, it is near enough; for it is as easy to multiply the price by 10 or 11, as by 2 or 3, and the addition is the same.

Example 6. Once more: What comes 110 cwt. $\frac{1}{4}$ of hops to, at 4l. 10s. *per cwt.*?

After.

l.	s.	d.
4	10	6
	10 and 10	

After having multiplied by 10 and 10, which makes 100, I multiply the price 4*l.* 10*s.* 6*d.* by 10, that is wanting, which gives the same with the first product, viz. 45*l.* 5*s.* 0*d.* which stands under the product by 100; and for the ¾ of a cwt. I take ¾ of the price, viz. first the half, and then the half of that half, that is 2*l.* 5*s.* 3*d.* and 1*l.* 2*s.* 7½*d*; which four lines added together make 501*l.* 2*s.* 10½*d.* for the answer.

45	5	0
	10	

452	10	0
45	5	0
3	5	3
1	2	7½

501	2	10½ Ans.

To prove Multiplication.

Whether of simple numbers, or of money, it is most surely done by *Division*; but before that is known, take this method, viz. As you multiply the *multiplicand* by the *multiplier*, so contrariwise multiply the *multiplier* by the *multiplicand*; and if the products are alike, the work is right; or otherwise one of them is wrong, and must be gone over again till they both agree.

Example 1.

365 days in a year.
24 hours in a day.

1460
730

8760 hours in a year.

Here (reversely) I say, 5 times 4 is 20; 0 and carry 2; 6 times 4 is 24, and 2 is 26; 6 and carry 2; and 3 times 4 is 12 and 2 is 14. Then 5 times 2 is 10; 0 and carry 1; 6 times 2 is 12; and 1 is 13; 3 and carry 1; and 3 times 2 is 6, and 1 is 7, which products added together make 8760, the hours in a year, without taking in the odd 6 hours which the year consists of, more than 365 days.

Example

Example.

56 gallons of spirits   I say here, twice 7 is 14; 2 and
at   *s.*   *d.*   carry 1*s.* and 3 times 7 is 21, and 1
   3   2 per gallon.   is 22*s.* or 1*l.* 2*s.* Again, twice 8
     7 and 8   is sixteen, 4 and carry 1*s.* and twice
    ——————   8 is sixteen, and 1 is 17, 17 and car-
   1   2   2   ry 0; and once 8 is 8*l.* Thus both
     8   these examples are the same in con-
  ——————   sequence as if you proceeded in the
  8 17 4 Ans.

common and regular method of Multiplication, and shows
the truth of the operation.

DIVISION.

THIS Rule, though accounted the hardest lesson in
Arithmetic, may be made easy and intelligible to the meanest capacity.

The use of this rule is to know how many times one number or sum is contained in another, as if it were asked how
often is 9 contained in 54? the answer is 6 times; or how
many times 12 is there in 144? Answer, 12 times

As by *Multiplication* great denominations are brought
into small, so contrarily by *Division* small denominations
are brought into greater; as farthings (from one gradation
to another) into pounds, pounds weight into tons, and gallons liquid into hogsheads, &c.

In this rule we are to take particular notice of the three
following terms, viz.

1 ⎫   ⎧ *Dividend,* or number to be divided.
2 ⎬ The ⎨ *Divisor,* or number by which we divide.
3. ⎭   ⎩ *Quotient,* or answer to the work; which shows
how often the divisor is contained in the dividend.

4. The *Remainder;* which is an uncertain branch of this
rule, because there is sometimes a remainder, and sometimes not. The remainder is always of the same name with
the dividend, and is less than the divisor, for if it be greater
than, or equal to, the divisor, the work is wrong.

To divide any number of one denomination by a number
not exceeding 12.

Rule—Write the divisor on the left hand side of the dividend, making a curve line, thus), between them, and find
how many times it is contained in a certain number of figures of the dividend, and place the result below.

Multiply the divisor by the quotient figure, subtract the
product from that part of the dividend, and carry the re-
                                   mainder

mainder, if any, as so many *tens* to the next figure of the dividend.

Then find how many times the divisor is contained in that number; place the result in the quotient, multiply the divisor, subtract the product, and carry the remainder, as so many *tens*, to the subsequent figure of the dividend. Divide again this number, as before, and so on, to the end of the dividend.

If the divisor consist of a number not greater then 12' and the dividend of a number not higher than 144, the answer is gained at once by the multiplication table; thus if 63 is to be divided by 9; the answer will be 7 times. Here 63 is the dividend, 9 the divisor, and 7 the quotient; and the operation will stand thus: 9)63

$$\overline{\qquad 7}$$

If 78 is to be divided by 9, the operation will be   9)78
Here the answer is 8, and 6 is the remainder, be- $\overline{8-6}$
cause in 78 there are eight nines and 6 over.

The general method of proving the truth of division is this " multiply the answer by the divisor, and take in the remainder, if any, and the result will be equal to the dividend, when the operation is right."—The following examples illustrate the foregoing rules.

	4)78906	5)34567	2)29702
Quotient	19726--2	6913--2	4950--2
	4	5	6
Proof	78906	34567	29702

In the first of these examples I say, the 4's in 7 once, and there remain 3, which considered as tens, and placed before 8, the next figure in the dividend, make 38; then the 4's in 38, 9 times; 9 times 4 is 36; 36 from 38, there remains 2; or two tens, which carried to the 9, the next figure in the dividend, make 29; then the 4's in 29, 7 times; 7 times 4 is 28: 28 from 29, there rests 1; which makes the 0, the next of the dividend, 10, and the 4's in 10 twice; twice 4 is 8; 8 from 10, there remains 2; which make 6, the last figure of the dividend, 26; lastly, the 4's in 26, 6 times, and 6 times 4 is 24; 24 from 26, leaves 2 the remainder: and so for the other two examples. And for proof of the work multiply the quotient by the divisor, and take in the remainder in the place

of

of units; and if the product be the same with the dividend, the dividend is right; for I say, 4 times 6 is 24, and 2 the remainder, make 26; 6 and carry 2, &c.

More Examples.

	3)54321	7)279060	9)234567
Quotient	18107	39865	26063
	3	7	9
Proof	54321	279060	234567

	8) 5987654	11) 9578651	12)8955674
Quotient	748456--6	870786--5	746306-2
	8	11	12
Proof	5987654	9578651	8955674

	11)72646206	12)76677240
Quotient	6604200—6	6389770
	11	12
Proof	72646206	76677240

	11)47627000	12(42007400
Quotient	4329727—3	3500616 - 8
	11	12
Proof	47627000	42007400

By being ready and dexterous in the above examples you may expeditiously divide by these numbers, viz. 110, 120, 1100, 1200, &c. for it is but cutting off, or separating the ciphers from 11 and 12, and cutting off and separating the like number of figures or ciphers from the right hand of the dividend, and then divide the other figures or ciphers towards the left hand, by 11 or 12, as it shall happen; as in the following examples, viz.

Divide 34567 by 110, and 890123 by 120, and 98765 by 1100, and 678901 by 1200.

	11,0)3456,7	12,0)890123
Quotient	314—27	7417—83
	11,00)987,65	12,00)6789,01
Quotient	89—865	565—901

When

When you divide by 10, 100, or 1000, 10000, &c. you have nothing more to do than to cut off, or separate so many figures or ciphers of the dividend towards the right hand, as you have ciphers in the divisor, and those figures toward the left make your quotient; and those cut off toward the right hand the remainder.

Examples.

Divide 123456789 by 10, 100, 1000, 10000
By 10 the Quotient is 12345678, and the Remainder is 9.
By 100 the Quotient is 1234567, and Remainder is 89.
By 1000 the Quotient is 123456, and Remainder is 789.
By 10000 the Quotient is 12345, and Remainder is 6789.

When the divisor consists of several figures, then there arises a little more difficulty in the work; but if the following directions are attended to it is easily overcome; as will be evident from the following example, viz.

Suppose I am to divide 78901 pounds among 32 parishes; or suppose an assessment of so much money was laid on so many parishes; what must each parish pay by an equal proportion towards raising such a supply?

Divisor 32)78901(.... Quotient.

The example thus set out, I begin at the left hand, seeking how often I can take 32 out of 78; or more easily, how many times 3 are in 7, and the answer is 2 times; which I place in the quotient thus 32)78901(2, and then according to the *General Rule*, I multiply the divisor 32, by the 2 placed in the quotient, saying, twice 2 is 4, and twice 3 is 6; so there is 64 to be taken out of 78, which should stand thus:

$$32)78901(2$$
$$\underline{461 \cdot}$$
$$14$$

Then I make a point under 9, the third figure of the dividend, and bring it down to the remainder 14, and then the work appears thus:

$$32)78901(2$$
$$\underline{64 \cdot}$$
$$149$$

Then I seek again, asking how many times 32 in 149, which is not readily to be answered; but how many times 3, the first figure of the divisor, is there in 14, the two first figures of the dividual 149, and the answer is 4 times; wherefore

wherefore, after placing 4 in the quotient, I multiply (as directed in the *General Rule*) the divisor 32 by the said 4, saying 4 times 2 is 8, placing it under 9 in the dividual; then 4 times 3 is 12, which set down under 14 ; so there is 128 to be taken out of 149, and then the work appears thus ;

```
32)78901(24
   64..
   ---
   149
   128
   ---
   210
```

And after subtraction there remains 21 ; then I make a point under 0 in the dividend and bring it down to the right of the remainder 21, and then there is 210 for a new dividend; then I seek again, saying, how many times 32, the divisor, is therein 210 ? Or easier, how many times 3 in 21 ? But observe, That whenever you have a place more in the dividend than in the divisor, then always try how often you can take the first figure of the divisor out of the two first of the dividend, and the answer is 7 times ; but it will not bear 7 times, for 7 times 32 is 224, and you cannot take 224 out of 210; or rather you cannot take 22 out of 21 ; wherefore try in your mind before you set down the answer, or figure of the quotient, whether it will go to the number of times as is most easily suggested; as here the question or demand is readily answered 7 times; and so many times 3 may be taken in 21 ; but when you come to multiply the whole divisor by the times you place in the quotient, you begin at the right hand; and go towards the left, carrying the tens that arise to the next place, which so increases the product, that sometimes subtraction cannot be made, because the under line is greater than the upper ; wherefore first try in your mind, as has been said ; and since it will not bear 7 times, try if it will go 6 times ; saying, 5 times 2 if 12, 2 and carry 1 ; and 6 times 3 is 18, and 1 is 19; and 19 may be taken out of 21 ; therefore set down 6 in the quotient, next to the 4, and multiply the divisor 32 by it, and the work will stand thus :

```
32)78901(246
   64...
   ---
   149
   128
   ---
   .210
   192
   ---
   181
```

Here the divisor 32, multiplied by 6, gives 192 to be taken out of 210, and the remainder is 18 ; to which, after a point made under it, I bring down the 1, the last figure of the dividend, and then there is 181 for a new dividend; then according to the rule, I seek again how many times 32, the divisor, may be taken out of 181, or how

many

many times 3 in 18, and the ready answer is 6 times: but on the trial I find it will not go 6 times; wherefore I try a quotient figure less by 1, viz. 5 times, and find it will bear it; and setting 5 in the quotient next to the 6, I multiply the divisor 32 by it, and it produces 160; which subtracted from 181, the last remainder is 21, and the quotient or answer is 2465; which shows that 32 is contained in 78901, 2465 times, and 21 over.

```
32)73901(2465
   64
   ---
   149
   128
   ---
   210
   192
   ---
   181
   160
   ---
    21
```

Again, If a nobleman hath 30,000*l. per annum*, what is his daily income?

If you divide 30,000 by 365 (the days in the year) the quotient will be the answer. Set it down for working thus :

$$365)30,000($$

First, seek how many times 365 can be taken in 300 ? (an equal number of places with the divisor) answer 0 times; wherefore I go to a place farther to the right hand in the dividend (for 0 must never begin the quotient, as was said before) and make a point under it, viz. under the last 0 but one, as may be seen in the example; and there being a place more in this dividual than in the divisor, I try how often the first figure of the divisor, viz. 3, is contained in the two first figures or places of the dividend, viz. 30, and the answer is 10 times; but you are never to take above 9 times at once, in any of these examples of division; wherefore try in your mind whether it will bear 9 times, before you set it down in the quotient (as noticed before) saying to yourself, 9 times 5 is 45, 5 and go 4 ; 9 times 6 is 54, and 4 is 58 ; 8 and go 5 ; and 9 times is 27, and 5 is 32 ; now 32 cannot be taken out of 30, wherefore take a figure less by an unit or one, viz. 8 times ; and finding it will go 8 times ; set down 8 in the quotient ; and then say 8 times 5 is 40 ; 0 and carry 4 ; and 8 times 6 is 48, and 4 is 52 ; 2 and carry 5, and 8 times 3 is 24, and 5 is 29 ; and then there is 2920 to be taken from 3000 ; and after subtraction the work will appear thus .

```
365)30000(8
    2920.
    -----
      80
```

Then

Then to the remainder 80 I bring down 0, the last figure of the dividend, and then there is 800 for a new dividual; then you must try how oft you can take 365 out of the said dividual-800, and the number of places being equal in both divisor and dividual, to wit, 3, try how oft 3 in 8; answer 2; so put in the quotient, and say twice 5 is 10, 0 and carry 1; and twice 6 is 12, and 1 is 13; 3 and carry 1; and twice 3 is 6, and 1 is 7; so there is 730 to be deducted from 800, and the remainder is 70, viz.

365)30000(82
2820.
———
800
733
———
(70)

Thus it appears that the nobleman hath eighty-two pounds *per diem*, and 70*l.* over; which, if multiplied by 20, the shillings in a pound, would produce 1400 shillings; and this divided by the divisor, 365, there would come out 3*s.* a day more, and there will be a remainder of 305, which multiplied by 12, the pence in a shilling, produces 3660; which divided still by 365, gives 10*d.* a day more: so 30000*l.* a year is 82*l.* 3*s.* 10*d.* a day.

Once more: divide 46242 gallons by 252, the gallons in a tun, thus set down:

252)46242(183
252..
———
2104
2016
———
882
756
———
(126)

In this example, after inquiry, I find that it will not go twice, therefore I set down 1 in the quotient, and place 252 under 462 of the dividend, and after subtraction the remainder is 210; to which bring down 4 from the dividend, which makes 2104; and then I find it will bear 8 times which put in the quotient, and the divisor 252 multiplied by it, the product is 2016 to be subtracted from 2104; which being done, the remainder is 88; to which 2, the last figure of the dividend, being brought down, there is 882, and then trying again, I find it will go 3 times; and the product of the divisor multiplied by 3, is 756; which subtracted from 882, there remains 126 for the true remainder: So that by this division I find there are 183 tuns in 44262 gallons, and 126 gallons remaining, or over and above, which being half of 252 the divisor, the remainder is half a tun more.

When you have a cipher or ciphers on the right hand of the divisor, in the first, second, or third place, &c. separate such cipher or ciphers, with a dash of the pen,

from

from the rest of the divisor; and also c..t off as many figures or ciphers from the right of the dividend as you cut off ciphers from the divisor, and divide the remaining figures towards the left hand, by the remaining significant figures of the divisor.

Example.

Divide 42952 square poles of land by 1£0, the square poles in an acre of land.

16,0)4295,2(268   Here the cipher is cut off from the di-
   32..   visor, and the 2 from the dividend;
    ———   then I ask how oft 16 in 42; answer
   109   twice; then the 16's in 109, answer 6
    96   times; then the 16's in 135, answer
    ———   8 times. So there are 268 acres, and
   135   almost half on acre in 42952 square
   128   poles.
    ———
   (7)

Divide 27,00)62746,20)2323

   54..   In this example two ciphers a e
   87   separated from the divisor, and
   81   also two places from the divi-
   ——   dend, and then 62746 is divided
   64   only by 27.
   54
   ——
   100
   81
   ——
   25

When the divisor is 3, 4, 5, 6, or more figures, there is a sure and easy way of performing the work truly, by making a table of the divisor; which may be done by addition, or by multiplying the divisor by 2, 3, 4, &c.

Suppose you are to divide 987654321 by 123456.

123456)987654321(8000 times.

987648...

(6321)

Here having noted the number of figures in the divisor, which here is 6, I make a point under the sixth figure, or place of the dividend, whereby 987654 becomes the first dividual.

1	123456
2	246921
3	370308
4	493824
5	617280
6	740736
7	864192
8	98764
9	1111104

The foregoing table is made by doubling the first line, which makes 246912; this added to the first or uppermost line, gives the third line 370368; which also added to the said first line, makes 493824 for the 4th line, or product, and so of the rest : still remembering to add the subsequent line or product to the first or uppermost line, till you come to the last line of 9 times, which is 1111104; the truth of which may be proved by multiplying the first or uppermost line by 2, 3, 4, 5, &c. and if you commit an error by *Addition* it may be found or corrected by *Multiplication*.

The Use of the said Table.

When you have pointed out your number of places in the dividend, ca t your eye on the table, and at the first view you may know how many times you can take, as in this example 7 times are too little, and 9 times too much ; wherefore I set down 8 in the quotient, and place 987648, the tabular number, which stands against 8 under the dividend; then I subtract that number from it, and the remainder is 6, to which I bring down 3, and place 0 in the quotient ; then to the 63 I bring down 2, and place 0 in the quotient ; then to 632 I bring down 1, the last figure of the dividend ; but still it will not bear any times or time, wherefore I put another 0 in the quotient, and so the work is done, and the quotient is 8000, and the remainder 6321, as in the work.

Thus having plainly, fully, and pertinently shown by verbal directions, the method of working Division, I think it unnecessary to give any more examples in that manner, but shall leave some few examples for practice sake, whose quotients and remainders are expressed, but the operation omitted, to save room, and for trial of the ingenuity of practitioners.

7400690042 divided by 987, the quotient is 7498166, and the remainder 200.

479679002742 divided by 4689 the quotient is 102298784, and the remainder 4566.

7969767002 divided by 976294, the quotient is 8163, and the r- mainder 279080.

456789012345 divided by 9876543, the quotient is 46249' and the remainder 8775138.

76469749 by 4500, quotient 16993, and the remainder 1249. And 8092320000 by 345000, quotient 23456, and remains (0). D 3 *The*

The Proof of Multiplication and Division.

These two rules reciprocally prove each other; for in proving *multiplication*, if you divide the product by the multiplier, the quotient will be like the multiplicand; or if by the multiplicand, the quotient will be the same with the multiplier.

Ex. No. I.   345
                24
          ─────
          1380
           690
       ─────
       24)8280(345
          72..
          ─────
          108
           96
          ─────
             0
           12 ●
          ─────
            (0)

Ex. No. II.   Or thus,
     345)8280(24
     690..
     ─────
     1380
     1380
     ─────
      (0)

To prove Division.

Division may be proved by Division thus:

If you divide the dividend by the quotient, the quotient will be your former divisor.

Ex. Divide 8280 by 345.

345)8280(24

Here the working again is needless, it being just done, and shows the truth of the assertion, that Division may be proved by Division.

But the most usual way of proving Division is by Multiplication, in this manner, viz. multiply the quotient by the divisor, and the product will be equal to the dividend. —See the preceding examples, No. 1.

345 *Quotient,*
 24 *Divisor.*
─────
1380
 690
─────
8280 *Proof.*

Note, That when there is any remainder, such remainder must be taken in or added to the product.

As I have given some examples of the utility of Multiplication in Money, I shall here give a few examples in *Division of Money;* whereby may be seen how expeditiously things may be done without having Recourse to Reduction, the Rule of Three, &c.   *Ex.*

Ex. 1. Divide 26*l.* 12*s.* 6*d.* equally among five men. For disposition of working set it down as follows:

$$
\begin{array}{ccc}
l. & s. & d. \\
5)26 & 12 & 6 \\
\hline
5 & 6 & 6 \\
& & 5 \\
\hline
Proof\ 26 & 12 & 6 \\
\hline
\end{array}
$$

In the working of this I say, the 5's in 26, 5 times; 5 times 5 is 25; 25 from 26 there remains 1, that is 1 pound, or 20 shillings; which, with the 12*s.* in the place of shillings, makes 32*s.* then the 5's in the 82, 6 times; 6 times 5 is 30; 30 from 32, there remain 2*s.* or 24*d.* which with 6*d.* in the place of pence, makes 30; then the 5*s.* in 30, 6 times, and so the work is done, and the answer is, that each man must have *l.* 5 6 6, for his equal share in the said division of *l.* 26 12 6 among 5 persons; and the truth of it is proved by Multiplication of Money, sufficiently shown in the rule of Multiplication; as here, 5 times 6 is 30, 6 and carry 2; and 5 times 6 is 30, and 2 is 32; 12 and carry 1; and 5 times 5 is 25, and 1 is 26, &c.

Ex. 2. Divide the charges of a country feast, amounting to *l.* 246 13 4 equally among 12 stewards, to know what each steward must pay.

$$
\begin{array}{ccc}
l. & s. & d. \\
12)246 & 13 & 4 \\
\hline
Ans.-20 & 11 & 1-4
\end{array}
$$

Here I say the 12's in 24 twice, and 12's in 6, 0 times, and there remains 6*l.* or 120*s.* and 13*s.* make 133, and then the 12's in 133 are 11, and there remains 1*s.* or 12*d.* and then 12 and 4 is 16; and the 12's in 16 once, and 4 remain : so that each steward must pay *l.* 20 11 1, and something more than a farthing; and this may be proved as above.

When any quantity is such a number that any two digits of the Multiplication Table multiplied together make the said quantity or number, then the quotient may be very expeditiously found at two divisions, and sooner than at one. Example: Divide 7872 by 32. In this example the component parts, which, multiplied together, make the divisor 32, are 4 and 8, or 8 and 4; for it matters not which of them you divide by first; for either way will give a true and the same quotient, as may be seen by the different methods of the following work.

$$
\begin{array}{ll}
4)7872 & \text{Or thus:}\quad 8)7872 \\
\hline
8)1968 & \qquad\qquad 4)984 \\
\hline
246\ Quotient & \qquad\qquad 246\ Quotient.
\end{array}
$$

Here

Here though the operations are different, yet the quotients are the same.   Again, divide 44184 by 56.

Example 3.

7)44184
8)6312

789 *Quotient.*

Here the Divisors are 7 and 8, or 8 and 7; for either will give the same quotient.

And thus may a great number of examples be wrought by numbers out of the Multiplication Table, with great dispatch and expedition, as by 15, 18, 25, 35, 64, 72, 96, and by many other numbers.

When it appears that there is any remainder in the first division, or the last, or both, to know the true remainder as if divided by the common way, take this method, *viz,* multiply the first divisor by the last remainder, and take in, or add the first remainder, if there be any, and the product will be the true or same remainder, as if you divided by the long way. *Example:* divide 1567, by 15.

3)4567

5)1522   1

304   2

(7)

Here I multiply 3, the first divisor, by 2, the last remainder, and take in 1, the first remainder, and it makes 7 for the true remainder, as may be proved at leisure by the other way.

The same method may be taken with respect to component parts in division of money, as in division of simple numbers: thus

Divide   3)463 18   6 into 18 equal parts.

6)154 12 10

Answer   25 15   5

By this method of *Division of Money* you may, by haveing the price of several things, know the price or value of one thing, at the said rate, as well as by the *Rule of Three ;* so doth *Multiplication of Money* answer questions in the *Rule of Three,* when the first number is a unit, or 1. Thus, If 84 lb. of coffee cost 31*l.* 10*s.* 0*d.* what costs 1*lb.* Here 7 multiplied by 12, gives 84; therefore proceed as follows :

l.   s.   d.

7) 31 10   0

12)   4 10   0

Answer   0   7   6

An

As in the Multiplication of Money, to have an answer, you multiply the price by the quantity, so in Division of Money you divide the price by the quantity, to have your answer.

The various uses of *Multiplication* and *Division* will be better understood by their application in the following Rule of *Arithmetic* called

REDUCTION;

WHICH shows how to reduce numbers of one denomination to another, thereby discovering the same value, though in different terms.

I. As first, all great numbers are brought into smaller by Multiplication, as pounds into shillings, pence, or farthings, by multiplying by 20, 12, or 4. Or hundreds weight into pounds weight, by multiplying by 4 and by 28, or by 112; or lower, into ounces or drams, by multiplying the pounds by 16 and 16.

II. And on the contrary, all small names are brought into greater by Division; as farthings into pounds, by dividing by 4, 12, and 20 : and pounds weight into hundreds weight, by dividing by 28 and 4; the drams into pounds by dividing 16 and 16.

But note, That pounds are brought into pence by multiplying by 240; or into farthings by multiplying by 960; and just the contrary by Division.

Ex. 1. In 240l. Sterling how many pence ?
            20 shillings 1 pound.

4800 shillings in 240l.   *Or thus* :
    12 pence 1 shilling.   240l.

Ans. 57600 pence in 240l.   240d. in 1l.
                                      9600
                                      480
                                Answer 57600

Ex. 2. In 226 tons of copper, how many pounds wt.
            20 cwt. 1 ton.   *Or thus :*

4520 cwt. in 226 tons.   226 tons,
        4 qrs. 1 cwt.   20

18080 qrs. of 1 cwt. in 226 tons.   4520
    28 lb. 1 qr. of a cwt.   112

144640   54240
36160   4520

506240 pounds wt. in 226 tons. 506240 pds.
            D 5   Th.

These foregoing examples are great names to be brought into small (as may easily be observed and understood) therefore as the rule directs, it is done by Multiplication, by multiplying the greater name by the number of the next lesser name that makes one of the said greater; as in the first example the lesser name to pounds is shillings : wherefore I multiply by 20, because 20 of that lesser name makes one of the said greater name, i.e. 20 shillings make a pound. And the same regard is had, and method observed, in the example of weight, as is very plain to be seen in the work, and is called *Reduction Descending*, because it brings higher or greater denominations into lower or lesser.

Ex. 3. Bring 4)494400 farthings into pounds.

· Or thus :

12)123600 pence   96 | 0)49440 | 0(515*l.*

             480 ..

2 | 0) 10300 | 0 shillings   144   In this way I

                                96   divide by 960,

     515 pounds   460   the farthings

                            480   in a pound,

                          (0)   &c.

In the first way I divide the farthings by 4, because 4 make a penny, and the quotient is pence; then the pence I divide by 12, because 12 make a shilling, and that quotient is shillings; these I divide by 20 to bring them into pounds, thus; I cut off the cipher in the dividend towards the right, for the cipher that is in the divisor 20, which is also separated from 2 with a dash of the pen; then I halve the figures one by one, as they are united with the remainder in the dividend; which half is pounds, and is a short way of dividing by 20; in the example I say the half of 10 (because I must not set down 0 at the beginning) is 5, and the half of 3 is 1, but there remains 1, which makes the next, which is 0, 10; and the half of 10 is 5; so that 10300 shillings make 515 pounds, or there are so many pounds in 494400 farthings.

Note, In dividing by 20, as above, if any thing remain it must be joined or annexed to the figure or cipher cut off; as suppose there had in the halving the last figure (excepting what you cut off) remained 1, then that 1 must have

                                               been

been added to the cipher separated or cut off, and there would have been 10 shillings.

Ex. 4. Reduce 27552 pounds weight into cwts.

$$4)$$
$$28)27552(984$$
$$252..$$
$$\overline{\qquad} 246 \text{ cwt. } Answer.$$
$$235$$
$$224$$
$$\overline{112}$$
$$112$$
$$\overline{(0)}$$

Or thus :

lb.		cwt.
112)27552(246 *Ans.*		

$$224..$$
$$\overline{515}$$
$$448$$
$$\overline{672}$$
$$672$$
$$\overline{(0)}$$

In the first of the two foregoing examples I divide the pounds by 28, to bring them into quarters; then I divide these quarters by 4, to bring them into hundreds weight, as above.

In the second way, I divide the pounds weight by 112, the pounds in 1 cwt. and it brings the pounds weight into hundreds weight at once.

The said examples are of small denominations to be brought into greater; and therefore it is done by Division, by dividing the lesser name by as many of them as make the greater name: that is by 28, because 28 of them make one of the next greater name, *viz.* a quarter of an hundred, and this reduction is called *Reduction Ascending,* because it brings low or small names to higher or greater denominations; by which may be observed, that all questions in Reduction, whether ascending or descending, are answered either by Multiplication or Division, or by both; as will plainly appear in the examples.

When it is required to reduce numbers of several denominations by *Reduction Ascending,* or by *Multiplication,* you are to work as before; but you must always remember to take in such numbers as stand in the place of the next inferior denomination, as when you multiply the pounds by 20, if there be any shillings to the denomination, or place of shillings, you must take them in; so likewise when you multiply the shillings by 12, if there be any pence in the place of pence, you must also take them in; and so when you multiply the pence by 4, to bring them into farthings, you must take in the farthings, if there be any in the

the place of farthings, as in the following work.

$$l. \quad s. \quad d.$$

Ex. 5. In 346 16 9½ how many farthings ?
20 shillings 1 pound.

6936 shillings in 346*l.* 16*s.*
12 pence 1 shilling.

83241 pence in 346*l.* 16*s.* 9*d.*
4 farthings 1 penny.

332966 farthings in 346*l.* 16*s.* 9½*d.*

The above example is so plain that it hardly needs any explication; but I begin to say 0 is 0, but 6 in the units of shillings is 6; then twice 6 is 12, and one in the tens of shillings is 13, 3 and carry 1 ; and twice 4 is 8 and 1 is 9, and twice 3 is 6: then by 12, saying 12 times 6 is 72, and 9*d.* (in the place of pence) is 81, 1 and carry 8; and 12 times 3 is 36, and 8 is 44, 4 and carry 4; and 12 times 9 is 108, and 4 is 112, 2 and carry 11 ; and 12 times 6 is 72, and 11 is 83: then by 4, saying 4 times 1 is 4, and 2 (in the place of farthings) is 6; 4 times 4 is 16, and so on.

$$C. \quad qrs. \quad lb.$$

Ex. 6. In 56 2 16 of tobacco how many pounds wt ?
4 qrs.

226 qrs. in 56 C. 2 qrs
28 lbs. 1 qr. of a C.

1814
453

Ans. 6344 pounds wt. in 56 *C.* 2 *qrs.* 16 *lb.*

In the foregoing example I multiply the 56 C. by 4, and take in 2 quarters; then I multiply the 226 qrs. by 28, saying 8 times 6 is 48, and 6 (the unit figure in the odd pounds) is 54, 4 and carry 5, &c. Then I multiply by 2, saying twice 6 is twelve, and 1 (that stands in the place of tens in the odd pounds) is 13, 3 and carry 1, &c. Then adding the two products together, they make 6344 pounds contained in 56 *C.* 2 *qrs.* 16 *lb.* as above stated.

Reduction

Reduction Ascending,

Is the bringing numbers from a smaller denomination to a greater, and is the reverse of *Reduction Descending ;* and each may serve as a proof to the other, one being performed by *Multiplication,* and the other by *Division.*

If at any time in *Reduction Descending* you take. in, or add to, the odd money, weight, or measure, as you multiply the several denominations, such quantities will be the remainders in *Reduction Ascending.*

4) *Examples,* (See *Ex.* 5 and 6.)

In 332966 farthing*, how many pounds ? D:vide by 4, by

12)83241—½d. remains.   [12, and by 20.

2,0)693,6—9d. remains.

346—16s. remains.

So that in 332966 farthings there are 346l. 16s. 9d¼.

Again, in 6344 pounds weight, how many hundreds weight ?   Here divide by 28, and then by 4.

           4)
28)6344(226 *qrs.* .
    56. ·   56 *C.* 2 *qrs.*
    74
    56
    184
    168
   (16) lbs. remain.

So that in 6344 pounds wt. there are 56 *C.* 2 *qrs.* 16lb. and these instances prove the preceding examples of descending to be right.

The following are promiscuous examples of both kinds of Reduction, one proving the other.

In 276l. 12s. how many pence?
        20
    ———
        5532
        12
Ans. 66384d.

        12
In 66384d. how many pounds ?
2|0)553|2
Ans. l. 276 | 12 and *Proof.*

In

In 47964 grains, how many pounds *Troy* ?

```
              2 | 0)
   24)47964 (199 | 8
      24...12)99  18 pwts.   Ans. 8lb. 3oz. 10pwts. 12grs.
```

```
      239     In 8lb. 3oz. 18pwts. 12gr. How many grains ?
      216          12
      ───          ──
      236          99
      216          20
      ───          ────
      204          1998
      192            24
      ───          ────
  Gr. (12)         7994
                   3997
                   ─────
```

Answer 47964 and *Proof.*

In 34 *C.* 3 *qrs.* of wool, how many pounds ?

```
      34    3 qrs.
       4                    Cwt.
      ───               112)3892(34   3 qrs.
      139                    336
       28                    ───
      ────                   532
      1112                   448
      278                    ───
      ────                   84lbs. or 3 qrs.
      3892
```

In 456 *cwt.* 3 *qrs.* 27 *lb.* of copper, how many pounds ? and what is the amount at 21 pence *per* pound ?

```
      Cwt.  qrs.  lb.
      456    3    72
        4
      ─────
      1827
        28
      ─────
      14623
      3656
      ──────
      51183 lb.
         21
      ──────
      51183
      102366
```

1074843 pence; which divide by 12 and by 20, give 4478*l.* 10*s.* 3*d.* the value of 456 *C.* 3 *qrs.* 27 *lb.* of Copper at 21 pence *per lb.*

Bring

Bring 4796 ells *Flemish* into ells *English*; multiply
by 3 and divide by 5, because 3 quarters
make an ell *Flemish*, and 5 an ell *English*.

```
       4796
          3
    5)14388
      2877¼
```

Reduce 456 ells *English* into yards; multiply by 5, and
divide by 4, thus

```
            456 English ells.
             5 qrs. 1 Eng. ell.    In 570 yds. how many Eng. e.
    4)2280 qrs.                            4 qrs. 1 yd.
Yds.  5˜0 Answer.                    5)2280
                            English ells 456, Answer and proof.
```

Bring 130 tuns of wine into gallons.

```
            4 hogsheads 1 tun.
          520                            Or thus:
           63 gallons 1 hogshead     252 gallons 1 tun.
         1560                         130 tuns.
         3120
Ans.    32760 gallons.                7560
                                      252
                                     32760
```

```
        Lasts.   Quarters.      Bushels.    Pecks.
Reduce   42        3               5          2 into pecks.
         10 qrs. 1 last.          Here multiply by 10,
        423                     and take in 3 qrs. and
           8 bushels 1 qr.      then by 8, and take in 5
        3389                    bushels; and lastly by 4,
           4 pecks 1 bush.      and take in 2 pecks.
       13558 pecks in 42 lasts, 3 qrs. 5 bushels, and
        4)                              2 pecks.
```

In 13558 pecks how many lasts, &c.

```
     8)3389          2 pecks taken in.
   1 | 0)12 | 3   5 bushels taken in.
Lasts    42      3   quarters taken in.
```

Answer 42 lasts, 3 quarters, 5 bushels, and 2 pecks.

By *Reduction* also
Foreign coins or exchanges may be reduced to Sterling
money, and on the contrary Sterling money to foreign.

Example

Example.

Reduce 246 *Venetian Ducats de Banco* into Sterling money, the exchange at 52*d.* Sterling *per* ducat, thus :

$$\begin{array}{r} 246 \\ 52 \\ \hline 492 \\ 1230 \\ \hline 12)12792 \\ \hline 2\ |\ 0)106(6 \end{array}$$

£. 53—6 to be paid in *London,*
for the 246 ducats drawn in *Venice.*

Reduce 53*l.* 6*s.* sterl. into ducats at 52*d.* sterl. *per* du.

$$\begin{array}{r} 20 \\ \hline 106 \\ 12 \end{array}$$

52)12792(246 ducats to be paid in *Venice* for 53*l.* 6*s.*
104   drawn in *London.*

23, &c.

To reduce *Flemish* money into *Sterling* money divide
the pence *Flemish* by the course of exchange, suppose 33*s.*
4*d.* and the quotient will be the *Sterling* money ; and what
remains, multiply by 20, &*c.*

Example.

In 242*l.* 13*s.* 4*d. Flemish,* how many
20   pounds *Sterling,* &*c.*

33*s.* 4*d. Flemish.*   4853
12   12

$$\begin{array}{r} 400 \qquad 4\ |\ 00)582\ |\ 40 \\ 145\ \text{remains}\ 240 \\ 20 \\ 4\ |\ 00)48\ |\ 00 \\ \hline 12 \end{array}$$

Answer 145*l.* 12*s.*

By the Above it appears that 145*l.* 12*s. Sterling* is
equivalent to 242*l.* 13*s.* 4*d. Flemish,* at 33*s.* 3*d. Flemish
per* pound *Sterling.*

Thus *Flemish* money may be reduced to *Sterling* money,
though the course of exchange may be at any other rate
of

of shillings and pence *Flemish;* but when the rate above, viz. 33s. 4d. then the answer is sooner found by multiplying by 3, and dividing by 5; for 400d. *Flemish* is the same to 240d. *Sterling*, (each being a pound) as 5 is to 3, for if you divide 400 by 5, it quotes 80; so 240, divided by 3, quotes the same.

The above *Example* done by the last proposed way.

l.242 13 4 *Flemish.*
              3
----
5)728 0   0
----
l.145 12   0

In 426 *French* crowns, each 54d.¼ *Sterling*, how many pounds *Sterling?*

                426
                 54¼

               1704
               2180
                106-2
            ----
            12)23110½
            ----
            2 | 0)192 | 5 10d.

            Ans. l.96 : 5 : 10d.½

In this Example the number of crowns is multiplied by 54d. and for the ¼d. I take the 4th part of 426, which is 106 ¾ of a penny, or a halfpenny, which added to the other pence gives for total 23110d. which divide by 12, quotes 1925, and 10d. remains: so the answer is 96l. 5s. 10d. ½ Sterling.

Note. To multiply a number by ¼, ½, ⅓, ⅛, &c. is the same as to divide the number by 4, 2, 3, 8, &c.

Again, bring 1600 pieces of eight, at 54d. ¼ *Sterling* into pounds *Sterling.*

                1600
                  54¼

               6400
               8000
                400
            ----
            12)86800 pence.
            ----
            2 | 0)723 | 3—4
            ----
            l.361 : 13 : 4.

Here the 1600 pieces of eight are multiplied by 54, to bring them into pence, and for the ¼ take the ¼ of 1600, &c. as in the work; and the answer is l.361 : 13 : 4.

This method is of use in reducing the exchanges of *Cadiz, Leghorn,* and *Genoa.* Or when the exchange is at so many pence and eights of a penny, (as often the exchanges

exchanges run) then multiply the given number to reduce it into pence, by the pence contained in a piece of
eight; and also multiply the said given number apart,
by the numerator or upper figure of the fraction, and divide by the denominator or under figure of the fraction,
and the quotient will be pence; which add to the other
pence produced by multiplying the given number by the
pence contained in one of the pieces for exchange, then
divide the total pence by 12, &c.

Example.

Bring 296 dollars at 52d. $\frac{5}{8}$ Sterling into pounds
Sterling.

```
            296
             52
          ------
            592          296 dollars.
           1480                5
          ------          --------
          15392          8)1480
            185          --------
          ------
       12)15577
       ------------
       2,| 0)129 | 8 : 1
```

Answer l. 64 : 18 : 1   Sterling money for
296 dollars, at 52d. $\frac{5}{8}$
Sterling per dollar.

But ducats, dollars, crowns, &c. are more expeditiously
cast up by rules of Practice, hereafter to be shown. The
next rule in Arithmetic is

The GOLDEN RULE, or RULE OF THREE.

It is called the Golden Rule from its excellent use
in Arithmetic, and in other parts of Mathematical learning.

And also denominated the Rule of Three, because by
three numbers given, proposed, or known, we find out a
fourth number required, or unknown, which bears the same
proportion to the third which the second does to the first
number: whence also the Rule of Proportion.

Of this Proportion there are two sorts; one named
Direct, and the other Indirect, or Reverse.

Direct Proportion is when the second and third numbers
are to be multiplied together, and their product divided by
the first.   Indirect,

Indirect, or *Reverse Proportion*, is when the first and second numbers are to be multiplied together, and their product divided by the third.

In *Direct Proportion*, the fourth number, or answer to the question, contains the third number as often (or as many times) as the second contains the first.

But in *Indirect Proportion* the greater the third number is the less is the fourth; and the smaller the third number is, the greater is the fourth.

Of the right placing of Numbers.

The chief difficulty that occurs in the *Rule of Three* is the right placing the numbers, or stating the question; for when that is done, you have nothing more to do, but to multiply and divide, and the work is done.

And to this end, we are to remember, that of the three given numbers, two of them are always of one denomination, and the other number is of the same name with the fourth number or answer required; and must always be the second or middle number. And the number that asks the question must possess the third or last place, and the other number of the same name with the third must be the first number; for the first and third numbers must always be of one name, viz. both money, both weight, both time, or both measure. And though they be of one kind, yet if one of them is altered by *Reduction* from a higher to a lower name, then the other must be reduced to the same name. That is, if either the first or third number consist of several denominations, that is, of pounds and shillings; or pounds, shillings and pence; or of pounds, shillings, pence and farthings; or of tons, hundreds, quarters, and pounds, &c. then must they be reduced to the lowest name mentioned. And if any one happens to be of divers denominations, and the other but of one name, then the number of one name must be reduced as low, or into the same name with the other. As suppose the first number is brought into farthings, the third number also, though but pounds, must be brought into farthings. Then you are to multiply the second and third numbers together, (when the Proportion is Direct) and divide the product by the first number, and the quotient thence arising will be the answer to the question, and in the same name with the middle number: and if in the small denomination, it must be brought by Division to the highest name for the

better

better understanding the answer. If the middle number be of several denominations, it must be brought into the lowest mentioned.

Example 1.

If 12 gallons of brandy cost 4*l.* 10*s.* what will 134 gallons cost at that rate ?

```
    Gall.    l.   s.      Gall.
If 15      4   10       134
             20            90
            ──           ──────
             90          15)12060
                          ────────
                          2 | 0)80 | 4
                          ──────────
                          £.40 | 4
```

Here the first and third numbers are of like names, viz. both gallons; and 134 being the number that asks the question, it hath the third place, as it always must, as before asserted; and 4*l.* 10*s.* the second number, being of two denominations, viz. pounds and shillings, it is reduced into the lowest mentioned, viz. shillings, as before directed, and then the three numbers are these, viz. 15--90-134; and 134 the third number being multiplied by 90, the second number produces 12060; which divided by 15, the first number quotes 804, which are shillings, because 90, the middle number, were shillings; and 804 shillings, divided by 20 give 40*l.* 4*s.* for the answer: for the proof of its truth, state it backward thus:

```
    Gall.     l.  · s.      Gall.
If 134 cost 40   4 what cost 15
             20
            ─────
             804
              15
            ─────
            4020
             804
            ─────
```

134)12060(90*s. Answer,* or 4*l.* 10*s.* the cost
1206   of 12 gallons, and this is a
────   proof of the first work; and
...0   the back stating and working
the proof is as much a question in the Rule of Three as the first.

By the foregoing rule and directions, and these examples, the nature of the rule, and method of working may
                                                            be

be understood; I shall therefore only give some few examples with a little of the work, and answers to the questions, leaving part of the operations to be performed by the ingenious practitioner.

Ex. 3. If 56*lb.* of indigo cost 11*l.* 4*s.* what will 1008*lb.* cost at that rate?

    lb.   *s.*   *lb*

If 56   224   1008? *Answer* 4032*s.* or 201*l.* 12*s.*

Ex. 4. If half an Cwt. of copper cost 4*l.* 18*s.* what quantity will 14*s.* buy at that rate?

    s.   *lb.*   *s.*

If 98 buy 56, what 14? *Answer* 8*lb.* of copper.

Ex. 5. If 4 *C.* 3 *qrs.* sugar cost 5*l.* 15*s.* 7*d.* what will 4 hogsheads come to, weighing 4 *C.* 1 *qr.* 14 *lb.*

    lb.   *d.*   *lb.*

If 532   13874   746? *Ans.* 12373 pence, or 51*l.* 11*s.* 1*d.* And the remainder, 226, multiplied by 4, gives a halfpenny more; so the whole is 51*l.* 11*s.* 1*d*$\frac{1}{2}$.

Either of these examples, or any other, may be proved by back-stating, according as the first example was proved; and each proof becomes another question in the Rule of Three, as stated before.

Ex. 6. If I have 50*l.* a year salary, how much is due to me for 144 days service at that rate?

    Days.   *l.*   *Days.*   *l.*   *s.*   *d.*

If 365   50   144? *Answer* 19 14 6 parts $\frac{90}{365}$ of a penny.

In this example, the product of the third by the second number is 7200; which divided by the first 365 (according to the rule) quotes 19 pounds, the name of the middle number; and there is a remainder of 265; which multiplied by 20, according to Reduction, the product still divided by 265, there comes out 14 shillings; and yet there is a remainder of 190: which multiplied by 12, and the product divided by 365, gives 6*d.* and there is a remainder of 90: which if multiplied by 4 (the last inferior name) and divided by 365, yet would not come to a farthing more; so that the answer is as above, 19*l.* 14*s.* 6*d.* $\frac{90}{365}$

When the first of the three given numbers is an unit or one, the work is performed, or answer found, by Multiplication only.

                                                             Ex.

Ex. 7. If I am to give 17s. for 1*lb.* of *Organzine* silk, what must I give for 264*lb.* at that rate?

```
    lb.         s.          lb.
If 1———17 ——— 264
                          17
```

Answer 4488s. or 224l. 8s.

Ex. 8. If I buy 49 bags of hops at 12l. 12s. 6d. per bag, what come they to at that rate?

```
   Bag           l.  s.  d.          Bags.
    1———————12 12  6——————— 49
Multiply by              7 and by 7
                   ————————
                   88  7  6
                          7
                   ————————
                   618 12  6
```

The foregoing work is performed by the component parts as taught in *Multiplication*, because 7 times 7 is 49.

When the third, or last of the three given numbers is an unit, or one, the work is performed by *Division.*

Ex. 9. If 12 ells of Holland cost 3l. 6s. what is the price of 1 ell at that rate?

```
   Ells.     12)  s.        Ell.
If 12 ——————66 ——— 1 Answer 5s. 6d.
             ————
             56 ⁶⁄₁₂ of 1s. or 6d.
```

Ex. 10. If 56 yards of broad cloth cost 40l. 12s. what is the price of a yard at that rate?

```
   Yds.      7)  l.  s.       Yd.
If 56————40 12———1 Ans. 14s. 6d. per yard.
         8) 5 16
         ————————
         0 14 6d. Answer.
```

This example is wrought by *Division of Money,* and by 7 and 8, the component parts; as shown in the *rule of Division.*

Ex. 11. If *A.* owes *B.* 296l. 17s. and compounds at 7s. 6d. in the pound; what must *B.* take for his debt?

```
    s.      d.       s.
If 20——90——5937.  Answer l.111 6s. 4½d.
```

Ex. 12. If a gentleman's income be 500l. a year, what may he expend daily, and yet lay up 12l. 15s. per month? First multiply 12l. 15s. by 12, the months in a year,

and

and it makes 153*l.* which is deducted from 500*l.* the remainder is 347*l.* Then say,

Days.   *l.*

If 365———347, what 1 day ? *Ans.* 19*s.* $\frac{5}{365}$

After you have reduced the pounds into shillings, which make 6940, you divide them by 365, and the quotient is 19*s.* *per* day, and 5 remains over, which being placed over the divisor 365, gives 19*s.* $\frac{5}{365}$

The RULE OF THREE, *Inverse or Indirect Proportion.*

In *Indirect Proportion,* the product of the third and fourth numbers is equal to the product of the fisst and second.

But the method of stating any question in this rule is the same with that of the *direct rule.*

For the first and third numbers must be of one name, and so reduced, as in that rule ; and the number that asks the question must possess the third place ; and the middle number will be of the same name with the answer as it is there.

To know when the question belongs to the Direct, *and when to the* Inverse rule.

When the question is stated as aforesaid, consider whether the answer to the question ought to be *more* or *less* than the second number : if more, then the lesser of the first and third numbers must be your *divisor.*

And if the first number of the three is your *divisor,* then the *Proportion* is *Direct ;* but if the last of the three is your *divisor,* the *Proportion* is *Indirect* or *Inverse.*

Or without regard to *Direct* or *Inverse,*

If more is required, the lesser }
If less, the greater } is the *Divisor.*

Examples for Explanation.

Ex. 1. If 4 men plane 250 deal boards in 6 days, how many men will plane them in 2 days ?

If 6 days require 4 men, what 2 days ? *Ans.* 12 men.

6

2)24

12 *Ans.*

Ex. 2. If a board be 9 inches broad, how much in length will make a square foot ?   In

In B.   In L.

If 12————— 12, what 9 inches broad?

$$12$$

$$9)\overline{144}$$

Answer 10 inches in length.

In these examples, the first and second numbers are multiplied together, and the product is divided by the third; for, in the first example, it is most certain, that 2 days will require more hands to perform the work than 6 days; therefore the lesser of the extreme numbers is the *Divisor*; and declares the question in the *Indirect Proportion.*

Likewise, in the second example, 9 inches in breadth, must needs require more in length to make a foot than 12 inches in breadth; wherefore it is the same *Proportion* with the first example, because the *Divisor* in the third number.

Ex. 3. How many yards of sarcenet, of 3 *qrs.* wide, will line 9 yards of cloth of 8 *qrs.* wide?

Qrs. wide.   *yds. long.*   *qrs. wide.*

If 8————9 what———3

         8   Here the narrower the silk, the
       ————   more in length is required, of course
    3)72   8 must be the multiplier, and 3 the
   ————   divisor.

Yards 24 *Answer.*

Ex. 4. If a loaf weigh 4*lb.* ½ when wheat is 5*s.* 6*d.* the bushel, what must it weigh when wheat is 4*s.* the bushel?

     d.   *Half lb.*   *d.*   *lb.*

If 66—————9————18 *Answer* 6¼

Ex. 5. If in 12 months 100*l.* principal gains 5 pounds interest, what principal will gain the same interest in 5 months?

     Months.   *Principal.*   *Months.*
      12 ————— 100————— 5

$$12$$

$$5)1200$$

Answer 240*l.* principal.

The Double RULE OF THREE *Direct.*

In this Rule there are five numbers given to find out a sixth, which is to be in proportion to the product of

the

the fourth and fifth numbers, as the third number is to the product of the first and second numbers.

Questions in this kind of *proportion* are wrought either by two operations in the *Single Rule of Three Direct*, or by the rule composed of the five given numbers, and the one may be a proof to the other : as may be seen in the following example :

Ex. 1. If 100 pounds principal in 12 months, gain 5 pounds interest, what will 246 pounds principal gain in 7 months?

If 100 gain 5, what will 246

5

1 | 00)12 | 30

20

1 | 00) 6 | 00 *Answer* 12*l.* 6*s.*

M.   *l. s.*   M.

Then say again, if 12 gain 12 6 what 7

20

246

7

12)1722

2|0) 14 | 3   6*d.*

l. 7   3   6*d.*

In the first stating, the answer is, that if 100*l.* gain 5 pounds, then 246*l.* will gain 12 pounds 6 shillings.

Then I say in the next stating, if 12 months gain 12*l.* 6*s.* what will 7 months? and the answer is 7*l.* 3*s.* 6*d.* And so much will 246 pounds gain in 7 months, if 100 pounds gain 5 pounds in 12 months.

You must particularly note, that in all operations where the answer to the question is found by two statings of the Rule of Three, the answer of the first stating is the middle number of the second stating; as in the preceding example.

This mark × when it stands between two numbers denotes that the numbers are to be multiplied into one another : thus 9 × 5 signifys that 9 is to be multiplied into 5, and the product is 45.

E

The

The foregoing question may be answered by a stating composed of the five given numbers thus :

(1)	(2)	(3)	(4)	(5)
L.	*M.*	*L.*	*L.*	*M.*

If 100×12————5————246×7

$$\begin{array}{r} 12 \\ \hline 1200 \end{array}$$

$$\begin{array}{r} 7 \\ \hline 1722 \\ 5 \\ \hline \end{array}$$

$$12,00)86,10$$

In this work, in stating the question, the first and fourth numbers are made of one name, as are the second and fifth; then the two first numbers are multiplied together for a divisor, and the last three numbers are multiplied together for a dividend,

$$L.\ 7.————210$$
$$\begin{array}{r} 20 \\ \hline \end{array}$$
$$12,00)42.00$$
$$\begin{array}{r} s.\ 3———600 \\ 12 \\ \hline \end{array}$$
$$12,00)72,00$$
$$d.\ 6$$

and the quotient, or answer, is of the same name with the middle numbers, viz. pounds, interest. In the work I find the first quotient 7 pounds interest : and so I proceed from one denomination to another, till I find the same answer as in the work at two statings, viz. $7l.\ 3s.\ 6d.$

This method of operation serves to answer all questions in the *Double Rule of Three Direct*.

The Double RULE OF THREE *Reverse.*

IN this Rule you must place your numbers in such order that your second and fourth number may be of one name or denomination, and your third and fifth.

Ex. If 100*l.* principal, in 12 months gain 6*l.* interest, what principal will gain 20*l.* interest in 8 months ?

Stated thus :

(1)	(2)	(3)	(4)	(5)
Principal.	*Mo.*	*Interest.*	*Mo.*	*Interest.*

If $100 \times 12———6 \times 8———20$

$$\begin{array}{r} 12 \\ \hline 1200 \\ 20 \\ \hline \end{array}$$

$$\begin{array}{r} 6 \\ \hline 6\ \text{the divisor.} \end{array}$$

$$48)24000(500l.\ \text{principal,}\ \textbf{\textit{Answer.}}$$
$$\begin{array}{r} 240 \\ \hline (0) \end{array}$$

In

In this work, the third and fourth numbers are multiplied together for a divisor; and then the first is multiplied by the second, and that product by the fifth number, and the product, 24000, is divided by 48, and the quotient is 500*l.* principal; which is the answer to the question, as before shown.

Rules of PRACTICE.

THESE Rules are so called from their frequent use and brevity in finding the value of most sorts of goods or merchandise; for any question in the Rule of Three, when the first number in the stating is 1, is more briefly done by these rules, called Practice.

But previously to these rules, it is necessary to have the following tables by heart :

Parts of a Shilling.	Of a Pound.	Parts of a Pound.
d.		*s. d.*
6 is $\frac{1}{2}$	$\frac{1}{10}$	10 0 is $\frac{1}{2}$
4 $\frac{1}{3}$	$\frac{1}{60}$	6 8 $\frac{1}{3}$
3 $\frac{1}{4}$	$\frac{1}{80}$	5 0 $\frac{1}{4}$
2 $\frac{1}{6}$	$\frac{1}{120}$	4 0 $\frac{1}{5}$
$1\frac{1}{2}$ $\frac{1}{8}$	$\frac{1}{160}$	3 4 $\frac{1}{6}$
1 $\frac{1}{12}$	$\frac{1}{240}$	2 6 $\frac{1}{8}$
		2 0 $\frac{1}{10}$
		1 8 $\frac{1}{12}$
		1 0 $\frac{1}{20}$

Parts of a Shilling.

6*d.* is $\frac{1}{2}$ | *Ex.* I. 426 pounds of sugar, at 6d *per lb.*
of 1s. | $\overline{2|0)21|3}$

l. 10 13 *Answer.*

Here 6*d.* being the price of each *lb.* and the half of a shilling; therefore the half of 426 is taken, and gives 213*s.* or 10*l.* 13*s.* for the value of the sugar.

4*d.* is $\frac{1}{3}$ | *Ex.* II. 512*lb.* of cheese, at 4*d. per lb.*
of 1s. | $\overline{2|0)17|0\ 8d.}$

l. 8 10 8 *Answer.*

Here 4*d.* is $\frac{1}{3}$ of a shilling; therefore the third part of 512 is 170*s.* and $\frac{2}{3}$ of a shilling, or 8*d.* remains.

The remainder is always of the same name with the dividend, which here is groats, for the pounds of cheese are at a groat each.

3d. is ¼ of 1s. | *Ex.* III. 246 yards of ribband, at 3d. per yard.

$$2|0)\ 6\ |\ 1\ 6d.$$

$$\overline{l.\ 3\ \ 1\ \ 6}\ Answer.$$

Here the yards are divided by 4, because 3d. is the 4th of a shilling, and it quotes 61 shillings, and 2 remains, or two 3 pences : so the answer is 3l. 1s. 6d.

And thus may any proposed question be answered, belonging to the first table, or parts of a shilling; that is, by dividing the given number by the denominator of the fraction; and the quotient will be always shillings, which (the remainders being known as above) bring into pounds, by dividing by 20, &c.

When the price of the integer is at a farthing, a halfpenny, or three farthings more than the value of the pence mentioned, then for those farthings take a proper part of the foregoing quotient found for the pence, and add them together.

Ex. 249 ells of canvas, at 4d.½ per ell.

4d. is ⅓
½d. is ⅛
of 4d.

$$83$$
$$10\ \tfrac{3}{8}\ or\ 4d.\ \tfrac{1}{2}.$$
$$\overline{2|0)\ 9|3\ \ 4\tfrac{1}{2}}$$
$$\overline{l.\ 4\ \ 13\ \ 4\tfrac{1}{2}}\ Answer.$$

In this example I divide by 3 for the groats, as being the third of one shilling, and it quotes 83s. then consider that a halfpenny is the eighth of 4d. therefore take the eighth part of the groat line, or 83s. and that produces 10s. and ⅜ of a shilling, or 4½d.; and the two lines being added together, make 93s. 4½d. or 4l.13s. 4½d. as in the work.

Parts of a Pound.

10s. is ½ | 254 yards of cloth, at 10s. per yard.

$$\overline{l.\ 127}\ Answer.$$

Here the half of 254 is taken ; because 10s. is the half of a pound.

s. d.

6 8 is ⅓ | 972 gallons, at 6s. 8d. per gallon.

$$\overline{l.\ 324}\ Answer.$$

Here the third part is taken, because 6s. and 8d. is the third of a pound ; and the Answer is l. 324.

And thus may any question proposed be answered, belonging

longing to the second table, or parts of a pound; that is, by dividing the given number by the denominator of the fraction, and the quotient will always be pounds; and if any thing remains, it is always so many halves, thirds, fourths, or fifths, &c. of a pound, according to the denominator that you divide by.

If the price be shillings and pence, or shillings, pence, and farthings, and no even part of a pound, then multiply the given number of the shillings in the price, and take even parts for the pence, or pence and farthings, and add the several lines together, and they will be shillings; which shillings bring into pounds as before.

Examples.

	lb.	s.	d.			Ells.	s.	d.
	426 at	4	9			216 at	2	3½
		4					2 *per ell.*	

6d. ½	1704		3d. ¼	432	
3d. ¼	213		½d. ⅛	54	
of 6d.	106½ or 6d.		of 3d.	9	

2|0)202|13 6   2|0)49 | 5s.

l. 101 3   6 *Answ.*   *l.* 24 15 *Answ.*

396 gal. of brandy, at 7s. 9d. *per* gal.

7

2772

6d. ¼ of 1s.	198
3d. ½ of 6d.	99

2,0)306|9

l. 153|9 *Answ.*

When the price is 10d. only; annex 0 to the right of the given number (which is multiplying by 10) and they are pence; which divide by 12 and 20.

Example: 426lb. of hops, at 10d. *per lb.*

12)4260

2|0) 35|5

l. 17 15 *Answer.*

When the price is 11d. set down the quantity twice in the form of Multiplication, and add the two lines together, then divide by 12 and 20.

E 3   *Example,*

Example.

426 *lb.* of copper, at 11*d. per lb.*

   426

12)4686 *pence.*

2|0) 39 | 0   6

      l. 19   10   6 *Answer.*

If the price be 11*d.*½ proceed as before, and take half the uppermost line, &c.

Example.

942*lb.* of tobacco at 11*d.*½ *per lb.*

   942

   471

12)10833

2|0) 90 | 2   9

     *l.*45   2   9 *Answ.*

When the price is 1*s.* only, divide by 20, and you have the answer at once.

Example.

2|0)96 | 4*lb.* of tobacco, at 12*d. per. lb.*

*l.*48   4 *Answer.*

When the price is 2*s.* it is done at sight, by doubling the last figure towards your right hand, and setting it apart for shillings ; and the figures towards the left are pounds.

Example.

596 gallons of spirits at 12*s. per* gallon,

l. 59   12 *Answer.*   Here the double of 6 is 12, and the 59 are pounds.

From this method of working by 2*s.* a multitude of examples may be most expeditiously wrought, *viz.*

	Els.	Yards.
	444 Cambric at 5*s.* 9*d.*	426 at 3*s.* 6*d. per* yard.
	44 8 at 2*s.*	42 12 at 2*s.*
	44 8 at 2*s.* 1*s.*½ 2*s.*	21 6 at 1*s.*
1*s.* ½ of 2*s.*	22 4 at 1*s.* 6*d.*½ 1*s.*	10 13 at 6*d.*
6*d.* ½ of 1*s.*	11 2 at 6*d.*	
3*d.* ½ of 6*d.*	5 11 at 3*d.*	74 11 at 3*s.* 6*d.*

Answer l. 127   13 at 5*s.* 9*d.*

The

The operation of these two examples is so plainly shewn that there is no need of further explanation.

Again, 548 yards broad cloth, at 12*s*. 6*d*. *per* yard.

l. 54 16 at 2*s*.

6 times 2 is 12*s*.

<table>
<tr><td>6*d*. is</td><td>328 16 at 12*s*.</td><td>Note, *That* 13*l*. 14*s*. is the</td></tr>
<tr><td>¼ of 2*s*.</td><td>13 14 at 6*d*</td><td>*fourth part of* 54*l*. 16*s*. *the*</td></tr>
<tr><td></td><td>*l*. 342 10 *Answer*.</td><td>*two shillings line.*</td></tr>
</table>

Or multiply by 12*s*. take half of the given number for the 6*d*. thus, and divide by 20, the answer is in pounds.

548 yards.

6576

½) 274

2|0)685|0

l. 342 10 *Answer*.

When the price is an even number of shillings, multiply these numbers of integers by half the price, and double the first figure of the product for shillings, and carry, as is usual in Multiplication, and the other figures towards the left will be pounds.

Example.

296 yards of cloth, at 14*s*. *per* yard.

7 the half of 14*s*.

l. 207 4*s*. *Answer*.

Here 7 times 6 is 42 ; the double of 2*s*. is 4*s*. &*c*:

When the price is an odd number of shillings, work for the even number as above, and for the odd shillings take the 1/20 of the given number, and add them together.

Example.

496 gallons of citron water, at 17*s*. *per* gallon.

8 half of 16*s*.

l. 396 16*s*.

24 16*s*.

l. 421 12*s*. *Answer*.

In this example I say, 8 times 6 is 48, then twice 8 is 16*s*. and carry 4 ; then 8 times 9 is 72, and 4 is 76, 6 and carry 7 ; and 8 times 4 is 32, and 7 is 39 ; then the half of 4 is 2, &*c*.

I have not here room to speak of the various and almost

E 4   infinite

infinite methods and rules of *Practice*, but I shall leave some general rules, which, if carefully noticed, will be of the greatest use to learners, these are

1. When the price is parts of a farthing, or of a penny, and $\frac{3}{4}$, $\frac{4}{6}$, $\frac{7}{8}$, &c. then multiply the integers by the numerator, and divide by the denominator, and the result will be either farthings or pence; which reduce to pounds, &c.

2. When the price is pence, and no even part of a shilling; as suppose 5d. 7d. 8d. or 9d. then it may be done by taking their parts, as 3d. and 2d. is 5d. and 4d. and 3d. is 7d. and 4d. and 4d. is 8d. and 6d. and 3d. is 9d. but it is an easy and sure way to multiply the given number by 5, 7, 8, or 9, then the product is pence, which bring to pounds by *Reduction*.

3. When the price is pence and parts of a penny; as 1d. $\frac{1}{4}$, 2d. $\frac{1}{2}$, or 6d. $\frac{3}{4}$, then work for the penny by taking the $\frac{1}{12}$; for 2d. the $\frac{1}{6}$; and for 6d. the $\frac{1}{2}$: then for the farthing take a $\frac{1}{4}$ of the penny line, and for $\frac{1}{2}$, $\frac{1}{4}$, of the two-penny line; and for $\frac{3}{4}$ take $\frac{1}{8}$ of the six-penny line; then add the results together, and the total will be shillings, which reduce to pounds by dividing by 20. Or by the sure way of bringing the mixed number into the lowest denomination; as 1d$\frac{1}{4}$, into 5 farthings 2d$\frac{1}{2}$, into 5 halfpence, and 6d$\frac{3}{4}$, into 27 farthings; then multiply the integers by 5, and the product is farthings; or by 5 halfpence, and the product will be halfpence; or by 27 farthings, and the product will be farthings; which, whether farthings, or pence, reduce to pounds, &c.

4. When the price is shillings and pence, or shillings, pence, and farthings; multiply the integers by the shillings of the price, and take parts of the pence, or pence and farthings, &c.

5. If the price be pounds and shillings, or pounds, shillings, pence, and farthings, multiply by the shillings in the price, that is in the pounds and shillings, and take parts of the pence and farthings.

6. When the number of integers hath a fraction annexed, or belonging to them, $\frac{1}{4}$, $\frac{1}{2}$, $\frac{3}{4}$, &c. then take $\frac{1}{4}$, $\frac{1}{2}$, $\frac{3}{4}$, of the price of one of the integers, and add that to the other results.

TARE & TRETT, &c.

Gross weight is the weight of the goods in hundreds, quarters,

Quarters, and Pounds, with the weight of the Hogshead, Cask, Chest, Bag, Bale, &c. that contains the Goods.

Tare is allowed to the Buyer for the Weight of the Hogshead, Cask, Chest, Bag, Bale, &c.

Trett is an Allowance made for Waste, Dust, &c. in sundry sorts of Goods, as Tobacco, Cotton, Pepper, Spices, &c. and is always 1*lb.* in each 104*lb.* Subtile, and found by dividing the Subtile Pounds by 26, because 4 times 26 make 104*lb.* When the Gross weight is brought into Pounds, and before the Tare is deducted, they are called *Pounds Gross*, and after the Tare is substracted the remaining Pounds are called *Pounds Subtile*, which divided by 26 (as before stated) quotes Pounds Trett, &c.

Tare at so much per Cask, Hogshead; Bag, &c.

The allowances for Tare variously wrought, as by the following examples:

In 12 Casks of Indigo, containing 45 *Cwt.* 1 *qr.* 14*lb.* Gross, Tare 30*lb. per* Cask, how many Pounds net?

```
   30lb.           Cwt. qr. lb.
   12               45   1  14
 ────────            4
 360 Pounds Tare   ────
                    181
                     28
                   ────
                   1462
                    362
                   ────
                   5082
   Subtract -       360
                   ────
   Answer. 4722
```

In this Example, the *lbs.* Tare of one Cask are multiplied by the Number of Casks, and the Product is 360 Pounds Tare; and the Gross Weight is reduced into Pounds by the method shown in Reduction of Weight; and then the Pounds Tare deducted from the Pounds Gross, and the remainder is Pounds net, *viz.* 4722, as above.

When the Tare is at so much *per Cwt.* multiply the Number of Hundreds by the Tare, and take parts for the odd Weight, adding to it the Tare found by Multiplication, and dividing by 112 to bring it into Gross Weight in order for Subtraction.

E 5

Example

Example.

What is the net Wt. of 12 Casks of Argol, Gross Wt.
84 *Cwt.* 2 *qrs.* 14*lb* ?

14 Tare per *Cwt.*		C. qrs. lb.

$$\begin{array}{l}\text{14 Tare per } Cwt.\\\hline 336\\84\\\hline 7 \text{ for half } Cwt.\\1\ \tfrac{3}{4} \text{ for 14lb.}\\\hline 112)1184\tfrac{3}{4}(10\ Cwt.\\112\\\hline64\text{lb. or half a } Cwt. \text{ and } 8lb.\end{array}$$

C. qrs. lb.
84—2—14
10—2— 8¼ Tare.
Answ. 74—0—5¼ net Wt.

The Tare in this example is to be found by the foregoing
Directions, 10 *C.* 2 *qrs.* 8*lb.* ¼, which subtracted as in the
work, leaves 74 *C.* 0 *qrs.* 5*lb.* ¼ for the Net Wt.

But this may be better performed by *Practice,* thus :

	Cwt.	qrs.	lbs.
14lb. is ⅛ of Cwt.	84	2	14 Gross.
Sub.	10	2	8¼ Tare
	74	0	5¼ net.

In this method the Gross Weight is divided by 8, because
14*lb.* is one Eighth of 112*lb.* and the remainder is reduced
into the next inferior Name, still divided by 8 to the end,
and then deducted as above, and the net Weight is the same
as by the other way. And so may any Tare *per Cwt.* be
found, if the Tare be an even part of 112*lb.* as 14 is one
Eighth, and 7*lb.* the Half of that, &c. that is, if the Tare be
at 7lb. *per C.* find it for 14*lb.* as before, and then take the
Half of that for 7*ld. per C.* Tare, the same for 8*lb. per Cwt.*
Tare ; taking one Seventh for 16*lb.* and then the Half of
that for 8*lb. per Cwt.* Tare.

Of TRETT, Example.

What *Trett* is, and how found, having been said already ;
now I shall give an Example for explanation, viz.

Bought six Hogsheads of Tobacco, containing Gross and
Tare as follows, viz.

No.		C.	qrs.	lb.	lb.
1	wt.	4	1	20 Tare	80
2		5	2	19	100
3		6	3	18	102
4		7	3	12	104
5		8	2	13	106
6		9	1	14	110
Subtile		42	3	12	602

26)4198(161*lb.* Trett

```
26)4198(161lb. Trett        42, 3  12        602
   26                        4
   ---                       ---
    159                      171
    156                       28
   ---                      ----
     38                      1380
     26                       342
   ---                      ----
     38                      4800 Pounds Gross.
     26           Subtract    602 Pounds Tare
   ---                       ----
26)192(7 oz.                 4198 Pounds Subtile.
   182           Deduct       161 7 Pounds Trett.
   ---                       ----
    10                       4030 9 Pounds Net.
```

There are a few other Rules, such as Barter, or exchange of Goods for Goods; for Coin, &c. but these being performed either by the Rule of Three, or by Practice, it is needless to enlarge upon them.

Of FRACTIONS, *Vulgar and Decimal.*

FRACTION is a Term for a part or parts of an Unit.

A VULGAR FRACTION is written with two Figures, or Numbers one above another, and a short line drawn between them. The *lower* number is called the Denominator, and this shows in how many equal parts the unit is supposed to be divided. The *higher* number is the Numerator, which shows how many of those parts are meant by the Fraction. Thus if I want to express 7d. as part of a Shilling, I write $\frac{7}{12}$. The Denominator 12 shows the number of Pence in a Shilling, and the Numerator 7 is the number given. If I would express 13 Shillings as a part of a pound, I write $\frac{13}{20}$: or if 35lb. as part of a Hundred Weight, I write $\frac{35}{112}$, because in the first case 20 Shillings make 1 pound, and in the second 112lbs. make 1 *Cwt.*

Fractions are thus set down and read, *viz.* $\frac{1}{4}$, one fourth; $\frac{1}{2}$, one half; $\frac{1}{3}$, one third; $\frac{1}{5}$ one fifth; $\frac{1}{6}$, one sixth; $\frac{2}{3}$, two thirds; $\frac{2}{4}$, two fourths; $\frac{5}{6}$, five sixths; $\frac{5}{7}$, five sevenths, &c.

Fractions are either proper or improper: A *proper* Fraction hath its Numerator less than the Denominator, as $\frac{5}{8}$, five eights; $\frac{24}{56}$, twenty-four fifty-sixths, &c.

An *improper* Fraction hath its Numerator *greater* than the Denominator; $\frac{7}{3}$, seven thirds; $\frac{48}{15}$, forty-eight fifteenths, &c.

Again

Fractions are either Simple or Compound ; Simple, when a Part of an Unit or Intreger, or thing, hath but one Numerator, and one Denominator ; as ¼ of a Pound Sterling, ¾ of *Cwt.* ½ of a Tun, of a Gallon, &c. Compound is a Fraction of a Fraction, as the ½ of a ¼ of a Pound Sterling, which is equal to Half a Crown ; or when one is divided into any number of parts, and those parts again subsided into parts, &c.

Again Fractions are of two kinds, *Vulgar* and *Decimal.* *Vulgar* Fractions are as before stated. *Decimal* Fractions are artificially expressed, by setting down the Numerators, only, the Nominators being understood ; and are always an unit, with as many Ciphers annexed as there are places in the Numerator ; and therefore may be either 10, or some power of 10, as 100, 1,000, 10,000, or 100,000, &c.

Decimal Fractions appear, and are worked as whole numbers, but are distinguished from them by a point or comma prefixed thus ; ,5 is read five tenths ; ,32 thirty-two Hundredths ; and ,256 two hundred fifty-six Thousandths ; but of *decimal* fractions, and their use, we shall treat hereafter.

REDUCTION *of Vulgar Fractions* is to prepare them for *Addition, Subtraction,* &c.

1. *To reduce a mixed Number to an improper Fraction.*

Multiply the Intreger by the Denominator, taking in the Numerator.

Ex. Reduce 12 Gallons ¾ to an improper Fraction, thus :

$$\frac{4}{51} \text{ New Numerator.}$$

Answer ⁵¹⁄₄ , or 51 Quarts.

2. *To reduce an improper Fraction to a whole or mixed Number.*

Divide the Numerator by the Denominator.
Ex. Reduce the above to a whole or mixed Number.
thus 51   4)5
    ——   ————
    4   12—3 remainder equal to ¾

Here 12 Gallons is the whole Number, ¾ the Fraction, the same with three Quarts.

3. *To reduce Fractions to a common Denominator.*

Multiply the Numerator of each Fraction into all the Denominators except its own, and the Product will be a Numerator to that Fraction; and so on by the others: The common Denominator is found by multiplying all the Denominators together.

Ex. Reduce $\frac{2}{3}$, $\frac{3}{4}$, and $\frac{5}{6}$ of any integer to a common Denominator; thus; twice 4 is 8, and 6 times 8 is 48, for a new Numerator to $\frac{2}{3}$; then 3 times 3 is 9, and 6 times 9 is 54; for a new Numerator to $\frac{3}{4}$; lastly, 5 times 4 is 20, and 3 times 20 is 60, the Numerator to $\frac{5}{6}$: Then to find the common Denominator, say 3 times 4 is 12, and 6 times 12 is 72, the common Denominator; so that $\frac{48}{72}$ is equal to $\frac{2}{3}$, $\frac{54}{72}$ is equal to $\frac{3}{4}$, and $\frac{60}{72}$ is equal to $\frac{5}{6}$. Which may be thus proved:

	s.	d.		
$\frac{2}{3}$ of a Pound is	13	4	48	72)162 (2 $\frac{18}{72}$ or 2 $\frac{1}{4}$
$\frac{3}{4}$ ditto	15	0	54	144
$\frac{5}{6}$ ditto	16	8	60	18
But 2*l.* $\frac{1}{4}$ = 2*l.* 5*s.* or	45	0	Common Denominator.	

Here the several Numerators are added together, and they make 162; which placed over the common Denominator 72, make the improper Fraction $\frac{162}{72}$; and its value is found as before shown in the Rule for reducing an improper Fraction to a whole or mixed Number.

4. *To reduce a Fraction into its lowest Terms.*

Rule. If they are even Numbers, take half of the Numerator and Denominator as long as you can; then divide them by any digit Number (*i. e.* 3, 4, 5, 6, *&c.*) that will leave no remainder in either.

Ex. Reduce $\frac{56}{84}$ into its lowest terms; thus the half of 56 is 28, and the $\frac{1}{2}$ of 84 is 42; then the half of 28 is 14, and the $\frac{1}{2}$ of 42 is 21: So the Fraction $\frac{56}{84}$ is reduced to $\frac{14}{21}$. And since these cannot be halved any further, for though you can halve 14, yet you cannot 21, without Remainder; try therefore to divide them by some other digit Number: you will there find, that 7 will divide both Numerator and Denominator without any remainder; then say the 7's in 14 twice, and the 7's in 21, three times: So the Fraction $\frac{56}{84}$ reduced into its lowest terms, will be $\frac{2}{3}$, which is of the same value as $\frac{56}{84}$. The working is performed in the following manner.

2	2	7	
56	28	14	2
84	42	21	3

And the Proof that $\frac{2}{3}$ is of equal value with $\frac{56}{84}$ appears by multiplying any Integer by the Numerator of each Fraction, and by dividing by the Denominator of each Fraction.

Ex. Let the Integer be £ 1. Sterling, or 20*s*. The Fraction $\frac{56}{84}$

```
   s.                      s.
   20                      20
    2                      56
 ----                 ----------
 3) 40                84)1120(13s.
 ------                   84
   13—4d.                ----
                          280
                          252           13s 4d.
                         ----
                           28
                           12
                         ----
                          336(4d.
                          336
                         ----
                          (0)
```

Here it is manifest, that by working by a Fraction in its lowest terms, much time and figures are saved. In one operation, 20 the Integer is multiplied by 2, and the Product 40 divided by 3, and there remains 1) or $\frac{1}{3}$ of a Shilling, or a Groat, as in the other work.

There are other Methods of reducing a Fraction into its lowest terms; but none so ready as the foregoing, where it can be used.

5. *To reduce a Compound Fraction into a Simple one of the same Value.*

Rule. Multiply the Numerators together for a new Numerator, and the Denominators for a new Denominator.

Ex. Reduce $\frac{2}{3}$ of $\frac{3}{4}$ of $\frac{5}{6}$ a Pound Sterling into a simple Fraction. Thus twice 3 is 6, and 5 times 6 is 30, the Numerator; then three times 4 is 12, and 6 times 12 is 72, the Denominator: so $\frac{30}{72}$ of a Pound is equivalent to $\frac{2}{3}$ of $\frac{3}{4}$ of $\frac{5}{6}$ of a *lb.* Thus proved, $\frac{5}{6}$ of a *lb.* 16*s.* 8*d.* and $\frac{3}{4}$ of 16*s.* 8*d.* is 12*s.* 6*d.* and $\frac{2}{3}$ of 12*s.* 6*d.* is 8*s.* 4*d.* the Answer. And multiplying 20*s.* by 30, and dividing by 72, gives the same Answer, as is seen in the following Work.

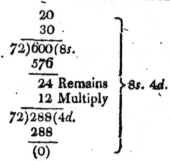

```
        20
        30
    72)600(8s.
       576
        ───
        24 Remains  } 8s. 4d.
        12 Multiply
    72)288(4d.
       288
       ───
       (0)
```

6. *To find the Value of any Fraction, whether of Coins, Weights or Measures.*

Multiply the Integer by the Numerator, and divide by the Denominator; and if any thing remains, multiply it by the Number of Units of the next inferior Denomination.

Ex. 1. What is 3/5 of a Pound, or 20s.? The Operation of the foregoing Example of Proof to the Compound Fraction 3/4 of 4/5, answers this Question, and need not repetition.

E. 2. What is the amount of 5/6 of a Ton Weight?

```
              20 Integer.
               5 Numeratorr
Denominator  6)100
              ─────────────────
              16  2  18  10 4/6
           Cwt. qrs. lb. oz.
  Answ.    16    2    18    10 4/6
```

Here the Integer 20 *C.* is multiplied by the Numerator 5; and the Product 100 divided by the Denominator 6, and the Remainder 4 is multiplied by the parts of the next inferior Denomination, &c. the Answer is 16 *Cwt.* 2*qrs.* 18*lbs.* 10*oz.* 4/6 or 2/3 of an Ounce Weight as above.

ADDITION of VULGAR FRACTION.

IF the Fractions to be added have a common Denominator, add the Numerators together for a Numerator, which place over the common Denominator, and the work is done.

Ex. Add 2/5, 3/5, and 4/5 of a Pound Sterling together. Thus 2 and 3 is 5, and 4 is 9, the Numerator; which place over 5 the common Denominator, thus 9/5, and this improper Fraction 9/5, is in value 36s. for 9 times 4s. (the 5th of a

Pound,

Pound) is 36s. for if the number 9 be divided by the Denominator 5, I say the 5's in 9 once, and 4 remains, which is $\frac{4}{5}$ of a Pound, or 16s.

$$5)9$$
$$\overline{\quad 1 \quad}$$

But if the Fractions to be added have unequal Denominators, they must be first reduced to a common Denominator, by the Rule before shown, before addition can be made ; and then proceed as above.

2. When mixed Numbers are to be added, work with the fractional parts as before, and carry the fractional value to the whole Numbers.

Example.

Add 25l. $\frac{1}{4}$ to 12 $\frac{1}{4}$, thus 26$\frac{1}{4}$
$$12\frac{1}{4}$$
$$\overline{\text{£. 38} \ \textit{Answer.}}$$

Here 1 and 3, the Numerators, make 4 ; and $\frac{4}{4}$ is 1, and 2 is 3, and 5 makes 8 ; and 1 and 2 is 3, the Answer is 38. Or they may be reduced to improper Fractions, thus:

25$\frac{1}{4}$	12$\frac{1}{4}$	103
4	4	49
103	49	4)152
4	4	38 Pounds.

Here the Numerators are added, and their Total is 152 ; which divided by 4, the common Denominator, quotes 38 Pounds, as above.

3. When compound Fractions are to be added to simple ones, reduce the compound Fractions to a simple one, as before directed ; and then proceed as above.

Ex. 1. Add $\frac{2}{8}$ and $\frac{3}{8}$ to $\frac{1}{2}$ of $\frac{4}{4}$ a Pound ; thus once 2 is 2, and twice 4 is 8, therefore $\frac{2}{8}$ is equal to the compound Fraction. Then saying, 2 and 3 is 5, and 2 is 7, the new Numerator; and $\frac{7}{8}$, equal to 17s. 6d. will be the Answer.

Ex. 2. Add $\frac{1}{4}$ to $\frac{2}{3}$ of $\frac{1}{4}$ of a Shilling. The work will be $\frac{1}{4}$ added to $\frac{2}{12}$, but these must be brought to a common Denominator, and the Fractions will then be $\frac{3}{6}$ added $\frac{2}{6}$ which will be $\frac{5}{6}$, or when brought to the lowest Terms $\frac{5}{8}$ of a Shilling; the 8th of a Shilling is 1d$\frac{1}{2}$. therefore $\frac{5}{8}$ is 7d$\frac{1}{2}$.

That this Answer is right is thus proved : I am to add $\frac{1}{4}$ of a Shilling, or 4d$\frac{1}{2}$. to $\frac{2}{3}$ of $\frac{1}{4}$ of a Shilling, now the third of a Shilling is 4d. and $\frac{3}{4}$ of 4d. must be 3d. of course 4d$\frac{1}{2}$ added to 3d. 7d$\frac{1}{2}$. according to the Answer as above.

Subtraction

Subtraction of Vulgar Fractions.

IN this Rule the Fractions must have a common Denominator, or be reduced to one, before any deduction can be made.

Ex. What is the difference between $\frac{1}{3}$ and $\frac{1}{4}$? Answer $\frac{1}{4}$ which may be proved by Addition, for $\frac{1}{4}$ and $\frac{1}{3}$ make $\frac{3}{4}$.

Note. The difference between the Numerators is the difference of the Fractions.

Again; from $\frac{3}{4}$ of a Pound take $\frac{5}{12}$: Here the Fractions are to be reduced to a common Denominator; 36 is the first Numerator, and 20 the second Numerator, their difference is 16; and 48 is the common Denominator: so that $\frac{16}{48}$ or $\frac{1}{3}$, in its lowest terms, is the difference between $\frac{3}{4}$ of a Pound, and $\frac{5}{12}$ of a Pound.

To subtract a compound Fraction from a simple one.

Rule. Reduce a compound Fraction to a simple one, and work as before.

Ex. From $\frac{13}{14}$ take $\frac{2}{3}$ of $\frac{8}{9}$. say twice 8 is 16, and 3 times 9 is 27, therefore $\frac{16}{27}$ is equal to a compound Fraction. Then the $\frac{13}{14}$ and $\frac{16}{27}$ must be reduced to a common Denominator, thus: 13 times 27 is 351s, the first Numerator; 16 times 14 is 224, the second Numerator; and 4 times 27 is 378s. the common Denominator. Subtract 224 the second Numerator, from 35; the first Numerator, and the remainder is 127, which place over 378, the common Denominator, thus $\frac{127}{378}$ Answer.

When a simple Fraction is to be deducted from a whole Number.

Rule. Subtract the Numerator of the Fraction from the Denominator, and place the remainder over the Denominator, carrying 1 to subtract from the whole Number, &c.

Example:

From 12*l.* take $\frac{5}{8}$ of a Pound; thus: 5 (the Numerator) from 8 (the Denominator) and there remains 3, which place over the Denominator 3, thus $\frac{3}{8}$; then 1 from 12 and there remains 11. So the Answer is, *l.* 11 $\frac{3}{8}$, or *l.* 11. 7. 6.

Multiplication of Vulgar Fractions.

Rule.—Multiply the Numerators into one another for the Numerator of the Product; and then do the same by the Denominators, for the Denominator of the Product.

Ex.

Ex. Multiply $\frac{3}{4}$ of a Pound by $\frac{5}{6}$ of ditto: say 3 times 5 is 15, the Numerator; and 4 times 6 is 24, the Denominator: So the Answer is $\frac{15}{24}$, or in the lowest term $\frac{5}{8}$.

You are to observe, that Multiplication in Fractions lessens the product, though in whole numbers it augments it; as above $\frac{5}{8}$, or 12*s.* 6*d.* is less than $\frac{5}{6}$, or 16*s.* 8*d.* and also less than the other Fraction $\frac{3}{4}$, or 15*s.*

2. *To multiply a whole Number by a Fraction.*

Rule. Multiply the Integer by the Numerator of the Fraction, and place the product over the Denominator.

Note. Multiplication by a Fraction implies the taking away some part or parts of the Multiplicand, and therefore, may be truly expressed by a Compound Fraction. Thus $\frac{1}{2}$ multiplied by $\frac{3}{4}$, is the same as $\frac{1}{2}$ of $\frac{3}{4}$ or $\frac{3}{8}$: and therefore though the rule is called Multiplication, it produces contrary effects from Multiplication in whole numbers.

Example: Multiply £ 56 by $\frac{3}{4}$.

$$\begin{array}{r} 56 \\ 3 \\ \hline 168 \\ \hline 4 \end{array} \Big\} \textit{ Facit.}$$

This improper Fraction $\frac{168}{4}$ reduced, according to rule, makes but 42*lb.* which is less than 56: and confirms what has been asserted, *viz.* that Multiplication of Fractions lessens the Product, &c.

To multiply a Simple by a Compound Fraction.

Rule. Reduce the Compound Fraction to a Simple one, according to the foregiong rules, and work as above.

Ex. Multiply $\frac{6}{8}$ of a Pound, by $\frac{2}{3}$ of $\frac{3}{4}$ of a Pound: say 6 times 6 is 36, and 8 times 12 is 96. So that the answer is $\frac{36}{96}$, or $\frac{3}{8}$ in its lowest terms; equal to 7*s.* 6*d.*

Division of Vulgar Fractions.

MULTIPLY the Numerator of the Divisor into the Denominator of the Dividend, and the Product is the Denominator of the Quotient; then multiply the Denominator of the Divisor into the Numerator of the Dividend, and the product will be the Numerator of the Quotient.

Ex. Divide $\frac{15}{16}$ by $\frac{2}{3}$. The work will stand thus:

$\frac{2}{3}$) $\frac{15}{16}$ ($\frac{45}{32}$ Quotient.

Here

Here 16, multiplied by 2, gives 32; and 15 by 3, gives 45! So the Quotient is $\frac{32}{45}$ equal to 1 $\frac{17}{45}$, as in the work.

Again, suppose $\frac{7}{4}$ was divided by $\frac{7}{4}$, the Quotient will be $\frac{7}{7}$, equal to 1 Integer, or whole thing. And so for any other Example.

Reduction of DECIMAL FRACTIONS.

What a *Decimal Fraction* is, has been already shown. The next thing is how to reduce a Vulgar Fraction into a Decimal, which is no more than to annex Ciphers at discretion. (that is 2, 3, or 4, &c.) to the Numerator, and then dividing by the Denominator.

$$\frac{4)3,00}{75}$$

Ex. 1 Reduce $\frac{3}{4}$ of a Pound Sterling to a Decimal that is, 75 hundredths, equal to 3 qrs. of any thing, whether Money, Weight, Measure, &c. as being $\frac{3}{4}$, and is written 75 of 100: and so 25 hundredths is, in Decimals, the Quarter of any thing, as being the $\frac{1}{4}$ of a 100; and is expressed ,25; and five tenths expresses the half of any thing, as being the $\frac{1}{2}$ of 10, as this, ,5.

In Reduction of Decimals it sometimes happens that a cipher or ciphers must be placed on the *left* hand of the Decimal, to supply the defect of the want of places in the Quotient of Division. In this case always remember that so many ciphers as you *annex* to the denominator of the Vulgar Fraction, so many places you must point off in the quotient towards the left hand; but if there be not so many places to point off, then you must supply the defect by placing a cipher to the left of the Decimal.

Ex. 2. Reduce 9d. or $\frac{9}{12}$ to the Decimal of a Shilling, thus:

$$\frac{12)9,00}{,75}$$

equal to ,75 or 75 hundredths of a Shilling, or to 9d.

Ex. 3. Reduce 9d. to the Decimal of a Pound Sterling.

In this case the Denominator of the Fraction will be 240, as 240 Pence make a Pound: and the work will stand thus:

$$240)9,0000(,0375$$
$$\underline{720}$$
$$1800$$
$$\underline{1680}$$
$$1200$$
$$\underline{1200}$$
$$....$$

Here are but three places in the Quotient, viz. 375; and therefore I cannot point off 4 for the four ciphers annexed to 9; wherefore I prefix 0 to the left of the Quotient 375, thus, ,0375, and then it is 375 ten thousand parts of an Integer; and in Vulgar Fractions it would stand thus $\frac{375}{10000}$

The

The more ciphers are annexed, when the Answer is not exact, the nearer will it bring the Decimal to the truth; in most cases, however, four. ciphers annexed are sufficient. But when you are to reduce $\frac{1}{4}$, $\frac{1}{2}$, or $\frac{3}{4}$ (as above) of an Integer to a Decimal, or any Number of Shillings to a Decimal of a Pound, two ciphers are sufficient.

Ex. 4. Reduce 3 Farthings to the Decimal of a Pound, that is the Vulgar Fraction $\frac{3}{960}$ Farthings in a Pound.

96|0)3,0000|0(,003125. The Work being performed according to the Division, with two ciphers prefixed, quotes ,003125, or 3125 Ten Hundred Thousandth Parts of a Pound; and in Vulgar Fractions it would stand thus; *viz.* $\frac{3125}{1000000}$

Ex. 5. How is 12 Pounds Weight expressed in the Decimal of 1 *Cwt. Avoirdupois*, or 112*lb*? The Vulgar Fraction is $\frac{12}{112}$, and the Decimal ,1071, found as before thus:

112)12,0000(,1071

112
80, &c.

The Remainder, 48, is not worth Noticing, being less than the 100000 part of a Unit, or 1.

Ex. 6. How is 73 Days brought to the Decimal of a Year? vulgarly thus expressed $\frac{73}{365}$ 36,5
365)730(,2 *Ans.* 2 tenths or ,2.   *Thus proved* 36,5
730   73
(0)

Here 365, the Days of the Year, are divided by 10, twice, and the Quotients added together make 73 Days.

Valuation of Dividends.

TO find the value of a Decimal Fraction whether of Corn, Weight, Measure, &c.

Rule. Multiply the Decimal given, by the Units contained in the next inferior Denomination, and point off as many places from the right hand as you have in your Decimal; those figures towards the left of the point are Integers, or whole Numbers; and those on the other side towards the right hand, are parts of 1. or Unity; that is, so many Tenths, Hundredths, Thousandths, or Ten Thousandths, of one of those Integers, whether a Pound, a Shilling, or a Penny, &c. of a Ton, a Hundred, a Quarter, or a Pound weight, &c. And so many of any other Integer, of what quality or kind soever.

Ex.

Ex. 1.   ,476 Parts of a Pound Sterling.
      23 Shillings a Pound.
     ————
   9,520
      12 Pence one Shilling.
    ————
   6,240 *Answer* 9s. 6d. ,240

Ex. 2.   ,476 Parts of a Ton. Wt.
           20 *Cwt.* 1 Ton.
           ————
         9,521
            4 *qrs.* 1 *Cwt*
Answer   2,080
9 *C.* 2 *lb.* 2 *lu.* 240 Parts   28 *lb,* 1 *qr.* of a *Cwt.*
           2,240

In the Example of Money multiply the Fraction by 20, and point off 520 for the three places in the Decimal, &c. and the Answer is 9s. 6d. and 240 over, or $\frac{240}{1000}$, which is nearly equal to a Farthing.

In the Example of Weight, proceed as in that of money, but differently with respect to the inferior Denominators, and the Answer is 9 *Cwt.* 2 *qrs.* 2*lb.* $\frac{240}{1000}$ of a *lb.*

To find the value of a Decimal in Money by a short method, *viz.*

Rule. Always account the double of the first figure (to the left hand) for shillings; and if the next to it is 5, reckon one shilling more: and whatever is above 5, call every one ten; and the next figure so many ones as it contains; which Tens and ones call Farthings; and for every 24, abate one. As in the last Example of Money, *viz.* 476, the double of 4 is 8, and there being one 5 in 7, (the next figure) reckon 1s. more, which makes 9s. and there being 2 (in the 7) above 5, they are to be accounted two Tens, or 20; which with the next figure 6 being so many Ones, making 26 Farthings; and abating 1 for 24, they give 6d. and a Farthing more.

Addition of Decimals.

IS the same in Practice as in whole Numbers, only in setting down, care must be taken that the Decimal Parts stand respectively under like Parts; that is, Primes under Primes, Seconds under Seconds, Thirds under Thirds, &c. and the Integers stand as in whole Numbers.

Example.

Example.

Inte-gers.	Primes	Seconds	Thirds		Parts			Primes	Seconds	Thirds	Fourths	Fifths
2 4 6	,4	2	6		,4	7 . 9	6	,4	7	9	6	2
˙7 4	,4	2			,4	2		,0	6	4	2	
9	,0	6			,0	7	6	,0	0	6		
6 5	,7	9	4		,0	0 0 .	4	,7				
4 2	,0 0	5			,5			,9				
4 3 7	,7 0 5				1 ,4 7 6 0			2 ,1 4 9 8 2				

Note. *There must be as many Places pointed off as there are in that Number which has most Decimal Places.*

The casting up of the foregoing Examples is the same with addition of one Denomination in whole Numbers, The total of the first (supposing them Pounds Sterling) is 437*l.* and ,705 Parts. The second is 1*l.* and 4760 Parts. And the third is 2*l.* and ,14982 Parts.

Subtraction of Decimals.

THE Number must be placed as before in *Addition*, and then proceed as in *Subtraction of Numbers of one Denomination.*

l. pts.	*l.* pts.	*l.* pts.
46,51	144,42	4762,0
9.24	91,7462	0,472
37.27	42,6738	4761,528

Multiplication of Decimals.

HERE the placing the Numbers and the Operation is the very same as in the whole Numbers; remember only to point off, towards the right hand, so many places for Decimals as you have Decimal places in both *Multiplicand* and *Multiplier.*

Example.

(1)	(2)	(3)
24,6	4602	,2796
2,5	075	26
1230	23010	16776
492	32214	5592
61,50	345,150	7,2696

(4)

(4)	(5)	(6)
,07214	,083	4,25
,006	,16	1,09
,00043284	498	3225
	093	4250
	,01328	4,6325

Note, That when there are not a competent number of figures, or places to point off, the defect is supplied with ciphers, to the left hand, as in the 4th and 5th examples, according to what has before been stated in reducing a Vulgar Fraction to a Decimal.

Division of Decimals.

IS the same in operation as in whole numbers, the only difficulty is to know how many Decimal places to point off, towards the left hand of the Quotient, to which end, remember this rule; observe how many Decimal places there are, both in the Divisor and in the Dividend, and find the difference; and whatever it is, so many places must be pointed off to the right hand of the Quotient.

Ex. 1. Divide 12,845670 by 6,789, and the work stands as thus :   6,789)12,345670(1,818 *Answ.*

In this example, the Dividend hath three Decimal places more than the Divisor, wherefore I point off three places to the right hand of the Quotient, *viz.* 118 ; so the Quotient is 1 Integer, and ,813 parts.

```
6,789 . . .
55566
54312
12547
 6789
57580
 54312
 3268
```

Ex. 2. Divide 3,46000 by 1,23 :

Here the difference between the Decimal places in the Devisor and Dividend is three places ; as in the foregoing Example, therefore 813 is pointed off for the Decimal Fraction; and the Quotient is 3 Integers, and ,813 Thousandths of an Integer.

```
1,23)3,46000(2,813
246 .·.
1000
 984
 160
 123
 370
 369
 (1)
```

The

The Reader, who has attended thus far, is recommended to look through the whole from the beginning; he will find but little difficulty, and much satisfaction and pleasure in treading over the same ground again, and amusing himself by working other examples which he may readily devise under every Rule.

OF BOOK-KEEPING.

BOOK-KEEPING is the Art of recording Mercantile Transactions in a regular and systematic manner.

A Merchant's Books should exhibit the true State of his Affairs. They should show at first sight, as it were, the particular State of each transaction, and exhibit also the general result of the whole: and they should be so arranged as to afford correct and ready Information upon every subject for which they may be consulted.

Books may be kept either by *single* or *double Entry*.

Single Entry is chiefly used in Retail Business; it is the most concise and simple method of Book-keeping, but not the most perfect.

Double Entry is generally used in Wholesale and Mercantile Affairs, whence it is usually called by way of pre-eminence *Merchants Accounts*. Of these we have now to give an Account: and it is not without good reason, that most people of business and ingenuity are desirous to be masters of this art; for if we consider the satisfaction that naturally arises from an account well kept, the pleasure that accrues to a person by seeing what he gains, by the species of goods he deals in, and his whole profit by a year's trade; and thereby also to know the true state of his Affairs and Circumstances, so that he may, according to discretion, retrench or enlarge his Expences, &c. as he shall think fit, the acquirement of this knowledge must surely be desirable.

The Books of principal use in the business of Double Entry are the *Waste Book*, (by some called the *Memorial*) *Journal*, and *Ledger*.

Waste Book.

IN this Book must be daily written in the order of time, in which it happens, whatever occurs in the way of trade; Buying, Selling, Receiving, Delivering, Bargaining, Shipping, &c. without omission of any one thing either Bought, Sold, Borrowed, &c.

The

The *Waste Book* is ruled with one marginal line, and three Lines for Pounds, Shillings, and Pence, and the Day of the Month, and Year of our Lord, is inserted in the middle of the page. In this Book any one may write, and on occasion, any thing may be blotted out, if not well entered, or any Error be made.

JOURNAL.

INTO this Book every article is brought out of the *Waste Book*, but in other terms, in a better style, and in a fairer hand, without any alteration of Ciphers or Figures: and every item is promiscuously set down without intermission, to make the Book, or the several Entries in it, of more Credit and Validity in case of any Law dispute, or any controversy that may happen between Merchant and Merchant. In this Book you are to distinguish the Debtor and Creditor (or in other terms, the *Debts* and *Credits).* And to this Book you must have recourse for the Particulars of an account which in the Ledger are entered in one Line. In this Book also, the day of the month is usually placed in the middle of the page: it is ruled with double Marginal Lines, for reference to the Ledger, and with three Lines for *£. s. d.* as the Waste Book.

Of the Ledger.

From the *Journal* or *Day Book* all matters or things are posted into the Ledger, which by the *Spaniards* is called *El Libro Grande,* as being the largest Book, or chief of Accounts. The left hand side of this Book is called the *Debtor,* and the right the *Creditor* side; and the *Numbers* or *Folios* of each side must be alike, as 45 *Debtor,* and also 45 *Creditor.* The day of the month (in this Book) is set in a narrow Column on the left hand, and the month on the left of that: But where I kept Books, the Number in the narrow Column referred to the Journal Page, and the Month and Day were placed in the broad Column, to the right of that; and at the head of each Folio the name of the place of residence, and the Year of our Lord; as thus:

London, Anno.................... 1810,

But the Example of these several Books hereafter following will make the foregoing hints of them much more intelligible. The following is a general Rule, upon which most of the Entries in Book-keeping depend, viz.

F   All

All things Received, or the Receivers, are Debtors to the Delivered, or the Deliverer.

	l.	*s.*	*d.*
Waste Book Entry.			
Bought of *John Wilks*, of *Norton Falgate*, 120 Yards of white Sarcenet, as 2s. 3d. per Yard, to pay in two Months	13	10	—
The Journal Entry of the same.			
Wrought Silk, Debtor to *John Wilks*, *l.* 13 10s. for 120 Yards of white Sarcenet at 2s. 3d. per Yard to pay in two Months - - - - -	13	10	—
In this Example the wrought Silks are received, and therefore Debtor to *John Wilks* the Deliverer.			
Waste Book Entry. *January* 4, 1810.			
Sold *James Chapman*, 246*lb.* nett of Indigo, at 6s. 6d. per lb. to pay in 3 Months -	79	19	—
Journal Entry.			
James Chapman Dr. to Indigo, for 246lb. nett, at 6s. 6d. per lb. to pay in 3 Months - - - -	79	19	—
Waste Book Entry.			
Bought of *George Goodinch*, sen. *viz.*			
Chesh. Cheese 430 Cwt. ½. at 23s. 4d. per Cwt £ 502 5			
Butter, 50 Firkins, qt. nett } 2800lb. at 3d. per lb. 35 0			
to pay at 6 Months - -	537	5	—
Journal Entry.			
Sundry Accounts, Cr. to *George Goodinch*, *l.* 537 5			
Chesh. Cheese, for 480 Cwt. } ½, at 23s. 4d. per Cwt. £. 502 5			
Butter, for 59 Firkins, qt. nett } 2800lb. at 3d. per lb. 35 0			
to pay in 6 Months.			
	537	6	—

Waste

Waste Book.

Sold to *James Jenkins*, viz.			
White Sarcenet, 50 Yards at 3s. per Yard -	7	10	0
Indigo, 50 Pounds, at 7s. per pound - -	17	10	0
		25	

6
7

Journal Entry of the last.

James Jenkins, Debtor to sundry Accounts, viz.

To white Sarcenet, for 50 yards, at 3s. per yard - -	l. 7	10	0
To Indigo, for 50 lb. at 7s. per lb. - -	17	10	0
		25	

From these few Examples of Entry, it may be observed, that a Person experienced in Accounts, and a good Writer, may keep a Journal without a Waste Book, or a Waste Book without a Journal, since they both import one and the same thing, though they differ a little in words or expression.

But, however, I shall give Methods of keeping each, as far as room will allow.

(1)

The Waste Book.

London, *January* 1st. 1810.

An Inventory of all the Money, Goods, and Debts, belonging to me A. B. of London, *Merchant, viz.*

In cash - -	3500—	—	
In Tobacco, 4726 lb. at 9d. per lb.	117	4	6
In Broad Cloth, 6 Pieces at 50s. per Piece	15	—	—
Dowlas, 1000 Ells, at 2s. 4d. per Ell	116	13	4
Canary Wines, 9 Pipes, at £ 30 per Pipe	270	—	—
Due to me from *Henry Bland,* per Bond	60	—	—
	4138	17	10

(1)

Journal.

Inventory, &c.   £   s.

			£	s.	d.
		Sundry Accts. Dr. to Stock—4138 17 10			
		viz.			
1	1	Cash———————	3500	—	—
		Tobacco, for 4726lb. at 9d. per lb.	177	4	6
	1	Broad cloths for 6 Pieces, at 5s. per Piece	15	—	—
		Dowlas, for 1000 Ells, at 2s. 4d. per Ell.	161	13	4
	1	Canary Wines, for 9 Pipes at £ 30 per Pipe.	270	—	—
	3	*Henry Bland,* due on Bond	60	—	—
			4138	17	

I shall make one Page serve for Waste Book and Journal
Entries, to save room, and also to have both Methods of
Entry under Eye, to make them more intelligibly useful to
the Reader, without being obliged to turn over to see their
difference of Entry.

Waste Book.

	London, January 1st. ————————1810.		£	s.	d.
	Owing to *William Webb,* by Note of Hand	50	—	—	
	Ditto to *Roger Ruff,* the balance of his Account	16	12	4	
	Ditto to *Henry Horn* due the 4th of May next	62	—	—	
			128	12	4
1	*Journal.*				
3	Stock Debtor to Sundry Accounts, £. 128 12 4. *viz.*				
	To *Henry Webb* by my Note of Hand	50	—	—	
	To *Roger Ruff,* for the Balance of his Account	16	12	4	
	To *Henry Horn,* due the 4th of May next.	62	—	—	
			128	12	4

Waste

Waste Book.

London, Feb. 2d.———— ————1810.	£.	s.	d.
Sold *Thomas Townshend, viz.*			
246 *lb.* of *Virginia* Cut Tobacco, at 14*d* per lb. } 14 7 —			
460 Ells of Dowlas, at 3*s.* per Ell } 69 — —			
	83	7	

Feb. 2.
Journal.

6 *Thomas Townshend* , Debtor to Sundries, *viz.*			
1 To Tobacco, for 246 lb. at 14*d.* per lb. } 14 7 —			
To Dowlas, for 460 Ells, at 3*s.* per Ell } 69 — —			
	83	7	—

Waste Book.
Ditto 24th.

Bought of *Leonard Legg*, four Pipes of Canary, at *£.* 28 per Pipe. To pay in 6 Months.	112	—	—

Ditto 24th.
Journal.

1 Canary Wines, Debtor to *Leonard Legg,* for 4 Pipes, at 28 Pounds per Pipe——			
2 To pay in 6 Months.	112	—	—

The short Lines ruled against the Journal Entries are, or may be, termed Posting Lines, and the Figure on the Top of the Lines denote the Folio of the Ledger where the Debtor is entered; and the Figure under the Line shows the Folio of the Ledger where the Credit is entered; and the other smaller Figures against the sundry Debtors, or sundry Creditors (whether Goods or Persons) show also in what Folios of the Ledger they are posted.

The Accounts of Persons and Things are kept in the Ledger, on opposite Pages, in which those, which in the Journal are said to be Debtors, are entered on the Left Hand Page, with the word *To*; and those, to which they are said to be Creditors, are entered on the Right Hand Page, with the word *By*. For instance, the last Journal Entry should be posted on the Left Hand, or Debtor's Side, of the Account of *Canary* Wines, thus:

F 5

1810. *Feb.* 24.   *To Leonard Legg*——4 Pipes—112 0 0
And the same should be posted on the right hand, or Cre-
ditor Side, of the Account of Leonard Legg, thus :
Feb. 24. By *Canary* Wines to pay in 6 Months, 112 0 0

There are several other Books used by Merchants, besides the three before mentioned: as the *Cash-Book*, which
is ruled like the Ledger, and in this all Receipts of Money
are entered on the left hand Folio, and payments on the
right; specifying in every Entry the Day of the Month
(the Year being set on the Top) for what and for whose
Account the Money was received, or paid; and the total
Debit or Credit on each side is to be posted into the Ledger
to the account of cash therein, in one line of either side, *viz.*
to, or by sundry accounts, as *per* Cash-book, Folio, &c.
which is to be done once a month, or at discretion, and
the Particulars of each Side, Article by Article, are to be
posted into the Ledger to the proper Accounts to which
they belong: with references in the Cash-book to the several Folios in the Ledger : and carry the Balance over
leaf into the Cash-book, by which you may know at any
time what cash you have, or ought to have by you,

Another Book, is a Book of Charges of Merchandize,
wherein is to be entered the Custom and petty Charges of
any Goods shipped; as porterage, wharfage, warehouse-
room, &c. which once a month is transferred into the Cash
book on the Credit Side, making reference to the Book of
Charges of Merchandise; and likewise 'the same in the
Debtor Side of the same Account in the Ledger for the
Amount thereof.

The next Book I shall name, is the Invoice-book, or
Book of Factories. In this Book is to be copied all Invoices
of Goods shipped, either for Accompts proper or portable;
and also of Goods received from abroad, which must always be entered on the left side, leaving the right side
blank; and on the advice of the disposal of goods sent
abroad, and also on the sale of goods received from abroad,
enter them on the blank or right side; so at first view may
be seen how the accompt stands, &c.

The next is a Bill-book, in which are entered Bills of
Exchange accepted, and when they become due ; and when
paid, they should be made so in the margin.

The next is a Book of Household Expenses, for the
monthly

monthly Charges of Housekeeping; likewise Apparel, House-rent, Servants Wages, and Pocket Expences; and this may be monthly summed up, and carried to the Credit of Cash.

Besides the above-mentioned, there must be a Book to copy all Letters sent Abroad, or beyond the Seas; in which the Name of the Person or Persons to whom the Letter is sent must be written full, for the readier finding it.

Then next, (and what is very necessary) a Receipt-book, wherein are given Receipts for Money, paid and expressed for whose Account or Use, or for what it is received; to which the receiving Person must set his Name for himself, or some other, with the year and day of the month on the top.

Lastly, A Note, or Memorandum-book, to minute down Affairs that occur, for the better help of memory, and is of great use, where there is a multiplicity of Business.

Having given an account of the several books and their use, the next thing will be to give some new Rules of Aid, to enable the Book-keeper to make proper Entries; and to distinguish the several Debtors and Creditors, *viz.*

First, For Money received, make Cash Dr. to the Party that paid it (if for his own account) and the Party Cr.

Secondly, For Money paid, make the Receiver Dr. (if for his own account) and Cash Cr.

Thirdly, For Goods bought for ready Money, make the Goods Dr. to Cash, and Cash Cr. by the Goods.

Fourthly, Goods sold for ready Money just the contrary, *i. e.* Cash Dr. and Goods Cr.

Fifthly, Goods bought for Time; Goods bought are Dr. to the Seller of them, and the Seller Cr. by the Goods.

Sixthly, Goods sold for Time, just the contrary, *i. e.* the Party that bought them is Dr. to the Goods, and the Goods Cr. by the Party.

Seventhly, Goods bought, part for ready Money, and the rest for Time; First make the Goods Dr. to the Party for the whole; Secondly, make the Party Dr. to Cash for the money paid him in part of those goods.

Eighthly, Goods sold, part for ready Money, and the rest for Time: First, make the Party Dr. to the Goods for the whole. Secondly, Cash Dr. to the Party received of him in part of those Goods.—Or either of these two last Rules may be made Dr. to Sundries; as Goods bought,

Dr.

Dr. to the seller for so much as is left unpaid, and to **Cash** for so much as is left unpaid, and to Cash for so much paid in ready Money: And so on the contrary for Goods sold.

Ninthly, When you pay money before it is due, and are to have discount allowed you, make the Person Dr. to Cash for so much as you pay him, and to Profit and Loss for the Discount; or make the receiver Dr. to Sundries as before.

Profit and Loss is Dr.

To Cash for what Money you pay and have nothing for it, as discount of Money you receive before due, and for abatement by composition, household expences, &c.

Per contra Cr.

By Cash for all you receive, and deliver nothing for it, as Discount for prompt Payment, any Legacy left you, Money received with an Apprentice, and by the Profit of every particular commodity you deal in, by Ships in Company, by Voyage, &c.

To balance, or clear an Account when full written.

FIRST, if the Dr. side be more than the Credit, make the old Account Cr. by the new; and if the contrary, make the new Account Dr. to the old. But if the Dr. side be less than the Credit, then make the old Account Dr. to the new; and the new Account Cr. by the old, for such a Rest or Sum as you shall find in the Account.

2. An Account of Company, wherein you have placed more received of another than his Stock; then add as much on the debit side as you find on the credit side; to the end that in the new Account you have so much debit as you put in, and so much credit as you have received.

3. In Accounts of Merchandise you must enter the gain, or loss, before you make the old Account Cr. by the new, and the new Dr. to the old, for the remainder of the goods unsold.

4. In the Foreign Accompts, which you are to keep with a double column for the Dollars, Crowns, or other Foreign Coins, as well as their Value in *l. s. d.* which have been received or paid, by Bills of Exchange for Goods sold by Factors or Correspondents, or bought by them for the Accompts before: here you must first balance the said inward column of Dollars, Crowns, &c.

T*

To remove an Accompt full written to another Folio.

Sum or add up the Dr. and Cr. sides, and see the difference, which place to its opposite: admit the Cr. side exceeds the Dr. then you are to write the line in the old Accompt to balance on the Dr. side, to answer the line on the Cr. side of the new Accompt.

How to balance at the Year's End, and thereby to know the State of your Affairs and Circumstances.

YOU must make an Accompt, of balance on the next void Leaf or Folio of your Ledger to your other Accompts; but after so done, do not venture to draw out the Accompt of Balance in the said Folio till you have made it exact on a sheet of paper, ruled and titled for that purpose, because of mistakes or errors that may occur or happen in the course of balancing your Ledger; which are to be rectified, and will cause erasements or alteration in that Accompt, which ought to be very fair and exact; and after you have made it to bear in the said sheet, copy fair the said accompt of balance in the Ledger.

The Rules for balancing are these, *viz.*

1*st.* Even your account of cash, and bear the net rest to balance Dr.

2*dly.* Cast up all your goods bought, and those sold, of what kind soever, in each account of goods; and see whether all Goods bought, be sold or not; and if any remain unsold, value them as they cost you, or according to the present Market Price, ready Money; and bear the net rest to balance Dr.

3*dly.* See what your Goods or Wares severally cost, and also how much they were sold for, and bear the net Gain or Loss to the accompt of Profit and Loss.

4*thly.* Even all the personal Accompts with your Drs, and your Crs. in order as they lie, and bear the net rest of them severally to balance.

5*thly.* Even your Voyages, your Factors Accompts, wherein is either Gain or Loss, and bear the net Gain or Loss to the accompt of Profit and Loss to the Goods unsold to Balance.

6*thly.* Even the accompt of Profit and Loss, and bear the net rest to Stock or Capital, as on advance to your Stock or Capital.

7*thly.* Even your Stock, and bear the net rest to Balance Cr. Then cast up the Dr. and Cr. sides of your Balance

lance; and if they come out both alike, then are your accompts well kept; otherwise you must find out your error
by pricking over your Books again to see whether you have
entered every Dr. and Cr. in the Ledger as you ought.

*Note. By pricking over the Book is meant, an examining every Arti-
cle of the Journal, against the Ledger, and marking it thus * or thus †;
and upon the second Examination thus ‡; and upon a third Examination thus §; or any other Mark.*

*Note also, In all Accompts of Goods you must keep a Column in
the Middle of the Leaf, of each Side, for Number, Weight, or Measure.*

Though all that hath been said in relation to Book-keeping, and the several Rules thereunto belonging, may seem
a little abstruse to the altogether unlearned therein, yet
there is no such mighty difficulty to instruct them as they
may imagine : The following hints may render what hath
been already said intelligible to an ordinary capacity ;

1*st.* Stick close to the Text, or general Rules before-
mentioned, *viz.* That all things received, or the Receiver,
are Debtor to all things delivered, or the Deliverer ; for this
Rule holds good in all Cases.

2*d.* When the Dr. (whether Person or Goods) is known,
the Cr, is easily understood without mentioning it ; for if
A. be Dr. to *B.* then *B.* is Cr. by *A.* for what Sum soever
it be : Also, if Goods be Dr. to *C.* then *C.* is Cr. by those
Goods for the Sum they amount to.

3*dly.* This Art of Book-keeping, is called *Book-keeping
by Double Entry,* because there must be two Entries ; the
first being a charging of a Person, Money, or Goods, and
the second a discharging of a Person, Money, or Goods.

4*thly. strictly note,* That if the first Entry be on the Dr.
or Left-hand side of your Ledger, the next or second Entry
must always be made on the right or Credit Side of your
Ledger ; for when one Person or Thing is charged, then
always another Person or Thing is discharged for the said
Sum, let it be what it will.

And so it is in balancing an Accompt, and carrying it to
another Folio ; for if the old Accompt be settled by the
Balance on the Credit Side, then the new Accompt must
be debited or charged on the Debit-side for the Sum that
balanced the old Account.

Much more might be said on this *Art of Book-keeping,* if
I had room ; but I have said what I hope may be sufficient
for the instruction and improvement of any Reader.

The

The next Matter I shall go upon is, to show, or give Examples of various Kinds of Receipts, and Promisory Notes; also Bills of Parcels in different Trades; likewise Bills of Book-debts, Bills of Exchange, with Remarks on them; and some other Precedents of Writings in Trade and Mercantile Affairs.

And first of Receipts of different Forms.

RECEIVED *September 9th,* 1809, of Mr. *Anthony Archer,* the Sum of Six Pounds Nine Shillings; I say received for my Master, *Bryan Barry, per* me

£ 6 9   *Caleb Catchpenny.*

London, September 14, 1809.

Received of Mr. *Kendrick Keeptouch,* Ten Pounds Eleven Shillings and Sixpence in full Payment, *per* me

£ 10 10 6   *Henry Hasty.*

Note. *The Sum received must always be expressed in Words at Length, and not in Figures, in the Body of the Receipt; but it may, and ought to be, expressed in Figures between two Lines on the Left-hand of the Name at the Bottom of the Receipt, as well as in the Body of the Receipt.*

When a Receipt is given in a Book, there is no occasion to mention the Man's Name of whom you receive the Money, because that is implied, he being the Owner of the Book.

Received the 24th of *September,* 1809, of Mr. *Timothy Trucklittle,* Fifty Pounds in part of *Indigo* sold him the 22d Instant, per me

£ 50 0 0   *Lawrence Lovemoney.*

A Receipt given in a Receipt-Book.

Received the 26th of September, 1809, the Sum of Forty-five Pounds, by the Order, and for the account of *George Greedy,* Esq. per me

£ 45 0 0   *Timothy Trusty.*

Received the 27th of September, 1809, of Mr. *Daniel Davenport* and Company, One Hundred Pounds, on account of Self and Partner, per me

£ 100 0 0   *James Jenks.*

Received the 28th of March, 1810, of Mr. *Peter Punctual*, Fifty Pounds sixteen Shillings and Nine-pence, in part for Tobacco sold him the 24th of August last.

£ 50 16 9   *Fabian Funk.*

Received the 29th of March, 1810, of the Honourable East India Company, Three Hundred and Fifteen Pounds Ten Shillings. per Order, and for the account of *Peter Pepper.*

£ 315 16 0   *Steven Storax.*

Received March 31st, 1810, of the Governor and Company of the Bank of England, One Thousand six Hundred Pounds Ten Shillings, for Self and Company, per me

£ 1600 10 0   *Leonard Longpurse.*

Received the 4th of April, 1810, of the Worshipful Company of Grocers, Forty-nine Pounds Fifteen Shillings, in full Payment for my Father Peter Plumb, per me

£ 49 15 0   *Peter Plumb*, junior.

Received the 6th of April, 1810, of Richard Cox, Esq. Chamberlain of London, the sum of Sixty Pounds, for the Use of the Worshipful Company of Joiners, per me

£ 60 0 0   *Caleb Careful.*

A Rent-Gatherer's Bill,

Received the 14th of November, 1809, of Mr. *Aron Arable* in Money, Eighteen Pounds, and allowed him for Land-Tax Five Pounds, and for Repairs Two Pounds, in all Twenty-five Pounds, in full for half a Year's Rent due at Michaelmas last; I say received for the Use of Lawrence Letland, Esq. by virtue of his Letter of Attorney, per me

£ 25 0 0   *Robert Rentroll.*

Received of Mr. *Timothy Tenant,* this 25th Day of November, 1809, Six Pounds for a Quarter's Rent due at Michaelmas last, for my Master Lancelot Letfarm, per

£ 6 0 0   *Francis Faithful.*

Received August 24, 1809, of Mr. Brook Bishop, Twenty-nine Pounds Six Shillings, in Part of a Bill of Sixty Pounds due the 3d of October next, to Mr. Samuel Shuffle.

£ 29 6 0   *Francis Fidell.*

A Receipt on the Back of a Bill of Exchange.

October 30, 1809, received the full Contents of the within mentioned, being Five Hundred Pieces of Eight.

500 Pieces of Eight   *Nathan Needy.*

Promissory Note.

I Promise to pay to Mr, *Timothy Teazer,* or Order, Sixty Pounds, on the 26th of this Instant October, Witness my Hand this 15th of October, 1809.

£ 60   0   0   *Daniel Dilatory.*

18th *October,* 1809.

I Promise to pay to the Honourable the Directors of the South Sea Company, or Bearer on Demand, Four Hundred and Fifty Pounds, for my Father, *James Jones.*

£ 450   0   0   *Joshua Jones.*

24th *October,* 1809.

I Promise to pay to the Governor and Company of the Bank of England, or Order, on Demand, Two Thousand Pounds.

£ 2000   0   0   *Nahum Neednothing.*

November 24th, 1809.

I Promise to pay to *Miles Man,* and Company, or Bearer on Demand, Seven Hundred Fifty-six Pounds Ten Shillings and Nine-pence, for my Master, *Robert Regular.*

£ 756 10   0   *Mark Martin.*

November 24th, 1809.

I Promise to pay to the Honourable East India Company, or Bearer, upon Demand, Five Hundred Pounds, for Henry Hudson.

£ 500   0   0   *Martin Moneybag.*

November 26th, 1809.

I promise to pay to Mr. *Christopher Cash,* or Order, Three Months after Date, Five Pounds for value received, Witness my Hand this 26th Day of November, 1809.

£ 5   0   0   *Robert Ruck.*

A Note given by Two.

WE, or either of us, promise to pay to Mr. *Matthew Mistrust,* or his Order, Six Pounds Sterling, on Demand, for Value received. Witness our Hands this 27th of September 1809.   *Nathan Needy.*

                                Samuel Surety.

£ 6   0   0

Witness Nicholas Notice,

A Bill of Debt.

Memorandum: That I *William Want*, of London, Weaver, do owe, and am indebted unto Mr. *Timothy Trust*, of Westminster, Watch-maker, the Sum of Twenty-five Pounds Six Shilings of lawful Money of *Great Britain;* which Sum I promise to pay to the said *Timothy Trust*, his Executors, Administrators, or Assigns, on or before the 19th Day of *December* next ensuing. Witness my Hand this 22d Day of March, 1810.

Winess, Titus Testis.   *William Want,*

Bill of Parcels.

It is usual when Goods are sold for the Seller to deliver to the Buyer, with the Goods, a Bill of Parcels, which is a Note of their Contents and Prices, with a Total of their Value cast up, &c. These Bills ought to be handsomely written, and in a methodical Order, according to the best and customary Way of each particular Trade.

I shall therefore give the Forms of Bills of Parcels in some Trades and Professions, with the shortest Methods of casting up the several Articles in each Bill.

A Mercer's Bill.

Richard Jones, Esq. London, *September* 26, 1809.
Bought of *Abel Atlas* and *Ben. Burdett, viz.*

	£	s.	d.
12 Yds. ½ of rich Satin, at 12s. 6d. per Yd. ..	7	19	4½
8 Yds. of sprigged Tabby, at 6s. 3d. per Yd.	2	10	0
5 Yds. ½ of Farringdon, at 6s. 8d. per Yd. ...	1	15	0
6 Yds. of Mohair, at 4s. 2d. per Yd.	1	5	0
17 Yds. ½ of Lustring, at 3s. 4d. per Yd.....	2	18	4
	£. 16	7	1½

If the Money is paid, then the Receipt is made as follows:

Received the 26th of September, 1810, Sixteen Pounds Seven Shillings and Eight-pence half-penny, for Abel Atlas and Company,   *Francis Fairspoken.*

A Woollen Draper's Bill.

London, *September* 24th, 1810.
Bought of Benjamin Broadcloth, 22d of September, 1810.

	s.	d.	
7 Yds. of fine Spanish black, at........	10	4	per Yd.
5 Yds. ¼ of ditto, at.................	12	4	ditto.
6 Yds. ¾ of fine mixed cloth, at......	15	4	ditto.
16 Yds. ¾ of Frieze, at	3	6	ditto.
4 Yds. of Drap-de-berry, at	13	5	ditto.
5 Yds. ⅞ of superfine Spanish cloth, at..	18	10	ditto.

The

The several articles of these Bills are purposely omitted being cast up, for the exercise of the reader in the Rule of Practice, or in those of *Multiplication of Money*, before shown; which indeed is the best method of all for the ready casting up the articles contained in any Bill of Parcels whatsoever.

We will take the last article of the Woollen Draper's Bill, *viz.* 5 yds. $\frac{7}{8}$, *&c.* at 18s. 10d. per yard.

	$5\frac{7}{8}$			18	10
l. 4	14	2			$7\frac{7}{8}$]
	16	$5\frac{1}{4}$		8) 12.1	10
Facit £ 5	10	$7\frac{1}{4}$		16	$5\frac{1}{4}$

In this example the price is multipled by the quantity, *viz.* 5 $\frac{7}{8}$, according to the Rules delivered in *Multiplication of Money*; and the product by 5 is 4*l.* 14s. 2d. Then for the $\frac{7}{8}$ of a yard, multiply the price of the Integer, *viz.* 18s. 10d. by the Numerator of the Fraction, *viz.* 7, and divide by the Denominator 8, and the Quotient is 16s. 5d. $\frac{1}{4}$, agreeably to the Rule in the Doctrine of Fractions.— Which 16s. 5d. $\frac{1}{4}$ added to 4*l.* 14s. 2d. gives 5*l.* 10s. 7d $\frac{1}{4}$, h   e foregoing operation.

A Hosier's Bill.

Mrs. James, Bought of *Abraham Sock*, *October* 5, 1809.

		s.	d.
To 5	Pair of Womens mixt Worsted Hose, at ..	5s.	7d.
3	Pair of Womens Silk Hose, at..........	9s.	4d.
22	Pair of Mens Woollen ditto, at.........	3s.	2d.
6	Pair of Womens ditto, at	2s.	2d.
21	Yds. of Flannel, at	1s.	11d.
8	Pair of Thread Hose, at	3s.	4d.

A Leatherseller's Bill.

Mr. Last, Bought of *Henry Sideboard*, the 17th of *October*, 1809.

		s.	d.	
To 15	Large oiled Lamb Skins, at ..	1	$3\frac{1}{2}$	per Skin.
13	Kipp of Goat Skins, at	3	4	
107	Alumed Sheep Skins, at	1	3	
19	Calf Skins, at	4	3	
85	Oiled Buck Skins, at	12	9	
10	Russia Hides, at	12	9	
60	Dicker of Hides, at..........	11	6	

Note

Note. 50 *Goat Skins make a Kipp; and other skins are five score to the hundred. A Dicker is* 10 *hides or skins ; and* 20 *Dickers a Last.*

A Pewterer's Bill.

Mr. *Johnson*, Bought of *Andrew Antimony*, October the 7th, 1809.

		l.	s.	d.
To	9 Metal Dishes, wt. 42lb. at 14d. per lb.	2	9	0
	1 Dozen of ditto Plates	0	17	0
	1 Standish of ditto	0	4	0
	2 Tankards of ditto	0	5	10
	8 Best Spoons	0	4	6
	13 Hard Metal Porringers	0	3	0
	1 Salt of ditto	0	1	10
	1 Set of Casters	0	10	0
		£ 4	15	2

A Mercer's Bill.

Madam *Deborah Doughty*, Dr. to *Bryan Brocade*.

1809		Yds.	s.	d.	
March	16	To 16½ of flowered Satin, at	14	9	per Yd.
April	14	14 of *Venetian* Silk, at	11	8	
	16	99 of Mohair, at	6	3	
May	16	14½ of flowered Damask at	9	7	
June	7	5¼ of *Genoa* Velvet, at	21	6	
	25	¾ of Lustring, at	4	7	

If part of the Bill only is paid, write thus:
Received of Madam *Deborah Doughty*, twelve pounds ten shillings, on account, for my Master, *Bryan Brocade.*

£ 12 10 0   *Henry Hunter.*

A Stationer's Bill.

Mr. *Samuel Scribe*, Dr. to *Philip Pott*, viz.

1809.			£.	s.	d.	
July	12	To 57 Reams Demy, at	1	2	0	per R.
	31	195 do. 2d Foolscap, at	1	2	0	
August	24	375 do. 2d Demy, at	1	4	0	
September	6	95 do. French Royal	1	15	0	
October	26	26 Rolls Parchment, at	0	2	6	

Note. A Roll of Parchment is 60 *Skins; a Ream of Paper* 20 *Quires; and a Bundle of Paper is* 2 *Reams.*

Bills

Bills on Book Debts.

A Woollen Draper's Bill.

Mr. Frank Fustian, Dr. to George Goose.

1809.		s.	d.	
April 20	To 16 Yds. ½ of Black Cloth, at	18	3	per Yd.
24	4 Yds. ¼ of Drap-de-berry, at	15	6	
May 4	35 Yds. of mixt Grey Cloth, at	10	5	
17	9 Yds. of fine ditto, at	17	3	
June 12	12 Yds. ½ of fine Broad Cloth, at	17	3	

If the whole Bill be paid, then make the Receipt thus
Received the 19th of *October*, 1809, of Mr. *Frank Fustian*, the sum of fifty-four pounds, for the above Bill, for my Master, *George Goose.*

£ 54   *Mark Goodmeasure.*

A Bricklayer's Bill.

Mr. Martin Topstone, Dr. to Peter Pantiles viz.

1809	
March 27	To 25 Thousand Bricks, 35s. per M.
30	11 Thousand plain Tiles, at 50s. per M.
April 1	28 Cwt. of Lime, at 14s. per Cwt.
9	20 Loads of Sand, at 5s. 6d. per Load.
May 20	140 Ridge Tiles, at 18s. per Hundred.
June 24	90 Days of work myself, at 5s. per Day.
	90 Days my Man, at 4s. 6d.
	90 Days another Bricklayer, at 4s
	90 Days for 2 Labourers, at 2s. 6d. each.

Note. 1000 *plain Tiles* is a *Load ;* and 25 *Bags* or *Bushels of Lime* 1 Cwt. *A Brick must be 9 Inches long and 4 Inches ½ broad. Bricks are of three Sorts,* Place-Bricks, Red, and Grey-Stock Bricks.

Here it will be proper to give a general rule for casting up any thing sold by the Thousand ; as Bricks, Tiles, &c. and other things mentioned in the Book of *Rates, viz.*

Barrel Hoops, Goose Quills, Oranges and Lemons, Squirrel Skins, Billets, &c. Which is as follows, *viz.*

Multiply the given number by the Shillings in the price (if the price be at so many Shillings per 1000), always

cutting

cutting off three Figures or places on the right hand; and the Figures towards the left hand are Shillings, which divide by 20, to bring them into Pounds; and those Figures separated toward the right hand multiply by 12, the next inferior denomination, and still cut off or separate three places towards the right hand, and the figures towards the left are pence; and cutting the three last Figures off, multiply by 4; still separating three places toward the right hand, and the Figures toward the left hand are Farthings.— If the price be Shillings and Pence, or Shillings, Pence, and Farthings *per* Thousand, multiply by the Shillings as before, and take the parts for the Pence and Farthings, as in the Rule of Practice; add these together, and proceed as before directed.

Ex. 1. 24650 Bricks, at 17*s. per* Thousand.

$$
\begin{array}{r}
17 \\
\hline
272550 \\
24650 \\
\hline
419|050 \\
1 \\
\hline
0600 \\
4 \\
\hline
2|400
\end{array}
$$

Answer 419*s.* 0½*d.* or 20*l.* 19*s.* 0½*d.*

Ex. 2. 6*d.*—½ 261324 plain Tiles, at 10*s.* 6*d. per* Thous.

$$
\begin{array}{r}
16 \\
\hline
1567944 \\
261324 \\
130662 \\
\hline
4311|846 \\
12 \\
\hline
10|152 \\
4 \\
\hline
608
\end{array}
$$

Answer 4311*s.* 10*d.* $\frac{608}{1000}$ ƒ. or 215*l.* 18*s.* 10*d.*

When any thing is sold by the Hundred, as *Dutch* and *English* Pantiles, then observe the following Rule, *viz.*

Multiply the given quantity by the Shillings in the price, and take parts for the pence and farthings (if there be any) as before; then from the right hand of the sum cut off two places, and proceed as in the last Rule.

Ex.

Ex. 3. 1726 Pantiles, at 7*s.* per Hundred.

$$\begin{array}{c} 7 \\ \hline 120|82 \\ \hline 12 \\ \hline 9|84 \\ 4 \\ \hline 3|36 \end{array}$$

Answer 120*s.* 9*d.* ¾ or 6*l.* 0*s.* 9*d.* ¾ and
$\frac{16}{100}$ of a Farthing.

Ex. 4. 6*d.*—½ 2964 Stock-Bricks, at 2*s. 6d. per* C.

$$\begin{array}{c} 2 \\ \hline 5928 \\ 1482 \\ \hline 74|10 \\ 1|20 \\ 4 \\ \hline 80 \end{array}$$

Ans. 74*s.* 1*d.* $\frac{40}{100}$ *f.* or 3*l.* 41*s.* 1*d.*
&c.

Of Bills of Exchange.

BILLS of Exchange are either Inland or Foreign. The *Inland* Bills are drawn by one trader in one city or town, upon another of another city or town, in the same kingdom ; as *London* upon *Bristol*, or *Exeter* upon *London, &c.* and these chiefly concern Shop-keepers, and wholesale Traders, either in town or country ; and the *Foreign* more immediately concern the merchants.

Bills of Exchange, if handsomely drawn, must be written in a fair hand, on a long piece of Paper, about three inches broad, and written in form after the following Precedents :

Form of a Bill payable at Sight.

London, 5th *April*, 1810.

At Sight pay to Mr. *Gregorius Grandy*, or his Order, the Sum of Fifty Pounds for Value received of *Christopher Cutpurse*, and place it to account, as per advice from

To *Mr.* Peter Palmer. —   Your humble Servant,
  Air-street,   David Drawwell.

                             York,

York, March 28, 1810.

Seven Days after Sight pay to Mr. *Nat. Needy*, or his Order; Twenty-four Pounds Ten Shillings for Value received of Mr. *Timothy Transfer*, and place it to account, as *per* advice from

To Mr. S. Surety, Your Friend and Servant,
Cheapside, London. *Mark Moneypenny.*

If Mr. *Needy* send his servant, *Abraham Honesty*, to receive the Money, after he has written his own name on the back of the Bill, (which is his Order) the servant must write a Receipt to his master's name, thus :

Received, for Nat. Needy,
Abraham Honesty,

USANCE is a determined time fixed for payment of Bills of Exchange, and reckoned either from the day of their being accepted, or from the day of their date. This is called Usance, because regulated by the Usage or Custom of places on which they are drawn.

A Foreign Bill of Exchange.

London, 28th *December*, 1809, for 460 Crowns, at 56d.¾ Sterling *per* Crown.

At Usance pay this my first Bill of Exchange, (my second or third not being paid) unto Mr. *Harry Vane*, or Order, Four Hundred and Sixty Crowns, at 56d.¾ *per* Crown, for value received of Mr. *Simon Thornhill*, and place it to account, as *per* advice from, Sir,

To Mr. Walter Watchful, Your humble Servant,
Merchant, Hamburgh. *Edmund Saveall.*

Note. It is usual to send two and sometimes three Bills of the same kind, in case the first and the second should not through any accident, arrive at their destined place.

Another.

London, 17th *October*, 1809, for 480 Dollars, at 55d.⅛ *per* Dollar.

At three Usance pay this my first Bill of Exchange unto Mr. *William Wealthy*, or Order, Four Hundred and Eighty Dollars, at 55d.⅛ Sterling *per* Dollar, for value received from him, and place it to account, as *per* advice from

To Messrs. J. & J. D'Costa, Your humble Servant,
Merchants, Aleppo. *Mark Mercator.*
  Usance.

Usance between *England* and *France*, or *Holland*, is one
Calander Month ; between *England* and *Spain*, or *Portugal*, two Months ; between *England* and *Italy*, Three
Months, &c.

Example.

Bristol, 10th *March*, 1810, for 600 pieces of
Eight, at 53*d*. ½ per Piece.

At double Usance pay this my first Bill of Exchange
unto Mr. *Lawrence de Luz*, or his Order, Six Hundred
Mexico Pieces of Eight, at 53*d*. ⅝ Sterling, for value received of *Henriques Gomes*, and place it to account, as *per* advice from youn's, &c.

To Mr. Solomon Silvester,   *Henry Hunt.*
  Merchant, Leghorn.

Remarks on Bills of Exchange.

1. THE Acceptor of any Bill is the absolute Debtor to
the person to whom the Bill is payable, for the contents
thereof :

2. The person to whom the Bill is payable must demand
the money the very day it becomes due, and if the Acceptor
dies before it becomes due it must be demanded of the Exe-
cutor or Administrator :

3. The Drawer of any Bill must always give his Correspondent a Letter of Advice, that he has drawn such a Bill
on him for such a particular Sum, &c. :

4. There is no obligation to pay a Bill without such Letter of Advice :

5. In *England* a Bill is due the third day after the expi-
ration of the time mentioned in the Bill.

Of Indorsing Bills and Notes.

IT frequently happens, that between the Acceptance
of a Bill and the time of Payment, the party to whom it
is first made payable has occasion to pay it away. In this
case he writes his name on the back of the Bill, which is
his Order, and gives it to the person to whom he is indebted ; he is then empowered to receive the Money :
And if the second person also wants to pay it away, then
he likewise writes his name under the other, and delivers
it to a third person to receive the money ; and it may
happen, the third does the same, and delivers it to a fourth
person,

person, &c.   All that thus do are Indorsers; and he that last has the Bill, if the Acceptor will not pay it, may sue him, or the Indorsers, or Drawer, or any of them, for the Money.

An Indorsement is sometimes in these words, *viz. Pay the contents of the within-mentioned Bill* to Henry Hasty.

George Greedy.

But generally the name only is accounted sufficient.

Of Protesting.

· WHEN a Bill is to be *Protested*, the party who is in possession of the Bill must go to a *Notary Public*, (not a common *Scrivener*) whose business it is; and he goes to the Acceptor's house and demands payment, &c.   He then draws up a *Protest* according to Law; which is to be returned to the Drawer, or the person from whom he received it, within the time limited, &c.

It is quite unnecessary to give the form of a *Protest*, as no person can do it for himself.

Charges of Noting and Protesting a Bill.

Noting $\begin{cases} \text{within the City} & 1 & 6 \\ \text{without the City} & 2 & 6 \end{cases}$ $\begin{array}{l} \text{Pro-} \\ \text{testing} \end{array}$ $\begin{array}{l} \text{within} \\ \text{without} \end{array} \begin{cases} 3 & 0 \\ 5 & 0 \end{cases}$

A Bill of Debt.

KNOW all Men by these presents, That I *Lawrence Luckless*, of *Southwark*, *Vintner*, do owe and am indebted unto *Claudius Careful*, *Brewer*, the Sum of One Hundred and Fifty Pounds of lawful Money of *Great Britain*; which sum I promise to pay unto the said *Claudius Careful*, his Executors, Administrators, or Assigns, on or before the 24th of *December* next ensuing the Date hereof.   Witness my hand and seal, this 6th Day of *March*, 1810.

Sealed and delivered   *Lawrence Luckless.*
·*in the Presence of*

A. B.

A Bill for Money borrowed.

Received and borrowed of *Oliver Forecast*, of *London*, Merchant, Fifty Pounds, which I do hereby promise to pay on demand.   Witness my Hand, this 6th Day of *April*, 1810.

£ 50.   *Launcelot Lackpenny.*

For

Form of a Bill of Lading.

Shipped by the Grace of God, in good Order and well-conditioned, by *Edward Export*, of London, Merchant, in and upon the good Ship called the *(Good Adventure of London)* whereof *(Martin Maintop*, of *London*, Mariner,) is Master, under God for this present Voyage, and now riding at Anchor in the Port of *London*, and by God's Grace, bound for *(Cadiz)*, that

T B
No.
1, 2

is to say, 1 (Bale of Stocking Baize, and 1 Trunk, containing Five Hundred Pair of Silk Stocking, Contents, &c. as *per* Invoice) being marked and numbered as *per* Margin, and are to be delivered in the like good Order at the aforesaid Port of *Cadix*, the danger of the Seas only excepted, under (Mr. *Martin Mercat*, Merchant there), or to his Assigns, he or they paying Freight for the said Goods (three pieces of Eight *per* Cwt.) with Primage and Average accustomed. In Witness whereof the Master or Purser of the said Ship hath affirmed to (three) Bills of Lading, all of this tenor and date, one of which (three) Bills being accomplished, the other (two) to stand void. And so God send the good Ship to her destined Port in safety. *Amen.*

Dated *London*, the 6th *March*, 1810; inside and Contents unknown to   *Martin Maintop.*

Note. The several words included in the Parentheses are to be put into the several vacant places that are in a Blank Bill of Lading.

Note also, Average is the general Allowance made to the Master of the Ship, of 1*d.* or 2*d.* in every Shilling Freight for Primage, as a small allowance to be distributed among the Sailors.

The Form of an Invoice.

Port-Royal, Jamaica, July 10, 1811.

Invoice of five Barrels of Indigo, five Hhds. of Sugar, and five Hhds. of Pimento, shipped on board the *Lune*, of *London*, *George Wright*, Commander, for account and risk of Messrs. *John* and *James Jones*, of *London*, Merchants, being marked and numbered as *per* Margin:

Contents,

Contents, Costs, and Charges, as in the following **Example:**

		l.	*s.*	*d*
viz. Indigo 5 B.				
FF. 143				
No. 143				
121 146				
to 152				
125 172				
750 *lb.* net. at 2*s.* 6*d. per lb.*		81	18	—

```
Sugar 5
Hhds.          Tare
C. pr. lb.  C. qr. lb.                C. qr. lb.
226  11-3-7—1-2-19          Gross  68-0- 0
·to  12-9-19—1-3- 0          Tare    8-3-12
130  13-2-13—1-2-16                 ——————
     14-1-15—1-3-11          Net  59-0-16        70 19  5
     15-1-10—1-3-22          at 24s. p. C.
     ——————————
     68 0- 0—8-3-12
```

```
Pimento            lb.
5 Hhds. Tare  2026 Gross
No.    lb.   lb.    389 Tare
131    432—84      ——
to     396—72 net 1637 at 11d. ½ per lb.    78  8  9½
135    410—81      ——
       376—70        Charges.
       412—80     To Cost of 5 Barrels and 10
       ——————         Hhds.  ........ 4-7-9
      2026-389    To Storage ........ 1-0-0     5  7  9
                                             236 13 11½
                  To Commission at 5 per C.  11 66  8¼
                  Errors excepted per A. B.
```

An Account of Sales.

Port-Royal, Jamaica, July 11, 1809.

Account of Sale of 2765 Ells of brown Osnaburghs, 1112 Yards of Blue Hartford, 2 Pieces of Grey Cloth, qt. 39 Yards, 50 Pair of fine Worsted Hose, and 157 Ells of Bag Holland, received from on board the Ship *Good*
Success

Success, Captain *Samuel Sharpe,* Commander, for Account of *Lawrence Lucky,* of *London,* Merchant, is Dr.

	l.	s.	d.	l.	s.	d.
To Portage of ditto............	0	17	6			
To Commission of Sales........	13	1	11			
To Storage, at ½ per C.........	6	10	11½			
				20	10	4½
To the net Product carried to the Credit of your Account, bad Debts excepted............				247	6	4½
				267	16	9

Per Contra, Cr.

	l.	s.	d.
By 2765 brown Osnaburghs, making 3456 Yds. ¼ at 8d. ½ per Yd. sold *Ambique Baker*......	122	8	2
By 1112 Yds. of blue Linen, sold at 7d. ¾ per Yard,.........................	35	18	2
By *James Smart,* for 39 Yds. of Cloth, at 15s. per Yard	29	5	0
By *Lawrence Monk,* for 50 Pair of Hose, at 7s. 10d. per Pair...................	19	11	9
By ditto for 175 Ells of Bag Holland, at 6s. 3d. per Ell	54	13	9
	261	16	10

Errors excepted, *July* 11th, 1809, per
Charles Careful.

Business on the Wharf, concerning Exporting and Importing of Goods, &c. Entering them at the Custom-house, &c.

When there are Goods to export, and ready packed, &c there must be first made a Bill of Entry, (as it is called) of the contents, after this Form, *viz.*

In the Loyal Briton, Abraham Handy, for Barbadoes.
Edwin Export.

Three Cases of Haberdashery.
Five Tuns of Beer, &c.

Of these bills there must be seven, one of which must be in words at length, and the other may be expressed in figures: These are by the Clerks of the Custom-house entered into several books kept for that purpose. If some of the articles pay Custom, and others not, then there must two entries be made; one for those that pay Custom, and another for those that do not; and you must likewise have two Cockets.

G

A *Cocket*

A *Cocket* testifies the payment of all Duties ; and is written on a small piece of Parchment as follows :

> *Know ye, that* Edwin Export, *Merchant, for three Cases of* Haberdashery, *and five Tuns of Beer, in the* Loyal Briton, Abraham Handy, *for* Barbadoes, *hath paid all Duties.   Dated the* 9th *of* November, 1809.

On the back of the Cocket must be set down the Marks, Numbers, and Quantity of the articles expressed in the Inside.   Then on clean paper transcribe your Bill of Entry, upon which a Shipping Bill will be made out, on the back of which signify the Marks, Numbers, and Contents, as before, on the *Cocket* ; both which being thus indorsed, are to be delivered to the Searcher at the Water-side, who deposits them in the Office till the going away of the Ship ; they are then delivered to the Captain or Master of the Ship.

If you have not knowledge or experience enough to enter your Goods yourself, application must be made to one of the clerks in the Long Room who make it their business to enter Goods ; they will write out Bills, and pass your Entries, without any further trouble, or your running a risk of making any false Entries, &c. for which you will pay him one shilling.

Entry Inwards.

ON a Ship's arrival, search the Entry Book in the Long Room, and you will find the name of the Ship and Captain, as also the Waiters that are to attend the Delivery of the Ship, and at what Wharf the Goods will be landed.   The Entry inwards runs thus :

In the Mercury, Jacob Keelson, *from* Antigua.

25 Hhds. of Sugar, &c.
56 Bags of Cotton, &c.

There must be eight of these Bills, (thought but seven Outwards) and one of these also must be in words at length, which is for the Warrant of Delivery, and must be signed by the person in whose name the goods were entered, and the mark also in the margin ; which being done, and the Fee for Entry and Custom paid, you will then have from the Land-Waiters a Warrant for the landing and receiving your Goods.

When Goods are to be exported by Certificate, *viz*
Foreign

foreign Goods formerly imported: these Goods being to be sent abroad, or exported to another place or country by a native of *England* within twelve, or a stranger within nine months after importation, entitles the exporter to a Drawback of part of the Custom paid on the Importation of the said Goods, upon producing a certificate from the Comptroller that they have paid the Duties inwards. And the Debenture of Custom Drawback runs thus:

Debenture.

Christopher Commerce, *natural born*, *did on*, &c. *make an Entry with us of Two Thousand* Ells *of broad* German Linen, *in the* Amazon, *Captain* Steven Stout, *for* Jamaica, *the Subsidy*, &c. *was paid inwards by*, &c. *as appears per Certificate of the Collector inwards*: And *for further Manifestation of his just dealing therein, he hath also taken Oath before us of the same.*

Custom-house, London, 12th November, 1809.

The Oath.

Jurat. C. C. *That Two Thousand Ells of broad* Germany linen, *abovementioned, was really shipped out, and hath not been relanded in any Port or Creek in* England *or* Wales *since last shipped.* Nov. 12, 1809.

The Certificate Cocket.

London: *Know ye, that C. C. for Two Thousand Ells of broad* Germany Linen, *paid per*, &c. *the Duty*, &c. *last, late unladen and now in the* Amazon, Stephen Stout, *for* Jamaica. *Dated the 12th of* November, 1809.

This *Certificate Cocket* is gained by applying to the books of the Importer, to know the day, &c. when the Custom inwards was paid, and by whom; which carry to the Long Room in the *Custom-house*, and deliver it to the Comptroller's Clerk of the Subsidy inward and outward, with an account of what you would export, &c.

As it has been mentioned that Goods must be landed at some Wharf or (Key) Quay, it may be proper to name them, viz.

Somer's Key, Smart's Key, Wiggen's Key, Bear Key, Dice Key, Custom-house Key, Potter's Key, Wool Key, Galley Key, Brewer's Key, Ralph's Key, Chester's Key, Lyon's Key, Cox's Key; Hammond's, Young's, and Gaunt's Key. And the Wharfs are, *Fresh Wharf and Botolph Wharf.*

G 2 Besides

Besides these, there are certain places called *Docks*, which are harbours cut into the land, where there is no current, but only a flow and an ebb, occasioned by the rise and fall of the Tide in the river *Thames* ; and these are convenient for the lying of Vessels, Hoys, Lighters, Barges and Boats ; and are as follow, viz.

Billingsgate Dock, Sabb's Dock, Tower Dock, St. Catherine's Dock, Wapping Dock, Hermitage Dock, Execution Dock, and *Limehouse Dock.* And above Bridge, *Queenhithe Dock, Puddle Dock, White Friar's Dock,* and *Scotland Yard Dock.* And in *Southwark,* on the *Surry-Side,* are *St. Saviour's Dock, Clink Dock,* and *Savery's Dock,* below the *Bridge Yard,* and several others for private Uses. But more particularly eminent on that Side of the Water is the *Bridge-Yard* for landing sundry sorts of Merchandises, but chiefly from the Ports of *England.*

Of Wharfage and Lighterage.

- WHARFINGERS have several Managers over them, and also a Committee to redress grievances, &c. and Clerks of the Stations, with Lighter Managers, and have the letting of many Warehouses, Cellars, &c. they have the privilege also of keeping Lighters for the carriage of Goods to and from Ships.

West-India Docks.

THESE immense Works, situated at Blackwall, are intended to receive all the Ships that trade to the West-Indies. The Northern Dock for unloading inwards, covers a Space of 30 Acres, and is capable of containing from 2 to 300 Ships. The smaller Dock contains an area of 24 Acres, and is devoted solely to the business of loading outwards. The proprietors of these great Works are styled the *West-India Dock Company.* The Expenses have not been short of a Million of Money. To re-imburse themselves, they lay a Tonnage of 6s. upon the burthen of every Ship which enters the Docks ; and for Wharfage, Landing, Weighing, Cooperage, Warehouse-room, &c. they are entitled to certain Rates upon all Goods that are discharged.

THE DOCKS AT WAPPING are upon a still larger Scale, and for more general purposes.

Of

Of Husbands of Ships.

WHERE several Persons are concerned in a Ship, there is usually a Husband chosen by them, to take an Account of every Merchant's Goods, &c. and pay the Wharfage, Lighterage, Porterage, &c. and these Husbands are to collect every Merchant's proportion, as also the Owner's Freight.

Of the MENSURATION of Planes and Solids.

THE several kinds of Measuring are three, viz.

1st. Lineal, by some called Running Measure, and is taken by a line, and respects length without breadth; the parts of which are,

12 Inches 1 foot, 3 feet 1 yard, 16 feet and a half 1 rod, pole, or perch.

All kinds of ornamental work, such as a Cornice, Frieze, &c. are measured by Running Measure.

2dly. Superficial or Square Measure, is that which respects length and breadth; and the parts are,

144 Inches 1 foot, 72 inches half a foot, 36 inches one quarter of a foot, 18 inches half a quarter of a foot, 272 feet and a quarter 1 rod, 136 feet half a rod; 1296 inches, or 9 feet, one superficial, or square yard.

3dly. Solid, or Cube Measure, which respects length, breadth, and depth, or thickness; and the parts are,

1728 Inches 1 foot, 1296 inches three quarters of a foot, 864 inches half a foot, 432 inches one quarter of a foot, and 27 feet one solid yard.

Superficial Measure.

TO measure things that have length and breadth, such as board, glass, pavement, wainscot, and land, is to take the dimensions of the length and breadth, according to the customary methods used in each particular; for instance, board and glass are measured by the foot, the dimensions are taken in feet and inches, and the contents given in feet.

The dimensions of wainscoting and paving, plastering, and painting, are taken in feet and inches, and the contents given in yards.

G 3 Of

Of the Square and Superficial Contents or Area.

The squaring of any number is multiplying it into itself, as 12 inches multiplied by 12 inches make 144 square inches. The superficial content or area of any thing is found four several ways, viz. by whole Numbers, by Decimals, by Practice, and by Cross Multiplication ; in each of which methods I shall give examples of operation.

A Rectangle hath its sides perpendicular, and those that are opposite equal; but the adjacent sides are unequal; boards, wainscots, ceilings, windows, doors, &c. are commonly of this figure.

When any thing is to be measured, it must be considered what form or fashion it is of; and then it must be measured according to the several Rules for each Figure.

First. If it be a square or oblong, then the length and breadth must be multiplied one by the other, which gives the contents in square measure, and that Product must be divided by its proper Divisor, according to the name in which the content or area is to be given.

Ex. Admit a board to be 12 inches broad, and 8 feet or 96 inches long, how many square or superficial feet doth it contain?

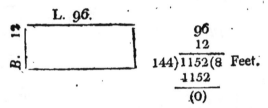

$$144)\overline{1152}(8 \text{ Feet.}$$

Here the length in inches is multiplied by the breadth in inches, and the product 1152 divided by 144, the square inches in a foot, quotes 8 feet square for the content of the board.

A Rule for Dispatch.

If the length of a board, or piece of glass, be given in feet, and the breadth in inches, multiply one by the other, (without any Reduction) and divide the product by 12 ; and the quotient will be the answer in feet, and the remainder will be parts of a foot. So the foregoing Example might have been done sooner by dividing 96 the length by 12 the breadth, and it quotes 8 feet for the content, by the former way.

Ex.

Ex. Suppose a board be 14 inches long, and 15 inches broad, what is the content in square feet?

14 Feet long.
15 Inches broad.

12)210
Feet 17 $\frac{6}{12}$ or $\frac{1}{2}$

Or thus:

14
by 1—3

14
3 is $\frac{1}{4}$ 3$\frac{1}{2}$ or $\frac{1}{2}$

Answer 17$\frac{1}{2}$

The Answer is 17 feet, and $\frac{1}{2}$. And so for any other Example of this kind.

Here 3 inches is the $\frac{1}{4}$ of a foot, wherefore $\frac{1}{4}$ of 14 is taken and added to 14, and it makes 17 feet, and $\frac{2}{4}$ equal to $\frac{1}{2}$.

Another Example worked four different Ways.

If a Board be 19 feet $\frac{1}{2}$, or 150 inches long, and 15 inches broad, how many square feet doth it contain?

Vulgarly.

Inches, 150 long.
15 broad.

750
150

2250

Decimally.

12,5
1,25

625
250
125

Feet, 15,625

144)2250(15 Feet
144

810
702

Rem. 90
Multiply by 12 Inch 1 Foot.
144)1080(7 Inches.
1008

Rem. .72
Multiply by .4 the Quarters in an Inch.
144)288(2 Quarters or $\frac{1}{2}$
288

. . .

Feet 15,625
12

Inches 7,500
4

Quarters 2,000

By

By Cross Multiplication.			By Practice.	
Feet.	*In.*		*Feet.*	*In.*
12	6		12	6
1	3		1	3
12	6		12	6
3	1 6	3 Inches is $\frac{1}{4}$	3	1$\frac{1}{2}$
Ans. 15	7 0		15	7$\frac{1}{2}$

The four methods here used are as follow : first, by
multiplying the inches together, and dividing by 144, &c.
The second work is performed Decimally ; the third method is by Cross Multiplication ; and the last and best is by
Practice.

Any of these methods may be easily understood by the
use of the Arithmetical part of this Book, except the
method by Cross Multiplication, which may be thus explained :

Rule. Under the Multiplicand write the corresponding
Denomination of the Multiplier.—Multiply each Term in
the Multipleand, beginning at the lowest, by the *Feet* in
the Multiplier, write each Result under each respective
Term ; carrying an unit for every 12 from each lower
name to its next higher.

Note. Feet multiplied by feet give feet :—Feet multiplied
by inches give inches : but inches multiplied by inches give
seconds.

In the same way mutiply all the terms of the Multipli-
eand by the *Inches* in the Multiplier, writing the result of
each term one place removed to the right hand of those in
the Multiplicand. Do the same with the *Seconds* in the
Multiplier, getting the result of each term two places removed to the right hand of those 'in the Multiplicand.
Thus in the Examples I say, once 6 is 6, and once 12 is
12 ;—then with the 3 inches I say, 3 times 6 is 18, that is
6 and carry 1, (putting the 6 to the right hand of the line
of inches) 3 times 12 are 36 and 1 are 37, but 37 inches
are 3 feet, 1 inch, which I put in their proper places.
I now add the two rows together, which make 15 feet, 7
inches, and 6 seconds.

If a board be wider at one end than the other, then take
the breadth in the middle, or add the measure of both ends
together, and take the half of the main breadth, which
multiply by the length.

Example

Ex. Suppose a board to be 120 inches long, and the narrowest end 10 inches wide, the broadest end 34 inches wide; what is its contents in superficial feet?

Add { 34 broadest end.
{ 10 narrowest.

Sum 44

its half ——

is 22 the medium between the least and greatest lengths.
120 the length

48
144)2640(18 feet ½ *Answer.*   12
144

1200   144)576 } 4 inches, or
1152   576 } ½ of a foot.

Rem. 48

Or thus :

Feet.	Inches.	
10	0	the length, equal 120 inches.
1	10	the mean breadth, or 22 inches.
10	0	
8	4 0	
18	4	*Answer.*

If a board or piece of glass be ever so irregular, it may be measured very near, by taking the breadth in five or six places, and adding the several breadths together, dividing the total by the number of places, and the quotient will be the main breadth; which multiply by the length, &c.

Having the breadth in inches of any board, or piece of glass; to know how much the length of that board or piece of glass will make a foot superficial.

Rule. Divide 144 by the inches in breadth, and the quotient will be the length of a board that will make a foot.

Ex. If one board be 9 inches broad, and another 24 inches; what length of board will make each a superficial foot?

9) 144   24)144(6 *Answer.*
———   144
Answer 16

One must be 16 inches long, and the other only 6.

G 5   *Prop*

Proper Directions for Joiners, Painters, Glaziers, &c.

Rooms being various in their forms, take this general rule in all cases, *viz.*

Take a line, and apply one end of it to any corner of the room ; then measure the room, going into every corner with the line, till you come to the place where you first began ; then see how many feet and inches the string contains, and set it down for the compass or round ; then take the height by the same method.

Glaziers are to take the depth and breadth of their work, and multiply one by the other, dividing by 144 ; glass being measured as board.

Having thus shown the methods of casting up dimensions, I come now to particulars ; and first of

Glaziers Work by the Foot.

If the windows be square, or rectangular, multiply the length by the breadth, which will produce the contents as has already been shown, *viz.*

By Cross Multiplication.	By Practice.
Feet. In.	*Feet. In.*
8—9 high	8 — 9
7—3 broad	7 feet 3
6₁—3	6₁ — 3
2—2 3 3 inches ¼	2 — 2¼
63—5 3	63 — 5¼ *Answer.*

Thus if the value of a window be required whose height is 8 feet 9 inches, and breadth 7 feet 3 inches, at 20*d.* per foot square, I first find the number of feet in the window, which in this case are 65 feet 5 inches, 3 seconds ; and to avoid fractions I call this 65 feet 6 inches, or 65 ½ feet, which I multiply by 20*d.* for the value of each foot, and divide by 12 and by 20.

$$
\begin{array}{l}
65,5 \\
20 \\
\hline
12)1310,0 \\
2,0)10.9..2\,½ \\
\hline
Answer\ £.\ 5—9—2
\end{array}
$$

Here it is convenient to throw the 2 ½ into the decimal, 5, and work as by the rule in decimals.

If the windows are arched, or have a curved form, no allowance is made, by reason of the extraordinary trouble, and waste of time, expenses or waste of glass, &c. And the dimensions taken from the highest part of the arch,
down

down to the bottom of the window, from the height or length ; which multiply by the breadth, and the product will be the answer in feet, &c.

Glaziers are often so very nice as to take their dimensions, and measure to a quarter of an inch.

Ex. How much does a window measure whose height is 4—3½, and breadth 2—7¼ ? Perform by Practice.

$$
\begin{array}{ll}
4 \text{ ---- } 3\frac{1}{4} & \text{long.} \\
2 \text{ ---- } 7\frac{1}{4} & \text{broad.}
\end{array}
$$

$$
\begin{array}{l}
6 \text{ inches is } \frac{1}{2} \\
1\ \frac{1}{2} \text{ is } \frac{1}{4} \text{ of } 6 \text{ inches} \\
\frac{1}{8} \text{ is } \frac{1}{4} \text{ of } 1\ \frac{1}{2}
\end{array}
\qquad
\begin{array}{ll}
8 \text{ ---- } 7 \\
2 \text{ ---- } 1\frac{3}{4} \\
\phantom{2 \text{ ---- }} 6\frac{1}{4} \\
\phantom{2 \text{ ---- }} 1 \\
\hline
14 \text{ ---- } 4
\end{array}
$$

The parts beyond the fraction of an inch are here omitted ; but the work may be performed with accuracy by Cross Multiplication, or as it is usually called, by Duodecimals, thus :

$$
\begin{array}{rrrrr}
Feet. & In. & & & \\
4 & 3 & 6 & & \\
.2 & 7 & 9 & & \\
\hline
8 & 7 & 0 & & \\
2 & 6 & 0 & & \\
 & 3. & 2 & 7. & 6 \\
\hline
11 & 4 & 3 & 1 & 6
\end{array}
$$

Here we see the accurate answer ; for Cross Multiplication is capable of being carried to thirds and fourths : as inches multiplied into inches give seconds, so inches by seconds give thirds, and seconds by seconds give fourths.

Glass is measured by the foot, and the price of it is as follows, *viz.*

			s.	d.	s.	d.
Newcastle crown, according to the size						
from	..	..	2	10 to	3	4
Second, ditto	..	..	2	5	2	11
Green glass	..	..	1	6	1	8

Painters Work by the Yard.

When the wainscot of a room is painted you are to measure round the room with a line, as hinted before, and the height is to be taken by girting a string over all the mouldings from the top of the cornice to the floor : then multiply the compass by the height, and you have the contents in feet and inches; which may be reduced into square yards by dividing by 9.

Example

Example 1.—A room painted,

     Feet In.

Being 45 — 8 in compass. What is the contents in

     10 f. 6 high.   square yards?

     ——————

     456 — 8

      22 — 10

     ——————

   9)479 — 6

Yards 33 — 2—6 *Answer.*

Example 2.—If the height of a room painted be 12 feet 4 inches; and the compass 84 feet 11 inches; how many square yards does it contain? Answer, 116 yards 3 feet 3¼ inches.

    Feet In.   *Note.* Double work is allow-

    84 — 11 compass ed in window shutters; sash

    12 — 4 high frames and mantle-pieces are

  —————————— reckoned separately unless the

                    mantle-pieces stand in the wain-

   1019 — 0 scot, in that case they are mea-

    28 — 3-8 sured as plain work, nothing be-

 9) 1047 — 3-8 ing deducted for the vacancies.

 ——————————

Yds. 116—3—3-8

Price of Painting in Common Colours.

	s.	d.
Clearcole and once in oil	0	4
————twice in oil	0	5½
————three times in oil	0	7½
Sash frames twice in oil, each	1	0
————three times, each	1	3
————Squares twice in oil, *per* dozen . .	1	3
Water trunk, gutters, &c. *per* foot running	0	1 to 2*d.*
Skirting, *per* foot running	0	1 to 2*d.*

Joiners Work.

In wainscoting, the dimensions are taken as in painting, *viz.* by measuring the height and then the compass; multiplying one into the other, and dividing the product by 9; the quotient is the answer in square yards.

Ex. 1.—What are the contents of a piece of wainscoting 9 feet 3 inches long, and 6 feet 6 inches broad?

Ft. In.

9 — 3
6 — 6
55 — 6
4 — 7—6
9)60—1½(6 yds. 6 feet 1½ inches answer.
54
6

The length and breadth being multiplied together brings it into square feet; which divided by 9. (the square feet in a yard) produces 6 yards two-thirds for answer.

Ex. 2.—What are the contents of a wainscoted room whose compass is 47 feet 3 inches, and height 7 feet 6 inches, in square yards? *Ans.* 39 yards ⅓.

Feet. In.
47—3 compass
7—6 the height.
330—9
23—7½
9)354—4½
39 yds ⅙ or ⅓.

Answer 39 yds. 3 feet, 4½ in.

Prices of Joiners Work.

	l.	*s.*	*d.*
Slit deal, wrought, 2 sides *per* foot	0	0	5
¾ deal ditto	0	0	6
Inch deal ditto	0	0	8
1¼ deal ditto	0	0	9¾
1½ deal ditto	0	0	9
2 inch deal ditto	0	0	11
¾ deal boards for slating, *per* square	1	10	0
¾ wrought weather-boarding	1	12	0
1½ wainscot ovolo sashes	0	0	9
2 inch ditto	0	0	10
1¼ 2-pannel square door	0	0	9
1½ 4-pannel ditto	0	0	11
2 inch deal 6-pannel moulded 2 sides	0	1	3
1½ square framed partition	0	0	8¾
Inch deal keyed dado....................	0	0	6¾
Deal mouldings *per* foot superficial	0	1	3

Carpenters Work.

Roofing, flooring, and partitioning, the principal parts of carpentery in modern buildings, are measured by the square of 10 feet each way, that is 100 square feet.

For

For rooffing, multiply the depth and half depth by the front, or the front and half front by the depth, and you will have the contents, if the roof is true pitch.

The dimensions are taken in feet and inches.

Ex.—How many squares are contained in a piece of work measuring 199 feet 10 inches in length, and 10 feet 7 inches in height ? *Ans.* 21 squares, 14 feet, $10\frac{3}{4}$.

Operation. Feet. In.   The division is performed

```
          199—10  long.       by pointing off two places
           10— 7              towards the right hand,
          ─────────           and the number on the left
          1992— 4             are squares.
          ·116— 6—10
          ─────────────
          22,14—10—10 An. 21 squares, 14 f. 10 in.
```

Again.—In a floor of 49 fet 7 inches 4 parts long, and 26 feet 6 inches broad, how many squares ?

The Operation performed by Practice.

Feet. In. Parts.

```
          49 —— 7 —— 4
          26
6 is ½  | 1289—10——8
        |  24— 9——8
       ─────────────────
        13,14— 8——8  Ans. 13 squ. 14 feet, 8 in. ⅓.
```

In measuring roofing no deduction is made for sky-lights, chimney-shafts, &c.

In measuring flooring, from the contents of the whole floor in feet, take the contents of the vacancy for the stairs in feet, and the remainder is the true contents; which bring into squares as before.

In partitioning, measure the doors, door-cases, and windows by themselves, and deduct their contents out of the whole, except they are included by agreement, in that case the doors, door-cases, and windows must be mentioned in the written agreement.

There are various sorts of carpenters work belonging to a building, *viz.* cornices, guttering, shelves, dressers, &c. all which are measured by superficial measure. There are also doors and door-cases, lantern-lights with their ornaments, cellar-doors, curbs, columns and pilasters, which are all valued by the piece, or superficial feet.

Carpenters measure the frames of any building, (which they call the carcass,) by the square of 10 superficial measure, or 100 square feet, as hinted before.

It.

Sawyers Work.

It may not be improper here to add something relative to the method used by sawyers in measuring their work, which when they perform by the Great, as they term it, they most commonly measure by the superficial foot; so that it is not difficult to take the dimensions; for they account the depth of the kerfs for the breadths, and the length for the length. The dimensions being thus taken in feet, the contents of one superficia kerf may be found by multiplying the length by the breadth, then having found the number of feet in one kerf, multiply it by the number of kerfs of the same dimensions, which gives the number of feet in them all.

When they have thus cast up the whole contents of their work in feet, they are paid for it by the 100 feet.

If the kerf be but six inches or less in depth, they have a custom to be paid for kerf and half, (as they express it,) *i. e.* for half as much more as it comes to by measure; the reason given for it is, that the trouble is so much the more on account of the often shifting, removing, and new binding the timber, and therefore they insist on it as a customary price.

The Prices of Sawyers Work.

	l.	s.	d.
12 Feet Deals sawed, *per* Dozen, cuts	0	3	6
10 Feet do. do.	0	3	0
12 Feet battens do.	0	2	4
10 Feet do. do.	0	2	9
Ends or half deals	0	1	9
Fir timber, at *per* load, 50 feet cube	0	6	6

{ All extra cuts are charged at the rate of 3s. 6d.
{ *per* 100 superficial feet

	l.	s.	d.
Oak timber *per* load	0	9	0
Elm, do. do.	0	8	0

Of Walling.

Walling is measured by the rod statute-measure, being 272 feet and ¼ superficial. The method of taking the dimensions for a wall round the orchard or the like, is by measuring the length by a line going over the buttresses: and for the height by measuring over the mouldings, (pressing the line into them,) even to the middle of the coping: likewise in taking notice of the thickness of the wall, *i. e.* how many half bricks in length the wall is in thickness; for three half bricks, that is a brick in length, and one in breadth,

breadth, is standard thickness ; and all walls, whether more,
or less, must be reduced to this standard by this rule, *viz.*
multiply the product of the length and height, by the number
ber of half bricks that the wall is in thickness ; which product being divided by 3, the quotient will be 272 (the $\frac{1}{4}$
being generally neglected,) and the quotient will be rods,
one brick and half thick, standard measure.

Ex.—Admit the face of a wall to measure 4085 feet, and
the thickness, two bricks and a half, or 5 half bricks thick,
how many rods does it contain ?

$$
\begin{array}{r}
4085 \\
5 \\
\hline
3)20425 \\
\end{array}
$$

262)6808)25 rod.
544
1368 rod.
1360 *Answ.* 25 $\frac{48}{175}$.
8

When the work is wrought Decimally, divide by 272$\frac{1}{4}$,
or 272,25, which gives the quotient somewhat less. But
the measuring of brick-work may be shortened by having
the rod of 16 feet $\frac{1}{2}$ divided into 100 equal parts, with
which you take the dimensions, and length of the wall in
those rods ; and 100 parts multiplied by the height give the
contents in rods of any wall that is a brick and half thick.
Deduction must be made for doors, windows, &c.

To reduce brick-work to standard-measure, *i. e.* a brick
and a half thick.

Brick.

Brick.		
1	Subtract	$\frac{1}{3}$
2	Add	$\frac{1}{4}$
3		
4$\frac{1}{2}$ } Multiply by	{ 2 } Reduces to a brick and $\frac{1}{4}$
6 }	{ 3
	{ 4

Example.—If a garden wall be 254 feet round, 12 feet
7 inches high, and three bricks thick, how many rods does
it contain ?

Feet. 251 0 In.   In this operation, the aggregate
    12 7   or total is multiplied by 2, because

In.   3048 0   twice 3 is 6, the number of half
6¼   127 2   bricks; which reduces the work
1½   21 2   to standard measure, as here shown.

    3196 2

        2

272)639 2 4(23, &c.

Of Chimnies.

This kind of brick-work is commonly agreed for by the hearth, and sometimes by the rod; and the method of taking dimensions thus: if the chimney stands not leaning against, or being in, a wall, and worked upright over the mantle-tree to the next floor, it is girt about the breast for the length, and the height of the story is taken for the breadth, and the thickness of the jambs for the thickness. But if the chimney stands against, or in a wall, which is before measured with the rest of the building, then the breadth of the breast or front, together with the depth of the two jambs, is the length; the height the story the breadth, and thickness of the jambs the thickness. But if the chimney stands in the corner of a room, and has 'no jambs, then the breadth of the breast is the breadth, the height of the story the length, and the thickness the thickness; and for the shaft, it is commonly girt in the smallest part for the length, and the thickness of both sides for the thickness, in consideration of the widths, pargetting, scaffolding, &c.

There is nothing to be deducted for the vacancy between the hearth and the mantle-tree, because of the width and the thickening for the next hearth above.

Of Gable Ends.

Take half the perpendicular for the breadth; the width of the house for the length, or half the width of the house for the breadth, and the perpendicular for the length, which brings the measure to an oblong, and the contents are found by multiplying the length by the breadth, &c.

Note. There are several other things in bricklayers work, as cornice, facias, straight arches, scheme arches, hips and valleys in tiling, and water-courses:—all which are measured

sured by the foot. Also piers, pilasters, rustic work, &c.
which are valued by the piece.

Prices of Bricklayers Work.	l.	s.	d.
Brick-work, all grey stocks, in walling, &c. per rod, including labour, materials, &c.	25	0	0
Labour and morter only	4	10	0
Grey stocks, per thousand	3	5	0
Plain tiles, per thousand	2	10	0
Pantiles, per 100	0	12	0
Bricklayers, per day, from Ma. 25, to Nov. 9,	0	5	0
Ditto do from Nov. 9, to Ma. 25,	0	4	0
Labourers, per day, from March 25, to Nov. 9,	0	3	0
Ditto do from Nov. 9, to Mar. 25,	0	2	9
Morter, per hod	0	0	9
New plain tiling, per square, including all materials	2	16	0

Of Paving.

Pavement for cellars, wash-houses, &c. is measured by
the square yard.

Example. If a cellar, wash-house, or court-yard be paved
with bricks, or pitched with pebble, being 9 yards 2 feet
long, and 6 yards 2 feet broad; how many yards square
doth it contain? *Answer*, 54 yards 1 and ¼ feet, as in the
following work, by Cross Multiplication.

```
Ft.   Yds.
9——2
6——2
58——0
6——1¼
46——1¼
```

Slating,

Is valued by the square of 100 feet, in some places by
the rod of 18 feet square : or 36 square yards, or 324 feet.

N. B. In tiling and slating, where there are gutters and
valleys, there is commonly an allowance, which is to take
the length of the roof all along the ridge, making the gut-
ter double measure; this is allowed in some places. Sometimes there is an addition for hollow ware, that is, ridge-
tiles, gutter-tiles, corner and dormar-tiles; and here
custom differ; for in some places one superficial foot is
counted for every lineal foot or running measure; then
100

roo feet lineal is reckoned a square. In other places, for every 100 of such tiles is reckoned square.

Prices of Slating in London, 1810.

Welch Slating, *viz.*		*l.*	*s.*	*d.*
Common double Welch slating, *per* square of 100 feet		2	10	0
Ladies ditto		2	6	0
Countess ditto		2	2	0
Welch rags		3	10	0
Westmorland slating, with iron nails		3	16	0
Ditto, with copper nails		3	19	0
Tavistock slating		2	16	0
Labour and materials, ripping old slating, and new laying complete, *per* square		1	4	0

Plasterers Work,

Is of two kinds, *viz.* First, Work lathed and plastered, sometimes called ceiling. *Secondly,* Plastering upon brickwork, or between the quarters in partitioning, by some called rendering; both which are measured by the yard square, as by the joiners and painters. In taking dimensions of a ceiling, if the room be wainscotted, consider how far the cornice bears into the room, by putting up a stick perpendicular to the ceiling, close to the edge of the uppermost part of the cornice; measuring the distance from the perpendicular stick to the wainscot, twice which distance must be deducted from the length and breadth of the room taken upon the floor, and the remaining is the true length and breadth of the ceiling. As if a floor be 24 feet long and 18 feet broad, and the cornice shoots out 6 inches, deduct 1 foot for both ends, and the length of the ceiling is 23 feet; the same for the breadth, and it leaves 17 feet broad; which multiplied together, gives the contents at 391 feet; or 43 pards and a half, nearly thus:

Example.—23 feet in length.
17 feet broad.
—————
161
23
—————
9)391(43 Yards, 4 feet.
36
—————
31
27
—————
4

If the ceiling of a room be 19 feet 10 inches one way, and 17 feet 6 inches the other, how many square inches does it contain?

By Cross Multiplication, thus:

$$
\begin{array}{r}
19 - 10 \\
17 - 6 \\
\hline
337 - 2 \\
9 - 11 \\
\hline
9)347 - 1(38 \text{ yds. } 5 \text{ ft. } 1 \text{ in.}
\end{array}
$$

How many yards square are in a piece of plastering feet 4 inches 7 parts long, and 18 feet broad?

F. I. Pts.

$$
\begin{array}{r}
47 - 4 - 7 \\
\text{3 times 6 is 18} \\
\hline
141 - 1 - 9 \\
6 \\
\hline
9)852 - 10 - 6(94 \text{ yds. } 6 \text{ feet, } 10 \text{ inches, } 6 \text{ parts.}
\end{array}
$$

The Prices.

	l.	s.	
Render 1 coat and sett, *per* yard	0	0	
Ditto floated	0	0	
Lath plaster sett	0	1	
Ditto floated	0	1	
Wash, stop, and white	0	0	
Straw colouring	0	0	
Lime whitening, *per* yard	0	0	
Plain cornice, *per* foot, superficial	0	1	
Plasterer, *per* day	0	4	
Labourer	0	3	
Boy	0	1	
A bundle of laths and nails	0	3	8
Lime and hair, *per* hod	0	1	0
Fine stuff, ditto	0	1	0

Of Masons Work.

Masons work consists of stone, and is of two sorts, viz. superficial and solid. Pavements and the face of stone walls, houses, &c. are measured as brick-work. If the work have ornaments, as capitals, pilasters, rails, and balusters, &c. they are then valued by the piece.

The Prices.

	s.	d.
Portland stone, *per* foot cube	4	3
Plain work, super.	0	11

nk or moulded,   super.   1   1
rtland chimney pieces per foot super.   1 10
e-stone, hearths, and covering, per foot super. 1   1
in marble chimney-pieces, set complete 6s. 6d. 7   6
rbeck paving in course, per foot super.   1   1
rbeck steps, per foot running   2   9
Inch York coping, per foot running   ..   1   8
rk window sills, per foot running   ..   1   3
bour and gravel, to pebble paving, per yard   0   8
nker paving all materials   ditto   6   6
w York paving, per foot 0 11
l paving relaid, per foot   0   2

Smiths work is done by the *lb. viz.*   *s.*   *d.*
imney bars, &c.   0   6
framed work, as gates, &c.   0   8
n bolts and nuts, &c. 0. 8
t-iron rails, &c. per cwt. 14s. to   ..   18   0

Price of Plumbers Work.   *l.* *s.* *d*

et lead, per cwt. 1 19   0
led lead   2   1   0
Rain pipes, per foot   ..,   ..   0   3   2
litto,   per foot   0   1   4
ints of solder   0   2   6
ints————   0   3   0
ipe————   0   2   0
ler per lb.   0   1   0
nber per day   0   4   0

Iem. Plumbers allow for old lead 4s. per cwt. less than
price of new cast lead; it is customary to deduct 2lb.
cwt. for dirt.

Land Measure.

and is usually measured by the acre. The dimensions
taken with a chain of four poles in length, which is di-
d into 100 parts, called *links*, and 10 square chains make
cre. Let them be 10 in length, and 1 in breadth, or 5
ngth and 2 in breadth, &c. or 160 square poles; but to
the contents, (if not regularly square,) it is generally di-
d into triangle: Thus a piece of land of 4 sides, (if not
re,) may be divided into two triangles, pieces of 5 sides
3, and a 6-sided piece into 4 triangles, and so on.

To

To measure a Triangle.

Admit the longest side of the following triangle, viz.
A D to be 76 poles; and the perpendicular or dotted line
B C to be 30 poles; multiply 76 (the base) by 15, the half
of the perpendicular B C, and it produces 1140; or multiply the whole perpendicular by half the base, (or longest
side,) it will produce the same; which divided by 160, (the
square poles in an acre,) the quotient gives the contents of
that piece of land in acres; multiply what remains by 4, dividing by the same divisor, and it gives roods, &c.

The perpendicular is always drawn from the opposite angle,
to the base, or longest side, as in the following figure.

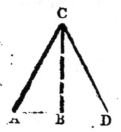

Operation thus: 76 the base.
15 half the perpendicular.

    16 ⌈0)114 | 0(7 acres $\frac{2}{160}$.
         612

          2

All pieces of land generally should be divided into triangles, and when measured their contents added together.

If an oblong plot of ground contains 35 poles broad, and
185 poles long, how many acres does it contain?

Rule. Multiply the length in poles by the breadth, dividing the product by 160, (the square poles in an acre,) and
the quotient will be the answer in acres, as follows.

            185 the length.
             35 the breadth.

            925
            555   The contents 40 acres
    160)6475(40 acres.   and 75 poles; or nearly
        640   acres and a half.

        75

By the Four Pole Chain.

Example 1. If a pole of ground contains 16 chains and 25 links in breadth, and 57 chains and 30 links in length, what are the contents thereof?

Ch. Link.
57,30 length.
16,25 breadth.

28650
11460
343 30
5730

Ac. 93 | 11250 cut of 5 places.
4

No roods ,45000
40

Poles 11 | 00000 93 a. 0 r. 18 p. *Ans.*

Four roods or rods make 1 acre, 40 poles 1 rood or rod, so that one rood or rod is a quarter of an acre.

The chain, commonly called *Gunter's* chain, contains 4 statute poles in 100 links, so that any number of chains are no more than so many 100 links, as 4 chains are 400 links, and 6 chains 600 links, &c. 160 statute poles are an acre, each pole being 16 feet and an half; therefore, in a square chain there are 16 square poles; and if you divide 160, the square poles in an acre, by 16, the square poles in a chain, the quotient is 10, the square chains in an acre.

A square chain contains 10,000 square links (or 100 multiplied by 100) hence it follows that 1 acre contains 100,000 square links.

To reduce the Statute to customary Measure.

According to a statute made in the 33d of *Edw.* I. and another in the 25th of Q. Elizabeth, a statute pole is 16 feet and a half long, but in some parts of England poles of 18, others of 21, and some of 24 feet long, are used, called customary measure, being in use according to the custom of the place where they are taken. Therefore to turn one kind of measure into another, admit statute measure to be turned into customary, as thus: multiply the number of acres, roods, and poles, statute-measure, by the square half yards, or square half feet in a square pole of statute measure, dividing the product by the square half yards, or square half feet contained in the pole of the customary
measure,

measure, and the quotient gives the answer in the latter, in acres, &c.

Example. In 172 acres statute-measure, how many acres of 18 feet to the pole or perch?

$$172 \text{ statute-measure.}$$
$$121 \text{ square half yards}$$
$$144)20812(144 \text{ acres } \tfrac{76}{144} \text{ customary measure.}$$

In a statute pole are 11 half yards, which squared, make 121 square half yards; and in a square pole of 18 feet, or 6 yards, there are 144 square half yards, &c. For the remainder, work as before, *viz.* by multiplying by 4, &c. and the next remainder by 40, &c. So that the answer is, that 172 acres, statute-measure, make 144 acres, 2 roods, and 4 poles of such customary measure.

An Example to the contrary.

In 548 customary acres of 18 feet to the pole, how many acres of statute-measure, of 16 feet and a half to the pole?

$$548 \text{ Customary.}$$
$$144 \text{ Square half Yards in customary acres.}$$
$$2172$$
$$2173$$
$$543$$
$$121)78192(646 \text{ statute acres.}$$
$$726$$
$$55, \&c.$$

The remainder 26 multiplied by 4 produces 104, which not amounting to a rood should be multiplied by 40, the product is 4160: this divided by 121 quotes 31 perches, 40 remaining: So that 543 customary acres, of 11 feet to the pole, make 646 acres 34 poles, and $\tfrac{40}{121}$ of a pole.

Note. Customary acres, as well as statute acres, contain 160 square poles or perches; the excess of size is by the size of the pole.

Solid Measure,

Is that of timber, stone, digging, &c. and the rule in working is to multiply the length taken in inches, and the breadth together, and the product by the depth or thickness, and the last product will be the contents in cubic inches, which, if timber or stone, divide by 1728, (the cubic inches in a solid foot) and the quotient gives the contents in a solid foot.

Example.

Place this at the end of Measuring.

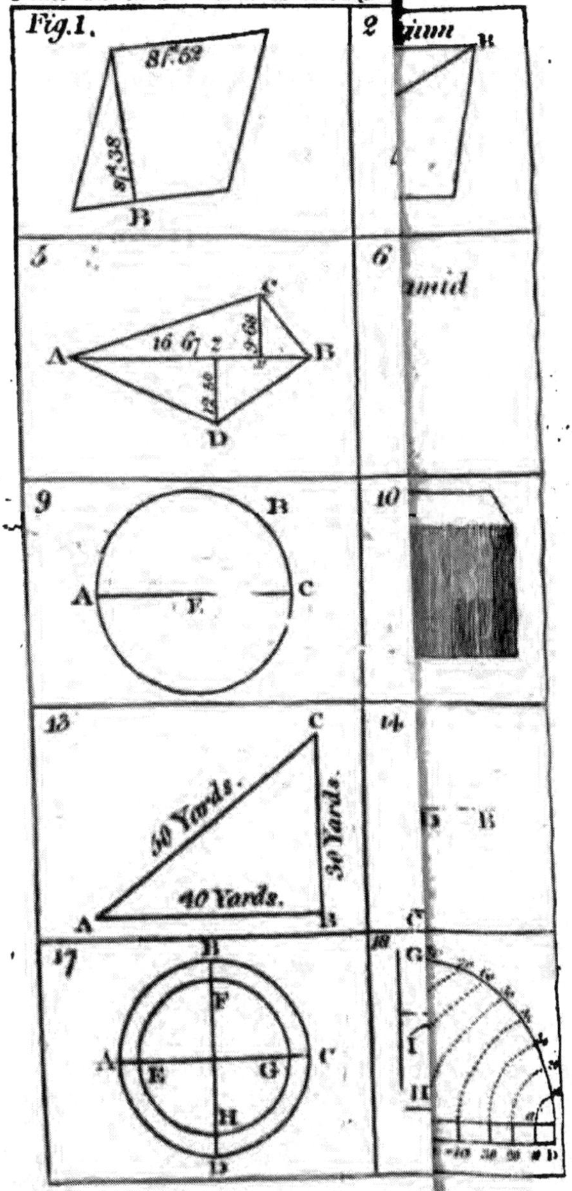

Fig.1.

81.52

84.38

B

2 ...ium B

5

C

16.67 z 9.68

A B

12.50

D

6 ...mid

9

B

A E C

10

13

C

50 Yards.

30 Yards.

40 Yards.

A B

14

D B

C

17

F

A E G C

H

D

18 G

I

H

Example. If a tree be 18 feet long, and 18 inches square, how many solid feet does it contain ?

Multiply $\begin{cases} 18 & 16 \\ 18 & 12 \end{cases}$

```
          324        192 length in inches.
                     324 breadth and thickness.
                     ───
                     768
                     384
                     576
            1728)62208(36  feet.
                  5184
                  ─────
                  10368
                  ─────
                    0
```

Solid Measure.

40 feet of round $\Big\}$ timber is a ton or load
50 —— of hewn

1728 inches is a foot of stone or timber.

27 feet is a yard.

282 inches is a gallon of ale or beer.

231 inches is a gallon of wine.

In an oblong piece of timber, whose breadth is 2,25 feet, thickness 1,64 feet, and length 36,5 feet, how many solid feet ?

```
        2,25 breadth.
        1,64 thickness.
        ────
         900
        1350
         225
        ─────
        36900
          36,5 length.
        ──────
        184500
        221400
        110700
        ──────
        134,68500
```
Ans. 134,685 solid feet, or 134, ¾ nearly.

Of Timber Measure.

To know the contents of a piece of timber by common or decimal arithmetic, observe as follows, *viz.* The tree being girted, and one-fourth part taken for the side of the square, multiply the length of the side of the square in inches into itself, and that product by the length in feet; which product divide by 144; but if you multiply by the

H   length

length in inches, then your divisor must be 1728, and if any thing remains, divide by 12, and the ·quotient will be the odd inches.

Ex. If a piece of timber be 15 feet long, and a quarter of the girt 42 inches ; what are the contents of that piece?

Thus : 42 inches in the side of the square.

$$\begin{array}{r} 42 \\ \hline 84 \\ 168 \\ \hline 1764 \end{array}$$

15 feet in length.

$$\begin{array}{r} \text{---} \quad F.\ I. \\ 144)26460(183\text{-}9\ Answer. \\ 144 \\ \hline 1206 \\ 1152 \\ \hline 540 \\ 432 \\ \hline 108 \\ 12 \\ \hline 144)1296(9\ \text{inches.} \\ 1296 \end{array}$$

In this example 1764 is multiplied by 15 in one line ; but it may be worked shorter by decimals, thus :

Squared $\left\{ \begin{array}{l} 3.5 \text{ the side of the square 42 Inches.} \\ 3,5 \end{array} \right.$

$$\begin{array}{r} 175 \\ 105 \\ \hline 12,25 \text{ the product are feet.} \\ 15 \text{ feet the length.} \\ \hline 183,75 \text{ the contents, or 183 feet, } \tfrac{7\,4}{1\,0\,0}, \text{ or 183} \\ \text{---} \quad \text{feet 9 inches.} \end{array}$$

But this common way of taking ¼ of the circumference for the side of the square, which is equal to the contents of the circle in round timber is erroneous, and gives the solidity somewhat less than the true contents ; for the true way is to multiply half the diameter into half the circumference, and then multiply that product by the length, which divide by 1728, and the quotient is the contents. If you cannot measure the end of the piece, you may know its diameter by this proportion, *viz.* as 22 is to 7, so is the circumference of the diameter.

Or you may find the side of
a square or a round piece of
timber, thus: multiply 2821
by the inches of the circumference, and cut off 4 figures
on the right hand for the
product

2821
Inch. 66 the compass.
18926
16926
18|6185 *Ans* 18 $\frac{6}{10}$. in.

Having the breadth 24 inches, and depth 18, of a piec
of timber or stone, to know how much in length will mak
a solid foot, multiply one with the other, and let the pro
duct be the divisor to 1728, thus

    24 broad.
    18 thick.
    ——
    192
    24
    ——
    432)1728(4 inches in length.
       1728

Thus you may make a table to serve all breadths and
depths, by which much labour may be saved, and yet mea
sure any piece of timber with accuracy.

In square timber you must make the inches squared a
divisor to 1728, and the quotient will be the answer in
inches of length, that will make a foot solid.

Ex. If a piece of timber be 8 inches square, what length
of it will make a foot?

    64)1728(27   *Answer*, 27 inches, or 2 feet 3
      128   inches in length.
      ——
      448
      441
      ——
      (0) Here the square of 8 is 64, &c.

Again, if a piece be 18 inches square, what length will
make a foot? *Answ.* 5 inches and one third.
The square of 18 is 324(1728(5$\frac{1}{3}\frac{2}{4}\frac{4}{4}$ equal to one third.
             1620
             ——
            (108)

The usual way of tapering timber is by taking the dimensions in the middle, and multiplying by the length; which
is not accurate; but if the dimensions are taken in several
places, and properly worked, the contents thus found will
be very near the truth.

H 2   *Digging*

Digging,

Is measured by the solid yard of 27 feet, that is, 3 times 3 is 9, and 3 times 9 is 27, by which are measured vaults or cellars, clay for bricks, &c. Other things are measured by the *floor* of 324 solid feet.

Ex. If a vault or cellar be 9 feet deep, 4 feet ½ long, and 3 feet 9 inches broad, what is its contents in solid yards?

```
            Feet. 4½ long
                  9  deep.
                 40½
                  3 F. broad
                121½
6 inches ¼       20¼
3 is ½ of 6      10⅛
         27)151⅞(5 Yards, 16 Feet ⅞
            135
            (16)
```

Ex. 2. How many yards of digging will there be in a vault that is 25 f. 4 long, 15 f. 8 broad, and 7 f. ½ deep?

```
 Ft. In.
 25—4
 15—8
386—0
 16—10—8
396—10—8
   7—6
2778—2—8
  98——4
              Yd. ft. in.
27)2976—8—0(110—6—8
   297
     6
```

Answer 110 Yds. 6 ft. 8 inches.

Ex. 3. In a mote 648 feet long, 24 feet broad, and 9 feet deep, how many floors?

648

648 long.
24 broad..

$$\begin{array}{r} 2592 \\ 1296 \\ \hline 15552 \\ 9 \\ \hline \end{array}$$

Divide by 324(139968(432 floors. *Answer.*

&c.

(O)

Most solid bodies being generally painted, it is necessary to know how to obtain the superficies. To find the superficial contents of a square, or many-sided, or round pillar, multiply the sum of the sides or circumference by the height in feet, and the product divided by 9 will be square yards.

Of a Globe.

Multiply the circumference in feet by itself, and then the product by this decimal 0,0353678, and this last product will be the contents in yards.

To find the superficial contents of a pyramid or cone, (see plate fig. 7 and 8) multiply for the pyramid, half the sum of the sides, or for the cone half the circumference of the base, by the slant height in feet; and the product divided by 9 will be square yards.

If the pyramid or cone be not complete, that is, if part of the top be wanting, add together the circumferences at top and bottom, and half their sum being multiplied by the slant height will be the superficial contents.

Note. A solid square yard of clay will make about 7 or 800 bricks: 3 bags (or bushels) and half of lime, and half a load of sand will lay 1000 bricks.

500 bricks
1000 plain tiles } make a load.
25 bags 1 cwt. of lime.

It may be proper here as well for refreshing the memory, as for improving the understanding and storing the mind with just notions and ideas of measuring, to give a short repetition by demonstrative geometrical figures, to explain what has been before expressed.

And 1st for *Planimetry*, or *superficial*, or *flat measure*, some parts of which are measured by the square foot; as

H 3

boards,.

rds, glass, marble, freestone, and pavements. The di-
nsions are taken in feet and inches, and the contents
en in square feet.

Ex. 1. In an oblong, or long square, whether board,
ss, or pavement, &c. and containing on the longest side
: length) 24 feet and a half, and the shortest side or
eadth, 14 feet ¼, as in the following figure. **Work as**
lows, *viz.*

F. 24½

14 F. ¼.

Area or contents
349 f. 125.

```
14,25 breadth.
24,5 length.
─────────
7125
5700
2850
─────────
319,135
```

Rule. Multiply the length by the breadth; and cut off as
any places to the right hand as there are decimals in the
ngth and breadth.

Ex. 2. Suppose a board or piece of glass, in the form of
g. 1 plate, called a Rhomboid, that is in the shape of a
ommon pane of glass, or diamond square. To measure
thich let fall a perpendicular at B, and multiply by the
ongth of any of the sides (for, they are all equal) and cut
ff as many places to the right hand as there are decimal
laces in both multiplicand and multiplier, as before hinted.
uppose the perpendicular height to be 8 feet 38 parts, and
he length of the side to be 8 feet 52 parts, then the work
rill be as under.

```
F. P.
8,52
8,38
─────
6816
2556
6816
─────
71,3976
```

Here the multiplication is as in whole
numbers, and the contents or answer
is found to be 71 square feet, and
$\frac{3976}{10000}$ of a foot, or something more
than 4 inches ¼.

3976 is separated by a comma, as above directed, and
re so many 10,000 parts of a foot.

Ex. 3. Again, suppose a solid body be in the form of fig. 2, called a Rhomboid; its length C. D. 17 feet 25 parts, and its breadth A. B. 8 feet 58 parts.

F. P.

17,25 length.

8,58 breadth.

13800

8625

13800

148,0050 *Answer*, the contents are 148 feet.

The forementioned figure hath its opposite sides equal, and its opposite angles a-like.

Again, suppose a board, piece of glass, pavement, or piece of land, to represent, or be in the form of a triangle, or three-cornered figure, expressed as in figure 3. Every triangle is half an oblong, whose length and breadth are equal to the perpendicular, and base.

The dotted line is the perpendicular, the bottom line the base, and the line from the top of the perpendicular A to the left angle of the base C, is called the hypotheneuse. If A B be 10 feet, and C D be 16 feet, the superficies of the triangle will be 80 feet.

Fig. 4. is called a trapezium, and consists of 4 sides: this figure, before it can be measured, must be divided into two triangles, thus: viz. by a line drawn from one angle or corner, to the angle opposite to it, as in the figure.—The line A B is called the diagonal.

Rule. Multiply the diagonal by half the sum of the two perpendiculars falling upon it from the opposite angles, and the product will be the area.

Ex. 4. Suppose the dimensions of the trapezium before described to be, viz. the diagonal A B 16 F. 67; the one perpendicular D z 12 F. 50, and the other C x 9 F. 68, (as in fig. 5.) what are its contents?

The Operation.

One perpendicular   12,50 ⎱ add
The other   -   -   -   9,68 ⎰
The sum is   22,18
The half sum is   11,09 which
multiply by the whole base   16,67
produces   184,8703

which is 184 feet, and $\frac{8703}{10000}$ of a foot, equal to 10 inches and a half.

H 4

1f

If two sides of a trapezium are parallel, equi-distant, add them together, and half the sum multiplied by the nearest distance, or a perpendicular between those two sides, gives the contents. Or measure in the middle between two sides or lines of equal length, and the answer will be the same.

The painting, plastering, &c. of irregular pieces, in forms of triangles or not, if divided as above, may be measured as before; and brought into yards (if the contents are to be so given) by dividing by 9, as before shown.

Of Regular Figures.

Figures having more than 4 sides are called polygons, and those that have their sides and angles equal are called regular polygons.

Regular figures have their names from the number of their sides; thus a figure having

3		Trigon, or equilateral triangle.
4		Tetragon, or square.
5		Pentagon.
6		Hexagon,
7	Equal sides, is	Heptagon.
8	called a	Octagon.
9		Nonagon.
10		Decagon.
11		Undecagon.
12		Dodecagon.

The area of a pentagon may be found by multiplying the square of its side by the number 1,7204774. Thus if the side of a pentagon be 11 feet, then the square thereof will be 11 times 11, or 121 feet.

Multiply   1,7204774
     by   121
            17244774
            34409548
            17204774
            208,1777654

Therefore the area of a pentagon will be upwards of 208 square feet.

In like manner, to find the area of the

Trigon

Trigon,			0,4330127
Tetragon,			1,0000000
Hexagon,			2,5980762
Heptagon,	Multiply the		3,6339124
Octagon,	Square of the		4,8284271
Nonagon,	Side by		6,1818212
Decagon,			7,6942088
Undecagon,			9,3656404
Dodecagon,			11,1961524

Note. The Multipliers in this Table are the Areas of the Polygons to which they belong; when the Side is Unity or One. See Bonnycastle's Mensuration, 2d. Ed.t. p. 55, where the demonstration is given at length.

Of a Circle. (Figure 9.)

A Circle is contained under one line cal'ed the Circumference or Periphery; as *ABC*. Plate Fig. 9. All right lines drawn from the centre *E*, to the circumference, are equal, and called Radii, or half Diameters: And the long line through the centre from *A* to *C* is the Diameter.

To divide a Circle into 6 equal parts extend the Compasses to half the Diameter, as from *A* to the centre *E*, and the extent applied to the Circumference will divide it into those parts.

The Diameter *AC* divides the Circle into two equal parts, each of which is called a Semicircle; and if a Semicircle be divided into two equal parts, those parts are called Quadrants.

The Questions relating to the measuring of the Circle and its parts may be solved as follows:

1. The Diameter being given to find the Circumference.
Rule. Multiply the Number 3.141597, by the Diameter, and the Product will be the Circumference. *Note.* The Number 3,1416 will be exact enough in most Cases.

Example. The Diameter of a Circle being 11 Inches, what is its Circumference?

$$3,1416$$
$$11$$
$$\overline{3,1416}$$
$$3,1416$$

Answer 345576 or something more than 34½ Inches.

H 5   2. Te

2. To find the Area of a given Diameter.

Rule. Multiply the Number 0,7853982 (or in common cases 0,7854) by the Square of the Diameter, and the Product will be the Area.

Ex. What is the Area of that Circle whose Diameter is 11 Inches? 11 times 11 is 121 0,7854

$$
\begin{array}{r}
121 \\
\hline
7854 \\
15708 \\
7854 \\
\end{array}
$$

Answer, 95,0334 Square Inches.

3. To find the Diameter of a given Circumference.

Rule. Multiply the Number 0,3183099 (or in common 0,31831) by the Circumference, and the Product will be the Diameter.

Example. What is the Diameter of a Circle whose circumference is 34¼ Inches, or 34,5

$$
\begin{array}{r}
0,31831 \\
34,5 \\
\hline
159155 \\
127334 \\
9459 \\
\end{array}
$$

Answer, 10,981695 (or almost) 11 Inches.

4. To find the Area of a given Circumference.

Rule. Multiply the Number 0,0795775 (or in common, 0,0796) by the Square of the Circumference, the Product will be the Area.

Example. What is the Area of a Circle whose Circumference is 34¼ Inches?

$$
\begin{array}{rr}
34,5 & 1190,25 \\
34,5 & 0,0796 \\
\hline
1725 & 714150 \\
1380 & 1071225 \\
1035 & 833175 \\
\end{array}
$$

1190,25 *Answer* 94,743900 (or almost 95.) sq. In.

5. The Area of a Circle being given, to find its Diameter.

Rule. Multiply the square Root of the Area by the Number 1,12837, and the Product will be the Diameter.

Example. What is the Diameter of a Circle whose Area is 95,0334 square Inches* ?

```
    95.0334)9,75 nearly.              1,12837
    81                                  9,75
187) 1403                             564185
     1309                             789859
  1945)9434                          1015533
  ....  9725                       11,0016075
```

Answer, The Diameter is 11 Inches.

6. To find the Circumference of an Acre of a Circle.

Rule. Multiply the Square Root of the Area by the Number 3,5449, the Product will be the Circumference.

Ex. What is the Circumference of a Circle whose Area is 95,0334 square Inches? The Square Root of

```
    95,0334)9,75          3,5449
    as before.             9,75
                         177245
                         248143
                         319041
                         4,562775
```

Ans. Circumference something more than 34¼ In.

7. To measure the Sector of a Circle. (See Figure 10.)

Case. 1. If the length of the Arc *D E*, and the Semidiameter *C E* be given, multiply the length of the Arc by ½ the Semidiameter; and the Product will be the Area.

Case 2. If the number of Degrees contained in the Arc and the Semidiameter be given, multiply the Square of the Semidiameter by the number of Degrees contained in the Arc, and that Product by the Number, 0,0087267, and the result will be the Area required.

Example. Let the Arc consist of 90 Degrees, or ¼ of the Circumference, and the Semidiameter be 3½.

```
    3,5        12,25          0,0087267
    3,5          90             11025
    175       1102,50          436335
    105                        174534
    12,25                      872670
                               8,7267
                             9,62118675
```

* Problems relating to the *Square Root* should be deferred till after the Reader has proceeded to that subject hereafter treated of.

Of

SOLID or Cube Measure has been already defined, as well as superficial Measure, some of the Figures of which are numbered 6, 7, and 8.

To measure a Solid in form of a Cube, which is in length, breadth, and thickness equal, multiply these into themselves; and the last Product will give the Solidity or Contents. A Cube has six Sides, and is in Shape like a Die.

Ex. What is the Solidity of a Cube whose Side is 12 Inches?

$$
\begin{array}{r}
12 \\
12 \\
\hline
144 \\
12 \\
\hline
1728
\end{array}
$$
the Solid Inches in a solid Foot.

To measure a solid of unequal length, breadth, and thickness, multiply the length by the breadth, and the product by the height; the last product will be the Solidity,

Ex. What is the Solidity of a block of marble whose length is 10 feet; breadth 5¾, and depth 3½ feet ?

By Cross Mult.	By Decimals.	By Practice.
5 ft. 9 In.	5,75	5——9
3——6	3,5	3
		6 is ¼
17——3	2875	17——3
2—-10—6	1725	2——10—6
20——1—6	20,125	20——1—6
10	10	10
201——3—0	201,25 the Sol.	201——3—0

The Cone is measured by finding the superficial Inches at the bottom or Base thereof; multiplied by one third of the Inches in length, and that Product is the solid Quantity in Inches; which divided by 1728, the Quotient gives the Answer in solid feet.

Example of finding the Solidity of the Cone Decimally without dividing by 1728.

Let the Diameter of the Base be 2 Feet 6 Inches, and the Altitude 10 Feet 6 Inches. The Area of a Circle is the Square of the Base multiplied by ,7854.

2,5 the

2,5the Diameter.
2,5

```
   125          4,908750  Area of the Base.
    50                3,5  Or third of the
  ----          --------      Height.
  6,25          24543750
  7,854         14726250
  ----          --------
  2500          17,1806250 = The solidity in
  3125                         feet.
  5000
  4375
  ------
  4,908755
```

This Method will serve for tapering timber, or for any Conical Figures.

To measure a Pyramid.

Multiply the Area or the Base or Bottom by one third of the perpendicular height, and the last Product will be the contents in solid feet : or one third part of the Area at the Base, multiplied by the whole Altitude, gives the contents also.

Examples of both Ways.

Suppose a square Pyramid (or figure resembling the spire of a Steeple) the side of whose base is 4½ feet, the perpendicular height 18 feet, what are its solid contents ?

```
   4,5        6,75 ⅓ of 20,250 the Area at the Base.
   4,5          18 The whole Height.
   ----        ----
   225         5400
   180          675
  -----        ----
  20,25      121,50 Answer, 121,50 as before.
   6⅓ of the Altitude.
```

121,50 Answer 121 Feet, and $\frac{49}{100}$ or ½.

When one Side of a Base is longer than the other, as suppose one to be 2 F. ½ and the other 1 F. ¼, then multiply the length of the Base by the breadth, and that Product by the height as before.

If the Base be a Polygon find its Area by the Rule given in page 168 ; multiplying it by ⅓ of its height.

To measure the Frustum or Segment, i. e. a piece or part of a Pyramid whose Ends are similar regular Polygons.

Rule. To the Areas of the two Ends of the Frustum add the Square Root of their Product, and this Sum being multiplied by ⅓ of the Height will give its Solidity.

To measure the Frustrum or Segment of a Cone.

Rule. Divide the Difference of the Cubes of the Diameters of the two Ends by the Difference of the Diameters, and this Quotient being multiplied by ,7854, and again by ⅓ of the Height, will give the Solidity.

Ex. What is the Solidity of the Frustrum of a Cone, the Diameter of the greater End being four Feet, and that of the lesser End two Feet; and the Height nine Feet?

```
            4                   2
            4                   2
           ──                  ──
           16                   4
            4                   2
Cube of 4. 64   Cube of 2.      8
Difference ⎫     8
  of the   ⎬  2)56  Difference of Cubes of the Diameters.
diameters. ⎭     28   Note. Multiply by 28.
            ,7854
           ──────
           62832
           15708
          ───────
          21,9912
            3 one third of the Cone's height.
          ───────
          65,9736
```

___

Of Gauging.

THERE is some kind of Affinity between the Art of Measuring Timber, and that of Gauging or Measuring Liquors; both being performed by cube or solid Measure. For as often as there is found 1728 solid or cubic Inches in a piece of Timber, (of whatever form,) it is said to contain so many solid feet; so likewise in Gauging; so many times as 282 (the solid inches in a Beer or Ale Gallon) are found in any vessel of such Liquor, that Vessel is said to hold so many Gallons; so of Wine; only in that the Divisor alters, it being 234 solid or Cubic Inches, instead of 282.

The Gal. of Dry Measure contains 272¾ cubical Inches.

Every cubical Foot in Beer or Ale-measure contains 6 Gallons and almost a Pint.

The same in Wine Measure is 7 Gallons, and almost 2 Quarts.

A cubical Foot of Dry Measure contains 6 Gallons and somewhat above one third of a Gallon.

141 Inches

- 141 Inches make 2 Quarts of Beer or Ale, 76 Inches $\frac{1}{2}$, one Quart, and 35 Inches $\frac{1}{4}$, a Pint.

Note. To find the Contents of any Vessel, as a Box, that has the form of a Cube, that is, a Figure whose breadth, depth, and length, are equal, and is well represented by the shape of a Die.

Multiply the Side into itself, and then again that Product by the Side; which last Product, if for Beer or Ale, divide by 282, the Inches in a Beer or Ale-Gallon; and for Wine, Brandy, &c. by 231, the Inches contained in a Wine-Gallon.

Ex. In a Cube, whose Side is 79 Inches, find the solid contents in Beer and Wine-Gallons. *Answ.* 1748 $\frac{123}{282}$ Beer or Ale-Gallons, or 2134 $\frac{85}{231}$ Wine-Gall.

```
   79      282)493039(1748 Beer or Ale Gall.
   79       282
  ────     ─────
  711       2110          231)493039(2134 Wine-Ga.
  553       1974               462
 ─────     ─────              ────
 6241       1363               310
   79       1128               231
 ─────     ─────              ────
56169       2359               793
43687       2256               693
──────     ─────              ────
493039 Cube In. 103           1009
                               924
                              ────
                                85
```

To find the contents of a Parallelopipedon, or Solid Figure, contained under six sides, of which the opposite are parallel, and of the form of Figure 12th.

Rule. Multiply the length by the breadth, and that Product by the depth; and then divide by 282 for Beer or Ale, and 231 for Wine,

Ex. If the length of a Chest be 95 Inches, the breadth 62 Inches, and the depth 23 Inches, what is its contents in Beer and Wine Gallons?

```
    95 Length.
    62 Breadth   282)135470(480 $\frac{110}{282}$ Beer-Gallons.
  ────
   190
   570
  ────
  5890
    23 Depth    231)125470(586 $\frac{124}{231}$ Wine-Gal.
  ─────
 17670
 11780
 ──────
135470 solid Inches.
```

To gauge a Buck or Square Tun.

Example. If its length be 112 Inches, its breadth 72 Inches, and its depth 48 Inches, what are the contents in solid Inches, and also the contents in Beer Gallons?

```
 112 Length      282)38072(1372 168/282 Galls. Ans.
  72 Breadth.    282...
 ───             ────
 224             1050
 784.             846
 ────            ────
8064             2047
  48 Depth.      1974
 ────            ────
64512             732
32256             564
──────           ────
387172 solid Inches.  (168)
```

To bring these Gallons into Barrels, divide them by 36, the Gallons in a Barrel of Beer :

```
thus; 35)1372(38    Answer. 38 Barrels and 4/36
      108           or 1/9 of a Barrel: and the Re-
      ───           mainder 168, is something more
      292           than half a Gallon.
      288
      ───
       (4)
```

How to gauge a Copper, Tub, or Cask.

If it be of equal size both at top and bottom, find its contents in Cube inches, and bring it into Gallons as before. But if it be wider at top than at bottom, or the contrary, then take the Width or Diameter somewhat above the middle, next to the broadest end, if it be taper; or find the mean Diameter thus; if the Bung Diameter be 26 inches, and the Head Diameter be 23 inches, the difference between which is 3 inches, two thirds of which make two inches; this added to the smaller of the two Diameters makes 25 for the mean Diameter sought. Having the mean Diameter, proceed to find the contents in solid Inches, thus: square the mean Diameter; and multiply that square by 0,7854, and the Product will give the Contents of the Liquor at one Inch deep, and this multiplied by the length will give the solid Inches in either Copper, Tub, or Cask.

Ex. Suppose the mean Diameter to be 72 inches, and the length 56 inches :

```
      72            4071,5136
      72                  56
     ―――         ―――――――――
     144            244290816
     504            203575680
    ―――         ―――――――――
    5184 square.    28004,7016
    ,7854
   ――――
   20736
   25920
   41472
  3628
 ―――――
```
4071,5136 Contents at one Inch deep.

The solid Inches as above found, 228004, brought into Gallons, make 808, and 148 solid Inches remain, something more than 22 ½ a Gallon; in all 22 Barrels, 16¼ Gallons of Beer. Again ;

If the mean diameter of a cask of wine be 14 inches, the length 72 inches, what is its contents in wine-gallons ?

```
      14            ,7854
      14             106
     ―――         ―――――
      56            47124
      14            70686
     ―――           7854
     196           ―――――――
                   153,9384
                         72
                  ――――――――
                   3078708
                  10775688
           231)11803,5048(47,9
                    924
                   ――――
                    1843
                    1617  Answer 48 Gal. nearly.
                   ――――
                    2265
                    2079
                   ――――
                    1866
                    &c.
```

The contents of a Spheroid may be found by multiplying the Square of the shortest Diameter by the longest Diameter, and dividing by 538 for Beer-Gallons, and by 441 for Wine-Gallons.

Ex. If a Spheroid in its shortest Diameter be 74 Inches, and the longest 125 Inches, what is its contents in Beer and Wine-Gallons?

74
74
———
296
518
———
5476 the square of the shortest Diameter.
125 the longest Diameter.
———
27380
65712
———
538)684500(1272 $\frac{164}{538}$ Gallons of Beer.

441)684500(1552 $\frac{68}{441}$ Gallons of Wine.

To find the Contents of a Frustrum of a Sp'eroid take twice the square of the Bung Diameter, and once the Square of the Head, and multiply the same by the length : Then for Beer divide by 1077 ; and for Wine Gallons, divide by 882.

Ex. In a Cask whose Bung Diameter is 23 Inches, Head Diameter 21 Inches, and Length 27 Inches, what are the Contents in Beer and Wine Gallons ?

23	21
23	21
———	———
529 Sp. Bung. Diam.	441 Sq. Head. Diam
2	
———	
7058	
441	
———	
1499	
27 Length.	

882)40473(45 $\frac{183}{441}$

3528

———

5193
4410
———
783

1077)40473(37 $\frac{624}{1077}$

3231

———

8163
7539
———
624

Answ. 46 Wine Gallons nearly ; and something more than 37½ Beer Gallons.

The Extraction of the Square and Cube Root, of great Use in Measuring, Gauging, &c.

Of the Square Root.

1st. A Square Number arises from the Multiplication of a Number into itself, the Number so multiplied being
called

led the Root; thus 4 multiplied by 4 produces 16, for 16
square Number, and 4 is the Root thereof; so also 4
the square of 2, for twice 2 is 4; and 9 is the Root of
for 9 times 9 is 81, &c.

lly. To extract the square Root of any Number, is to find
ther Number, which multiplied into itself produces the
mber given; and after the Root is found, such a Multi-
ation is a proof of the work.

3dly. Square Numbers are either single or compound.

4thly. All the single square Numbers, with their respec-
Roots, are contained in the following Table, *viz.*

ts	1	2	3	4	5	6	7	8	9
uares	1	4	0	16	25	36	49	64	81

5thly. When the Square Root of any Number less than
is required, and that Number is not expressed in the
going Table, then take the Root of that Square Num-
in the Table which is the least nearest to the given
mber. Thus if the Square Root of 50 be required, then
9 is the nearest Square Number in the Table, its Root
will be the Root of the given Number, nearly.

6thly. A compound square Number is that which is pro-
ed by a Number consisting of more places than 1, multi-
d by itself, and is never less than 100; so 709 is a com-
nd square Number, produced by the multiplying 27 into
lf, and 961 is the square of 31.

7thly. The Root of any Number under 100 may be easly
wn by the foregoing Table of single squares; but to ex-
t the Root of a compound Number of several places,
erve the following directions:

Ex. To find the square Root of the Number 45796.

. Set a point over the place of the Units thus, 45796,
o successively over every second Figure towards the
hand, as thus 45796; and thus, 45796. But in Deals you must point from the place of Units toward the
t hand, omitting one place, as above; and if the
es of Decimals are odd, put a cipher toward the right
d of them to make them even. The Number thus
ared, draw a crooked Line on the right of the Num-
, as in Division; (and, indeed, the operation of the
re Root, not much unlike Division, only there the
isor is fixed, but in the square Root we are to find a
Divisor for each Operation.) Having made a crooked

Line

Line thus, 45796 (, seek in the foregoing Table for the nearest square to the first point on the left hand, here is 4 the Root of which is 2, which Root place on the right hand of the crooked Line, and set its square 4 under the said point as under:.

$$45796 \ (2.$$
$$4$$
$$\overline{(0)}$$

Then subtract it, and 0 remains: To the Remainder, bring down the next point 57, thus:

$$45796$$
$$4$$
$$\overline{057}$$

Which call the Resolvend; then double the Root of the first point, and place it on the left hand of the Resolvend, thus:

$$45796 \ (2$$
$$4$$
$$\overline{057}$$

Call the 4 the double of the Root 2, thus placed on the left hand of the crooked Line, the Divisor, and seek how often 4, the Divisor, can be taken in 5, the first Figure of the Resolvend 57 (for you are to omit the last Figure towards the right hand) which here is once, place 1 at the right of the Root 2, and also to the right of the Divisor 4, thus:.

$$45796 \ (21$$
$$4$$
$$\overline{40)057}$$

Then multiply the Divisor (now 41) by the Figure last placed in the Root, viz. 1, place it under the Resolvend and subtract it therefrom.

$$45796(21$$
$$4$$
$$\overline{41)057}$$
$$41$$
$$\overline{16}$$

Then bring down the next point, viz. 96, and place on the right of the remainder 16, for a new Resolvend or Dividend: next double the Quotient, or part of the

oot, viz. 21, and place it for a new Divisor to the new
esolvend 1696, thus :

$$45796 \quad (21$$
$$4$$

$$41) \quad \overline{057}$$
$$41$$

$$42) \quad \overline{1696}$$

hen try how often 42 be in 169, (still reserving or omit-
ng the Unit Figure of the Resolvend or Dividend as afore-
id) and it will be found 4 times, which 4 place to the
Quotient and in the Divisor; and proceeding as before, the
Work will appear thus :

$$45796 \quad (214 \text{ Root.}$$
$$4$$

$$41) \quad \overline{037} \text{ Resolvend.}$$
$$41$$

$$424) \quad \overline{1696} \text{ Resolvend.}$$
$$1696 \text{ Product.}$$

$$\overline{(0)}$$

In this last Operation 4 is placed in the Root, and like-
be in the Divisor 42, which makes the new Divisor 424,
the Resolvend 1696; this Divisor multiplied by 4, the
gure placed in the Root, produces 1696; equal with the
ividend or Resolvend aforesaid, as in the Operation.
herefore the square Root of 45796, is 214; for 214 mul-
plied into itself produces 45796, the Number whose square
oot was sought.

Example 2.

hat is the square Root of 12299049 (3507 the Root.

$$9$$

$$1\text{st Divisor } 65) \quad 329 \text{ Resolvend.}$$
$$325 \text{ Product.}$$

$$2\text{d Divisor } 700) \quad \overline{490} \quad \text{Resolvend.}$$

ere it is evident 49 cannot be divided by 70, of course put
wn an 0 in the Divisor, and also in the Root, and bring
wn the next point.

$$3\text{d Divisor } 7007) \quad 49049 \text{ Resolvend.}$$
$$49049 \text{ Product.}$$

$$\overline{(0)}$$

Example

Example 3, performed Decimally.

160,0000009 (12,649 Root.
     1

1st Divisor 22) $\overline{000}$
             44

2d Divisor 246) $\overline{1000}$
             1476

3d Divisor 2524) $\overline{12400}$
             10096

4th Divisor 25289) $\overline{230400}$
             227601
             $\overline{2799}$

When the Divisor cannot be had in the Resolvend, th
place a ciper in the Quotient, and also on the right of
Divisor, bringing down the next square, &c. as in the
cond Example.

If any Remainder happen after extraction, proceed by
nexing pairs of ciphers to the right of the given Num
and then come to what Exactness you please.

Such Numbers given for Extraction that leave Rem
ders, are by some called *Irrationals*, because their Roots
not be exactly discovered, but still there will something
main, though you work by whole Numbers or Fracti
As in the Example above, where the Remainder is 2
For here you may proceed for ever and not come to an
act Root, because no Figure multiplied into itself
give 0.

The Extraction of the Cube Root.

TO extract the Cube Root of any number is to find
other number, when multiplied by itself, and that
duct by the number found, produces the number given
Extraction.

All single Cube Numbers, with their respective Roots,
contained in the following Table:

Roots.	1	2	3	4	5	6	7	8	
Square.	1	4	9	16	25	36	49	64	
Cube.	1	8	27	64	125	216	343	512	

1st. To prepare any Number for Extraction, make a point over Unity, and so successively over every third Figure towards the left hand in Integers, missing two between each point; but in Decimals point from the place of Units to the right hand, &c.

Ex. Extract the Cube Root of 46656, prepared as above directed;

thus: 46656

Here are but two points, therefore the Root will have but two places.

2*dly.* The Number being prepared, find in the foregoing Table the nearest Root to the first point or period 46, which you will find to be 3, which place in the Quotient thus, 46656(3; the Cube whereof is 27, which place under your first period 46, as in the Margin; subtract it from 46, and there remains 19; this is your first Work, and no more to be repeated. Then to the Remainder 19 bring down the next period, viz. 656 (which is the last) and place it on the right of the Remainder 19.

$$46656(3$$
$$27$$
$$10$$

$$46656(3$$
$$27$$
$$\overline{19656} \quad \text{Resolvend.}$$

Then draw a Line under the Resolvend; next square the 3 placed in the Quotient, which makes 9; which multiplied by 300 makes 2700 for a Divisor, which place accordingly thus:

$$46656(3$$
$$27$$
$$2700)\ \overline{19656}$$

Then try how often 2 may be found in 19, which is only 6 times; because of the Increase that comes from the Quotient, and place 6 in the Quotient: then multiply the Divisor by 6, and the product will be 16200; which place orderly under the Resolvend thus:

$$46656(36$$
$$27$$
$$2700)\ \overline{19656}$$
$$1600$$

Then proceed to find the Increase coming from the Quotient thus: Square your last Figure 6, and it makes 36;

which multiplied by three, the other Figure of the Quotient, gives 108; which multiplied by 30 makes 3240. This place also orderly under the last number set down, viz. 16200, and the Work will appear thus:

$$
\begin{array}{r}
46556\ (36 \\
27 \\
\hline
2700)\ 19656 \\
16200 \\
\hline
3240
\end{array}
$$

Then cube the Figure last placed in the Quotient, viz. 6, and it makes 216; which place orderly likewise under the Line 3240; add the three Lines together, and they make 19656; which is equal to the Resolvend above, viz. 19656, and there being no more periods to bring down, the Work is finished, and the Cube Root of 46656 will be found to be 36.

This will appear to be right if the Root 36 be multiplied by 36, and that product again by 36, for then the Result will be 46656 as under.

$$
\begin{array}{r}
36 \\
36 \\
\hline
210 \\
108 \\
\hline
1296 \\
36 \\
\hline
7776 \\
3888 \\
\hline
46656\ \text{proof}
\end{array}
$$

Having separated the given Number into periods, and from the first period substracted the greatest Cube it contains, put the Root as the Quotient, and to the Remainder bring down the next period for a Dividend.

Find a Divisor by multiplying the Square of the Root by 300; try how often it is contained in the Dividend, the Answer is the next Figure in the Root.

Multiply the Divisor by the last Figure in the Root. Multiply all the Figures in the Root by 30 except the last, and the product by the Square of the last. Cube the last Figure in the Root. Add these three last found Numbers together, and subtract their Sum from the Dividend: to the Remainder bring down the next period, proceeding as before.

To Extract the Cube Root of 52313624.

```
    3                    52313628(374 Root.
    3                    27
    ──                   ─────
    9                    25313
  300                    23653
  ────                   ─────
 2700                     1660624
    7                     1660624
  ─────                   ─────────
18900                    ........
 4410=3×30×49
  343=7× 7 × 7
 ──────
23653
```

37 × 37×300=410700 Divisor.

```
            4
         ────────
         1642800
          17760=37×30×
             64= 4×  4× 4.
         ──────────
          1660624
```

Let the Reader try his Skill by answering the following Questions.

What is the Cube Root of 389017 ? *Ans.* 73.

What is the Cube Root of 5735339 ? *Ans.* 179.

What is the Cube Root of 32461759 ?

What is the Cube Root of 84604519 ?

Uses of the Square and Cube-Root.

1. *To find a mean Proportional between two Numbers.*

Rule. THE Square Root of the Product of the given Numbers is the mean Proportional sought, so the mean Proportional between 16 and 64, will be 32, for 16 multiplied by 64 produces 1024, and the Square of 32 is also 1024. This is the use in finding the side of a Square equal to any Parallelogram, Rhomb, Rhomboid, Triangle, or Regular Polygon.

2. *To find the Side of a Square equal to the Area of a given Superficies.*

Rule. The Square Root of the contents of any given Superficies is the Side of the Square. So if the Content of a given Circle be 160, the side of the Square equal will be 12,649, &c

5. *The Area of a Circle being given, to find the Diameter.* See Page 178.

I   *The*

6. *The Area of a Circle being given, to find the Circum-ference.* See Page 179.

Any two Sides of a Right-angled Triangle being given, to find the third Side.

This depends upon a mathematical Proposition, in which it is proved that the Square of the Hypotenuse, or longest Side of a Right-angled Triangle, is equal to the Sum of the Squares of the Base and Perpendicular, that is, of the other two Sides.

1. Let the Base or Ground *B A*. Fig. 13, represent the Breadth of a Moat or Ditch, and the Perpendicular, *B C*. the Height of a Castle, Tower, or Wall; and the Hypotenuse *A C*. the Length of a scaling ladder.

, In this Figure the Base *A B* is supposed to contain 40 Yards; and the Perpendicular, or Height of the Tower or Wall 30 Yards; what Length will the Hypotenuse *AC*, or Scaling Ladder be?

Rule. The *Square Root* of the sum of the squares of the Base and Perpendicular is the Length of the Hypotenuse, thus:

1600 the Square of the Base 40..

900 the Square of the Perpendicular 30.

The Sum 2500 (50 Yards the Root or Length of the Scaling
    25   Ladder.

    (0)

2. If the Length of the Base or Breadth of the ditch be re-quired, then the Square Root of the Difference of the Squares of the Hypotenuse and Perpendicular is the length of the base, or breadth of the ditch or moat, thus:

2500 the Square of the Hypotenuse *AC*.

900 the Square of the Perpend. *BC*.

The Differ. 1600(46 Yards the Root or Breadth of the
    16   Ditch.

    (0)

3. If the Height of a Tower or Perpendicular *B* were re-quired, then the Square Root of the Difference of the Squares of the Hypotenuse and Base is the height of the Perpendicular *BC*, thus:

2500   900 (30 Yards.
1600   9
—————
900

7. *If*

7. *Any Number of Men being given to be formed into a Square Battalion, to find the Number of Rank and File.*

Rule. The square Root of the Number of Men given will be the Number of Men to be placed in Rank and File.

Example. If an Army of 32400 Men be formed into a square Battalion, the square Root of 32400 will be found to be 180, and so many Men must be placed in Rank and File.

8. *To find the Side of a Square, Polygon, or the Diameter of a Circle, which shall be to any other given Square, similar Polygon, or Circle, in a given Proportion.*

Rule. Since similar surfaces are to each other in a duplicate proportion of their like sides, therefore,

As the given Circle, Square or Polygon,
Is to the required Circle, Square or Polygon;
So is the Square of the Diameter, or Side of the first,
To the Square of the Diameter, or Side of the second.

Then the Square Root of the Result of the above Proportion will be the Diameter or Side required.

Ex. 1. In a Circle whose Diameter is 11, what will the Diameter of that Circle be whose Area is four times the Area thereof?

Here 11 times 11 is 121 : and

As 1 ———— 4 ———— 121

$$\begin{array}{r} 4 \\ \hline 484 \\ 4 \\ \hline 48)84 \\ 84 \end{array}$$ (22 the Answer.

Ex. 2. In two similar Polygons, whose Areas are as 9 to 25, and the Side of the smaller is 12 Yards, what is the Side of the larger?

Here 19 Times 12 is 144 ; and

As 9 ———— 25 ———— 144

$$\begin{array}{r} 25 \\ \hline 720 \\ 288 \\ \hline 9)3600 \\ \hline 400 \\ 4 \\ \hline 000 \end{array}$$ (20 the Answer.

I 2

9. Th

9. *The Uses of the Cube Root are to find the Dimensions of similar Solids, as Globes, Cylinders, Cubes, &c.*

Rule. Since similar Solids are to each other as the Cubes of the like Sides or Diameters : therefore,

As the Content or Weight of a given Solid,

Is to the Content or Weight, of another like Solid ;

So is the Cube of the Side, or Diameter, of the one,

To the Cube of the Side, or Diameter, of the other.

Then the Cube Root of the Result will be the Length of the Side or Diameter required.

Ex. 1. If a Ball weighs 72*lbs.* and is 8 Inches in Diameter, what will be the diameter of a ball that weighs 9*lbs.* Here the Cube of 8 is 512 ; and

As 72———9————512

$$
\begin{array}{r}
9 \\
\hline
72) \ 4608 (64 \\
432 \\
\hline
288 \\
288 \\
\hline
\end{array}
$$

Then the Cube Root of 64, *viz.* 4, is the Diameter required.

Ex. 2. If a Ship of 100 Tons be 44 Feet long at the Keel, of what Length must the Keel of a Ship be that carries 220 Tons ?

Say as 100 is to 200, so is the Cube of 44, *viz.* 85181, to 187401,8 ; whose Cube Root is 57,226, the Length of the Keel sought.

Ex. 3. A Cubical Vessel has its side 12 Inches, and it is required to find the Side of a Vessel that holds three times as much. Here the Cube of 12 is 1728, which

multiplied by ————————————— 3

Produces ——————————————— 5184

the Cube Root of which is 17,306 the *Answer* required, or Side sought.

An easy Rule to find the Length of the Mast of a Ship.

The Mast always bears a certain Proportion to the Breadth of the Ship ; whatever be the Breadth of the Vessel multiply it by 12, and divide the Product by 5, which gives the Length of the Main-mast. Thus a Ship 30 Feet broad, in the widest part, will have a Mast 72 Feet long. And a Ship 40 Feet broad will have a Mast 96 Feet high, for 40 × 12 = 480, and 480 divided by 5, gives 96.

To find the Thickness of Masts.

The Thickness of Masts are estimated by allowing one Inch for every three Feet in Length; accordingly a Mast Seventy-two Feet long must be Twenty-four Inches in Diameter.

SOME USEFUL GEOMETRICAL PROBLEMS.

At a given Point near the Middle of a Right Line, to erect a Perpendicular.

Let $C D$ (Fig. 14.) be the Line given; to have a Perpendicular erected on it from the Point B, with the Compasses (opened at a convenient distance) place one Foot at the point B, and with the other make the two marks E and F, on each Side of B, and at equal Distance from it; then, with the same, or any other Distanace in the Compasses, set one Point on E, and with the other describe the Arc $G G$; which being done, without altering the Compasses, set one Foot at F, and with the other describe the Arc $H H$, crossing the former at the Point A; through which Intersection with a Ruler draw a Line from A to B, which will be perpendicular to the Line $C D$.

To raise a Perpendicular at or near the end of a Line.

This is effected several Ways; but I shall instance only two, which are very easy.

1st. Suppose the Line $A B$ (Fig. 15.) be given to raise a Perpendicular near the End, A.

First open your Compasses to a convenient Distance, and set one Foot on the Point A: and with the other describe the Arc $F E D$; then with one Foot of the Compasses in D, (they being kept to the same Distance) cross the Arc in E; and then setting one Foot in E, with the other make the Arc $A F G$, crossing the first Arc in F. Again set one Foot in F, and with the other describe the small Arc $H H$, crossing the former in the Point C; so the Line $A C$ being drawn, will be the perpendicular required.

2d. Let B be the given point on which to draw the Perpendicular $B I$. Open the Compasses to any convenient Distance; and setting one Foot on the Point B, pitch down the other Foot at random, as suppose at K, then the Foot resting in K, turn the other about till it cross the Line $A B$ in L; then draw the Line $K L$, and continue the same beyond K, setting off the same distance $K L$, (at which the Compasses already stand) from K to M, so a Line drawn from B, though M will be the perpendicular required.

I 3

3. How to divide a Right Line into two equal Parts.

Suppose the Line *A B* (Fig. 16) be given to be divided into two equal Parts. Take in the Compasses any Distance above half the Length of *A B*, and setting one Foot on the Point *A*, with the other draw the Arc *F D E*; then (with the Compasses unaltered) set one Foot in *B*, and with the other cross the former Arc both above and below the Line, in the Points *F* and *G*, then a Line drawn from *F* to *G* shall intersect, or cut the given Line in *H*, and divide the Line *A B* into equal Parts, *A H* and *D B*.

4. *A Line being given, how to draw another Line parallel thereto, at any Distance required, or through any Point assigned.*

Of parallel Lines there are two Sorts, viz. *Straight* or *Circular*. And all Circles drawn on the same Centre, whether greater or less one than the other, are said to be parallel or concentric, that is, having one common Centre.

In this Figure the Circle *A B C D* (Fig. 17.) is concentric or parallel to the Circles *E F G H*, because both of them are drawn from the same Centre. The Line *A C* is the Diameter of the greater Circle, and the Line *E G* of the lesser Circle. And all right Lines drawn from the Centre to either of the Circumferences, are equal with respect to their Periphery; and such Lines are called half Diameters, and sometimes the Radius of the Circle, and will divide the Circle into six equal Parts, each containing 60 Degrees, and the whole Circle 360; into which all the great Circles of the Sphere are supposed to be divided.

Of Parallel Right Lines.

Right-lined Parallels are Lines drawn on a Plane of equal length and distance; and though infinitely extended will never meet, and in all Parts retain an equal distance as underneath.

B ——— —— —— ——————— C
C ——— —————— ——— — D

To draw a Right Line parallel to another Right Line at a Distance given.

- Take in your Compasses the given Distance *G H* (Fig. 18.) then setting one Foot in *E*, draw the Arc *I K*; then moving to *F*, describe the Arc *L M*; then laying a Ruler on the Top of the two Arcs, just touching them, draw the Line *N O*, which will be parallel to the given Line *E F*.

5. Through

5. *Through any three Points (not in a straight Line) to describe a Circle.*

Let the Points given be *A, B,* and *C,* (Fig. 19.) through which it is required that a Circle be drawn First, set one foot of the Compasses in one of the given Points, as suppose in *A,* and extend the other Foot to *B,* another of the Points, and draw the Arc of a Circle *G F D;* then (the Compasses not altered) set one Foot in *B,* and with the other cross the said Arc with two small Arcs, in the Points *D* and *E;* and draw the Line *D E.* Thirdly, set one Foot in *C* (the Compasses being at the same distance) and with the other Foot cross the first Arc *G F D* in the Points *F* and *G,* and draw the Line *F G,* crossing the Line *D E* in the Point *O,* which is the Centre sought for; in which, place one Foot of the Compasses, and describe the Circle at the distance *O A,* and it will pass through all the given Points *A, B,* and *C.*

Another Method. Join the three Points, and bisect any two Sides of the Triangle, and on the Points of Bisection erect Perpendiculars crossing each other, and the Point of Intersection is the Centre of the Circle sought.

How to make the Line of Chords geometrically to any assigned Length or Radius.

As in the Art of Dialling frequent use is made of the Line of Chords, it is proper here to show the making thereof.

A Line of Chords is 90 Degrees of the Arc of a Circle transferred from the Limb of the Circle, to a straight Line; now every Circle, whether great or small, is divided (or supposed to be divided) into 360 equal Parts, called Degrees; so the Semi-circle contains 180; the Quadrant or Quarter 90, and the Radius or Semi-diameter (which is that Line with which the Circle or Semi-circle is drawn or described) is always equal to 60 Degrees of that Circle which it describes, and therefore 60 Degrees of a Line.

To make the Line of Chords.

First draw a Line to any Length, *C B D* (Fig. 20.) and on the Middle thereof erect the Perpendicular *A B;* next open your Compasses to the Radius or Length that you would have your Line of Chords be, which admit *A B,* and with that distance on *B* as the Centre, describe or draw the Semi-circle *C A D,* which is divided into two equal Parts

I 4

or Quadrants by the Perpendicular Line *A B*; thirdly, divide the Arc or Quadrant *A D*, into 9 equal Parts, each of which will be 10 Degrees, according as the Numbers are seen and set apart to them. The Quadrant *A D*, being thus divided into Parts of 10 Degrees each, set one Foot of the Compasses in *D*, and open the Foot to 90 and describe the Arc 90 *A*, touching the Line *C*, *D*, in *A*, so is the Point *A* upon the right Line *C D* the Chord of 98 Degrees. Open the Compasses from *D* to 80 Degrees, and describe the Arc 80 *b*; so shall the point *b* be the Chord of 80 Deg. Open the Compasses from *D* to 70, describe the Arc 70 *c*, the Chord of 70 Degrees, and so of the rest, and then you will have the Line *D A* divided into 9 unequal Parts, called Chords, as in Figure 20, and if the Quadrant be large enough, each of the Parts may be subdivided into ten others, in the same manner, and then you have the Chords for 90 Degrees.

Thus much for the Line of Chords, frequently made use of in dialling, where there is not the Convenience of having a Mathematical Instrument Maker near at Hand.

Note. *A Degree is the 360th Part of the Globe, or of any Circle, and each Degree is supposed to be divided into 60 Parts, called Minutes; so that 45 Minutes is three Quarters of a Degree, and 30 Minutes half a Degree, and 15 Minutes one Quarter of a Degree.*

Instrumental Arithmetic.

As all Problems or Questions in Measurement, &c. are solved or answered arithmetically by the Pen, so are they Instrumentally taken by the Compasses, from certain Lines, &c. or Rules made for that Purpose, for the help of those that are deficient in Arithmetic, or for a quicker Dispatch of Business; and such Performances are called *Instrumental Arithmetic;* and of these Instruments, the most in use are the three following : 1. The carpenter's Plain Rule : 2. Gunter's Line : 3. *Coggeshall's* Sliding Rule.

Description and Use of the *Carpenter's Plain Rule.*

This Rule is made use of in measuring Roads and Timber, being two Feet in Length, and divided into twenty-four Parts or Inches, and every one of those Parts or

Inches

inches subdivided into half inches, and each of these halves into quarters, and each quarter into two parts ; so that every inch is divided into eight parts, and the whole length into 192 parts.

As this rule is well known, it is not necessary to represent it ; but, however, for the better understanding it, I shall give one thus :

Under-board measure thus described :

1	2	3	4	5	6	1		7
12	6	4	3	3	2			
0	0	0	0	0	0			

This line begins at 6, and goes on to 36, within 4 inches of the rule on the right hand. Its use as follows : ·

$$\text{If a board be} \begin{cases} & \textit{In. dp.} & \textit{Feet. In. Pts.} \\ 1 & 12 \quad 0 \quad 0 \\ 2 & 6 \quad 0 \quad 0 \\ 3 & 4 \quad 0 \quad 0 \\ 4 & 3 \quad 0 \quad 0 \\ 5 & 2 \quad 4 \quad 5 \\ 6 & 2 \quad 0 \quad 0 \end{cases} \text{in length make a foot square.}$$

By this table it will be easily understood that a board of 4 inches requires 3 feet in length to make a foot square, and a piece of 3 inches broad will require 4 feet in length to make a square, &c.

At the other end of the rule is a table called Under-timber Measure ; and described thus :

· 1	2	3	4	5	6	7	8	
144	36	16	9	5	4	2	2	
0	0	0	0	9	0	11	3	

This line begins at 8½, going on by divisions to 36.

$$\text{In a piece of timber of} \begin{cases} & \textit{In. Square.} & \textit{Feet.} \\ 1 & 144, \quad 0 \\ 2 & 36, \quad 0 \\ 3 & 16, \quad 0 \\ 4 & 9, \quad 0 \\ 5 & 5, \quad 9 \\ 6 & 4, \quad 0 \\ 7 & 2, \quad 11 \\ 8 & 2, \quad 13 \end{cases} \text{In length make a solid foot}$$

So that if a piece of timber be six inches square, four feet in length of such piece will make a solid foot.

I 5   It

It is a common method with carpenters to add the breadth and thickness of a piece of timber in inches together, and call the half thereof the side of the square of that piece ; but this method gives the contents more than it is ; and the greater the difference the larger the error. But the true square may be found in Gunter's Line, thus : place one point of the compasses upon the line at the thickness, and the other at the breadth ; then half of that extent will reach, from either the breadth or thickness, to the side of the true square in inches.

2. *Gunter's Line.*

This Line is commonly set on the carpenters plain rule, and consists of two lines, numbered 1, 2, 3, &c. one set at the end of the other, and it is somewhat of the following form :

Gunters's Line.

To prove the line by the compasses observe that the

$$\text{Distance} \begin{Bmatrix} 1 \text{ to } 2 \\ 4 \text{ to } 10 \\ 5 \text{ to } 8 \end{Bmatrix} \text{is equal to the distance} \begin{Bmatrix} 2 \text{ to } 4 \\ 4 \text{ to } 8 \\ 3 \text{ to } 6 \end{Bmatrix} \&c.$$

To Number on Gunters's Line.

Observe, that the figures 1, 2, 3, 4, 5, 6, 7, 8, 9, sometimes signify themselves simply, or alone ; at other times 10, 20, 30, 40, &c. Again, at other times 100, 200, 300, or 1000, &c.

To find a Number on the Line, as suppose 134.

For the figure 1, account 1 on the line ; and for 3, take 3 of the largest divisions ; and for 4, take 4 of the smaller divisions ; and that is the point : Again, to find 750 on the line, for 7 take 7 on the line ; for 50 take 5 of the great divisions, and that is the point.

To find a small Number on the Line, as suppose 12.

For 10, take 1 as before, and for 2 take 2 of the larger divisions, and that is the point.

In measuring boards or timber it is best to have a line of two feet long, and compasses one foot long.

Note.

Note.---Let the measurement be by the inch, foot, yard, pole, rod, &c. it is best to have it decimally divided, or so supposed, that is, into 10th parts.

Note also, That if one point of the compasses reach beyond the line in the work, remove the other point to the same figure or place on the other line.

Multiplication by Gunter's Line.

To multiply 5 by 7, set one foot of the compasses on it in the left-hand line, and extend the other to 5 upwards, or toward the right hand, and with the same extent place one foot in 7, and the other foot will fall on 35 in the right-hand line, which is the answer.

Division in Gunter's Line.

Example 1. Divide 63 by 3 ; extend from 3 to 8 downwards, or towards the left hand, and the extent will reach the same way from 63 to 21, the quotient.

N.B. *In multiplying you must always extend upwards, that is, from* 1, *to* 2, 3, 4, &c. *and on the contrary, in dividing extend downwards.*

Example 2. Divide 288*l.* equally among 16 men : extend from 16 to 1 downwards ; and that extent will reach the same way, from 288*l.* to 18*l.* for each man.

Again :

Example. Suppose 750*l.* were to be divided among 25 men, extend from 25 to 1 downwards : and that extent will reach the same way, from 750*l.* so 30*l.* each man's share.

RULE OF THREE DIRECT.

Example 1. If 5 bushels of barley cost 11 shillings, what will 40 bushels cost ?   Extend from 5 to 11 upwards ; and that extent will reach the same way, from 40 to 88, the shillings required.

Example 2. If three ells of Holland cost 10*s.* 6*d.* what will 40 ells cost ? Extend from 3 to 10¼ upwards, and that extent the same way will reach from 40 to 140*s.* the answer.

The Use in Board-Measure.

Example. If a board be 9 inches broad, and 19 feet long, what is the contents superficial square feet ?   Extend from 12 (the centre of foot measure) to 9 downwards, and that extent the same way will reach from 89 to 14 and ¼.

In

In Timber-measure.

Example. In a piece of timber 24 inches square, and 8 feet long, what is the contents in solid feet ? Extend from 12 the centre, to 24 upwards, and that extent twice the same way will reach from 8 to 32 feet the contents.

Brick-Work.

How many rods of work are there in 4085 feet ? Extend from 272 downwards to 2, and that extent the same way from 4085 will reach 15 rods, the answer.

3. Description of Coggeshall's Sliding-Rule.

This rule is framed three ways; sliding by one another as the glaziers rule; sliding on one side of a two-feet joint-rule; one part sliding on the other, in a foot of length; the back part being flat, on which are sundry lines and scales.

Upon the aforesaid sliding side of the rule are four lines of numbers, three are double lines, and one a single line of numbers, marked with *A B C* and *D*, the three marked *A B* and *C* are called double lines of numbers, and figured 1, 2, 3, 4, 5, 6, 7, 8, 9. Then 1, 2, 3, 4, 5, 6, 7, 8, 9, and 10, at the end. That marked *D* is the single line of numbers, and figured 4, 5, 6, 7, 8, 9, 10, 20, 30, and at the end 40, even with and under 10, in the double line next to it; and that is called the Girt-line, and so marked in the figure.

The figures on the three double lines of numbers may be increased or decreased at pleasure ; thus 1 at the beginning may be called 10, 100, or 1000 ; and 2 is 20, 200, or 2000 ; so that when 1 at the beginning is 10, then 1 in the middle is 100, and 10 at the end is 1000 ; but if 1 at the beginning is accounted for 1, then 1 in the middle is 10, and 10 at the end is 100.

And as the figures are altered, so must the strokes or divisions between them be altered in their value, according to the number of the parts they are divided into; as thus, from 1 to 2, it is divided into 10 parts, and each tenth is divided into 5 parts ; and from 2 to 3 it is divided into 10 parts, and each tenth into 2 parts, and so on from 3 to 5 ; then from 5 to 6 it is divided into 10 parts only ; and so on unto 1 in the middle of the rule, or at the end of the first part of the double line of numbers. The second part of the double line is divided like the first.

The

The Girt-line marked *D* is di
parts, and each 10th into 2 parts
and then from 10 to 20 it is divid
tenth into 4 parts; and so on all
the end, which is right against 1
line of numbers.

The lines on the back-side of
side, are these, *viz.* a line of th
12, each divided into halves, qu
another line of inch-measure fron
to 12 equal parts, and a line of f
divided into 100 equal parts, and
50, 60, 70, 80, 90, and 100,
measure.

And the back-side of the sli
inches, halves, quarters, and half-
12 to 24, so that it may be slid o
length of a tree, or any thing e
measure.

Example of the Use of

Suppose there is a geometrical
feet $\frac{1}{4}$ each : set 1 foot on the lin
and then against $3\frac{1}{2}$ on the line *B*
which is the contents of such a s

$$
\begin{array}{c}
F.\ Pts. \\
3-6 \\
3-6 \\
\hline
10-6 \\
1-9 \\
\hline
10-3 \ \text{Proof.}
\end{array}
$$

Suppose the side of a rhomb be
breadth of the line *A B* 8 feet 4
Set one foot on the line *B*. to 8 fe
again 8 feet $\frac{4}{100}$ on the line *B*, is
on the line *A*, and to know the
part of the foot, look for $\frac{10}{100}$ on t
against it 4 inches $\frac{1}{4}$, so that the
71 feet 4 inches $\frac{1}{4}$.

Again, suppose the length of
or 17 $\frac{6}{10}$ and the breadth 8 fe

contents ? Set, one foot on the line *B* to 17, 25 on the line *A*, then against 8; 58 on the line *B*, is 148 feet on the line *A*. The figure has been represented before, and worked arithmetically, therefore it is here unnecessary.

Let the base of a triangle be 4 feet 1 inch ¼, and the perpendicular 2 feet 1¼; the half of the one, in 2 feet 7 parts; and of the other 1 foot 7 parts. Set one on the line *B*, to 4, 15 on the line *A*; then against 1, 07 half the perpendicular on the line *B*, is 4 feet and almost half a foot for the contents. Or, if you set 1 on the line *B* to 1, 07 on the line *A*, against 4, 15 on the line *B*, is 4, and almost half a foot on the line *A*.

Again, another way : If you set 1 on the line *B* to 4, 1 on the line *A*, then against 2, 25 on the line *B* is 8 feet $\frac{9}{10}$ (which is about 11 inches) on the line *A*, the half whereof is 4 feet 5 inches ½, which is the contents of the triangle.

Of GEOGRAPHY.

Geography is the art of describing the surface of the earth, the constituent parts of which are land and sea.

Many arguments may be produced to prove that the earth and seas are of a spherical or globular figure ; one of them may be sufficient in this place, *viz.* that ships in sailing from high capes or headlands lose sight of the lower parts first ; and continue gradually also to lose sight of those which are situate higher and higher, till at last the top disappears, which could not be unless the surface of the sea were convex ; now this convexity of the sea is found to be uniform in all parts thereof, therefore the surface of the waters is spherical, which being granted, that of the land must be nearly so, because its extremity sets limits to the waters.

The whole body of the earth and seas is therefore called the Terraqueous Globe.

Since, as has been before observed, all circles are divided into 360 Degrees, therefore any great circle surrounding the terraqueous globe is usually so divided. Our ingenious countryman, Mr. Richard Norwood, about the year 1635, by an accurate measurement of the distance between
London

London and York, found that a degree of a great circle was about 69¼ statute miles in length, and consequently that the circumference of the terraqueous globe was 25,020 miles, whence its diameter will be 7964 miles.

The sea covers the greater part of the terraqueous globe, out of which the land rises with very slow ascents, the height of the loftiest mountains being Chimboraco in South America, and this is not quite four miles perpendicular above the surface of the sea.

Geographers have found it necessary to imagine certain circles to be drawn on the surface of the earth, for the better determination of the positions of places thereon.

These are either greater or lesser circles ; great circles divide the globe into two equal parts, the lesser circles divide it into two unequal parts.

There are six kinds of great circles ; two of them, *viz.* the Equator, or Equinoctial, and the Ecliptic, are fixed ; but the others, *viz.* the Meridians, the circles of Longitude, the Horizons, and the Vertical circles, are variable, according to the part of the globe they are appropriated to.

There are two points on the surface of the terraqueous globe, called the Poles of the Earth, which are diametrically opposite to each other; the one is called the North, and the other the South Pole.

The Equator is that great circle which is equally distant from both the above-mentioned poles, and is so called from its dividing the terraqueous globe into two equal parts, named from the poles which are situated in each, the northern and southern hemispheres. It is also called the Equinoctial, because when the sun enters it the days and nights are of equal length in all parts of the globe. Seamen commonly call this circle the Line.

Meridians, or Circles of Terrestrial Longitude, are supposed to be drawn perpendicular to the equator, and to pass through the poles : they are called Meridians, or Mid-day Circles, because when the sun comes to the meridian of any place it is noon, or mid-day, at that place.

Hence every particular place on the surface of the terraqueous globe hath its proper meridian, and consequently a traveller who doth not directly approach to, or recede from one of the poles, is continually changing his meridian.

With

With respect to the two circles above described, every place upon the earth is said to have its particular latitude and longitude.

The latitude of any place upon earth is its distance from the equator, in a direct line towards one of the poles ; and since the meridians proceed in such a direct line, therefore latitude is reckoned in degrees, and parts of degrees, on the meridians of the place.

The longitude of any place upon earth is the east or west distance of the meridian of that place, from some fixed meridian, at which longitude is supposed to begin. Now, since all the meridians pass through the poles, they coincide with one another at those points, and their greatest distance from each other will be when they are farthest from those points of coincidence, viz. at the equator ; therefore, longitude is reckoned in degrees, and parts of a degree, of the equator.

Geographers have differed very much in the meridian from whence they have assumed the beginning of longitude ; the ancients chose the meridian of the Canaries, which they called the Fortunate Islands ; others have pitched upon the Azores, or the Western Islands ; but the most usual way is now to reckon longitude from the capital of that country in which an author writes, and accordingly the longitude is reckoned in this work from the meridian of London.

Parallels of latitude are small circles drawn parallel to the equator at any assigned distance therefrom ; therefore every particular place on the surface of the terraqueous globe hath its proper parallel of latitude.

There are four of these parallels of latitude that are particularly remarkable, viz. the two tropics, and the two polar circles ; but for the better explanation of those properties it will be necessary, first, to define the ecliptic.

The Ecliptic is that great circle in which the Sun seems to perform its annual motion round the earth ; this circle makes an angle with the equator of $23^\circ 29'$; it intersects it in two opposite points, called the Equinoctial Points ; and those two points in the ecliptic, which are farther from the equinoctial points, are called the Solstitial Points.

The Tropic of Cancer is a parallel of latitude $25^\circ 29'$ distant from the equator in the northern hemisphere, passing

ing through the northern solstitial point of the ecliptic, as before described : And,

The Tropic of Capricorn is a parallel of latitude, as far distant in the southern hemisphere, passing through the southern point.

The Arctic Polar Circle is a parallel of latitude 23° 29' distant from the north pole : and the antarctic polar circle is a parallel of latitude as far distant from the south pole.

The tropics and polar circles divide the globe into five parts, called, Zones ; that is to say, Girdles or Belts; one of them is called the Torrid ; two temperate ; and two frigid.

The Torrid Zone, so called from the great heat of the Sun, which passes directly over the heads of the inhabitants twice in the year, is situated between the two tropics, and is therefore about 47 degrees in breadth; the inhabitants are called Amphiscians; that is, such as have their shadows cast both ways, the sun being seen at noon sometimes to the north, and at other times to the south of them.

The Northern temperate zone is situated between the tropic of Cancer, and the arctic polar circle ; and the southern temperate zone, between the tropic of Capricorn, and the antarctic polar circle ; they are each of them about 43 degrees broad : the inhabitants are called Heteroscians, that is, such as have their shadow but one way ; for at noon the shadows of the inhabitants of the northern temperate zone are always cast northward ; and those of the inhabitants of the southern, southward.

The Frigid Zones contain all that space between the polar circles and the poles themselves ; the northern frigid zone being surrounded by the arctic circle, and the southern by the antarctic. The inhabitants are called Periscians, because, when the sun is on the same side of the equator as those inhabitants are, their shadows are, in the space of 24 hours, cast of all sides, or quite round them. The sun does not act in the places within these zones during several successive revolutions or days in the summer : and in the winter he doth not rise for a like space of time. To the inhabitants of the poles, if there be any, the sun is visible for one half the year, and invisible for the other half.

If any place on the globe, except the poles and equator, be particularly considered, there will be three other places

on

on the same meridian which have more immediately a relation thereto, viz. 1. That place which has the same latitude on the other side of the equator. The inhabitants of this place are called Antiscii. They have mid-day and mid-night at the same time with those of the place assumed ; but the seasons of the year are different, the summer of the one being the winter of the other.

2. That place which is on the same parallel of latitude, but is 180 degrees different in longitude. The inhabitants of this place are called Periscii. They have summer and winter at the same time with those of the place assumed ; but the times of the day are different, the mid-day of the one being the mid-night of the other.

3. That place, which has the same latitude, on the other side of the equator, and is 180 degrees different in longitude. This place is diametrically opposite to the place assumed : its inhabitants are called Antipodes, and their seasons of the year, as well as times of the day, are totally opposite.

The Horizon is that great circle which divides the upper or visible hemisphere of the world, from the lower or invisible, the eyes of the spectator being always in the centre of the horizon. Hence every particular place on the terraqueous globe hath a different horizon ; and consequently a traveller, proceeding in any direction is continually changing his horizon.

The Circle is by mariners divided into four quarters, containing 90 degrees : the four points quartering this circle are called Cardinal Points, and are named East, West, North, and South : the East and West are those points on which the Sun rises and sets when it is in the equinoctial ; and the north and south points are those which coincide with the meridian of the place, and are directed toward the north and south poles of the world.

Each quarter of the horizon is further divided into eight points, which are very necessary to the geographer for distinguishing the limits of countries ; but the use of those divisions is much more considerable when applied to the Mariners Compass.

Before the invention of this excellent and most useful instrument it was usual, in long voyages, to sail by, or keep along the coast, or at least to have it in sight ; as is manifest and plainly evident by the voyages of St. Paul, Acts xx, 13, and xxviii. 2, which made their voyages long, and
very

very dangerous, by being so near the shore. But now, by the help of a needle, touched by the magnet, or load-stone, which, by a wonderful and hidden quality, inclines its point always northerly, the mariner is directed in his proper course of sailing through the vast ocean, and unfathomable depths, to his intended port ; and if the wind is favourable, can sail more than 333 leagues, or 1000 miles, in a week, through the darkest weather, or darkest nights, when neither land, moon, nor stars, are to be seen, which before were the only guides ; and, if not seen, the mariners were at a great loss, and exposed to the most imminent danger.

The following figure is a representation of the said Compass, with the Cardinal and other Points.

The Mariners Compass.

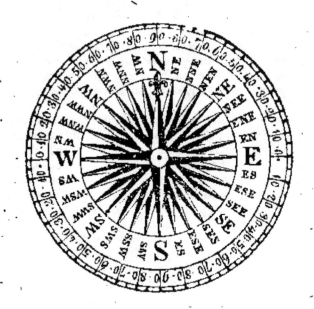

The

The Compass in the preceding page is a representation of the Horizon on a circular piece of paper, called a Card, which card being properly fixed to a piece of steel, called the Needle, and placed so as to turn freely round a Pin that supports it, will show the position of the Meridian, and other points; and consequently towards which of them the ship sails.

Note. The letters *N* by *E*, *N N E*. *N E* by *N*, &c. are to be read, North by East, North North-East, North-East by North, &c.

A Climate is a space of the terraqueous globe contained between two such parallels of latitude, that the length of the longest day in the one exceeds that in the other by half an hour.

There are sixty Climates, thirty to the North, and thirty to the South of the Equator; twenty-four of each thirty being situate between the Equator and the Polar Circle, differ in the length of their longest day by 24 hours; but in the remaining six, between the Polar Circles and Poles, the differences of the lengths of the longest day are each a month.

A Table of the Climates between the Equator and the Polar Circles,

Climate.	Longest Day.	Begins Latitude.	Ends Latitude.	Breadth.
1	12½ Ho.	0° - 0′	8° - 34′	8° - 34′
2	13	8 - 34	16 - 43	8 - 09
3	13½	16 - 43	24 - 11	7 - 28
4	14	24 - 11	30 - 45	6 - 34
5	14½	30 - 45	36 - 30	5 - 45
6	15	36 - 30	41 - 22	4 - 52
7	15½	41 - 22	41 - 31	4 - 09
8	16	45 - 31	49 - 01	3 - 30
9	16½	49 - 01	51 - 58	2 - 57
10	17	51 - 58	54 - 29	2 - 31
11	17½	54 - 29	46 - 37	2 - 08
12	18	56 - 37	58 - 26	1 - 49
13	18½	58 - 26	59 - 59	1 - 33
14	19	59 - 59	61 - 18	1 - 19
15	19½	61 - 18	62 - 25	1 - 07
16	20	62 - 25	63 - 21	0 - 49
17	20½	63 - 21	64 - 09	0 - 48

Climate.

Climate.	Longest Day.	Begins Latitude.	Ends Latitude.	Breadth.
18	21 Ho.	64° - 09′	64° - 49′	0° - 40′
19	21¼	64 - 49	65 - 21	0 - 32
20	22	65 - 21	65 - 45	0 - 24
21	22¼	65 - 45	66 - 06	0 - 21
22	23	66 - 06	66 ′ 20	0 - 14
23	23½	66 - 20	66 - 28	0 - 08
24	24	66 - 28	66 - 31	0 - 03

A Table of the Climates between the Polar Circles and the Poles.

Climate.	Longest Day.	Begins Latitude.	Ends Latitude.	Breadth.
25	1 Mo.	66° - 31′	67° - 21′	8° - 50′
26	2	67 - 21	69 - 48	2 - 27
27	3	69 - 48	73 - 37	3 - 49
28	4	73 - 37	78 - 30	4 - 53
29	5	78 - 30	84 - 05	5 - 35
30	6	84 - 05	90 - 90	5 - 55

The Terraqueous Globe, or Globe of the Earth and Water, is divided by Nature into continents, islands, peninsulas, isthmusses, mountains, promontories or capes, hills and vallies ; oceans, seas, lakes, gulphs or bays, streights, ports or harbours, and rivers ; rocks, shelves, banks, marshes and bogs.

A Continent, called sometimes the main-land, is a large tract of land, containing several contiguous countries, empires, kingdoms, or states.

An island is a piece of land wholly surrounded by the ocean, sea, or other water, and so divided from the Continent.

A Peninsula is a piece of land encompassed by water, except on one side, where it is joined to the continent, or other land.

An isthmus is a neck, or narrow piece of land, that joins a peninsula to the continent.

A Mountain is a part of the earth which is considerably higher, or more elevated, than other lands near it.

A Promontory is a mountain running out into the sea, the extremity of which is called a Cape or Headland.

A Hill is a smaller kind of mountain ; and a valley is that

that land which is situate at the bottom of a mountain or hill, or between two or more hills or mountains.

The Ocean is a vast body of salt water, which separates some of the continents, and washes their borders or shores.

A Sea is a branch of the ocean flowing between some parts of the continents, or separating islands from them.

A Lake is a body of water every where surrounded by the land.

A Gulph or Bay is a part of the ocean or sea contained between two shores, and is encompassed by the land, except on one side, where it communicates with the other waters.

A Strait is a narrow passage whereby seas, gulphs, and bays, communicate with the ocean, or with one another.

A Port or Harbour is a part of the ocean, or sea, so inclosed by the land that ships may ride in safety.

A River is a running water, descending in a narrow channel from the mountains, or high lands, and emptying itself into some ocean, sea, lake, or other river.

Rocks are immense stony masses; shelves and banks are eminences consisting of stones, sand, or other matter, which obstructs the passage of ships at sea, and often prove fatal to those who do not keep clear of them.

Marshes are lands lying low, and liable to be overflowed by the sea or rivers; and Bogs are mixtures of earth and water, over or through which it is dangerous to attempt a passage.

The known parts of the Earth are commonly divided into four parts, *viz.* Europe, Asia, Africa, and America; the first three were known to the ancients, and are for that reason called the Old World: the fourth was discovered something more than 300 years since, and therefore called the New World.

The lands which lie toward the north and south poles are very little known; that toward the north pole is called Terra Arctica, and that toward the south pole, Terra Antarctica, or Terra Australis Incognita; the latter is supposed by some to be nearly as large as Europe, Asia, and Africa.

The ocean assumes different names in different parts of the earth; and the seas, gulphs, and bays, are named mostly from the lands to which they adjoin; it is thought therefore most convenient in this short sketch to describe the land and waters together; and first,

Of Europe, with the adjacent Waters.

Europe is bounded on the north by the northern or frozen ocean; on the west by the north Atlantic, or western ocean, which separates it from America; on the south by the Mediterranean sea, separating it from Africa; and on the east by Asia, to which it joins, without any visible limit, toward the northern parts; but on the southern it is separated by various rivers, seas, &c.

The length of Europe, from Cape St. Vincent to the Uralian Mountains, is about 3,300 miles; and the breadth from Cape North in Lapland, to Cape Matapan in Greece, may be about 2,350 miles.

Europe contains the following empires, kingdoms, regions, or states, viz. Spain, Portugal, France, Italy, Turkey, Great Britain, the Netherlands, Germany, Hungary, Poland, Denmark, Sweden, and the Russian Empire.

Of Spain and Portugal.

Spain and Portugal are surrounded by the sea on three sides; on the south and south-east by the Mediterranean, which communicates with the Western or Atlantic ocean, by the Straits of Gibraltar; on the west by the said ocean; and on the north by the same, or a part thereof, called the Bay of Biscay: on the north-east by the Pyrenean mountains, which, reaching from the Mediterranean to the Bay of Biscay, separate it from France.

Portugal is now a kingdom separate from Spain, to which it was formerly subject: it is situated on the ocean, which washes it on the west and south; it is hardly 300 miles in length from north to south, and about 100 in breadth. The capital city is Lisbon, which was till lately in a ruinous condition, having been almost totally destroyed by an earthquake, and a fire which succeeded it in November 1755. The city of Oporto is also a place of great trade, particularly famous for its wine.

Most of the provinces of Spain were all formerly separate kingdoms; such were Andalusia, in which Gibraltar is situated, as are the cities of Seville and Cadiz; Granada within the Straits, the principal city has the same name, and on the Mediterranean are situated the ports of Malaga and Almeria, Murcia more eastward in the Mediterranean, in which, besides a city of the same name, is the city and port of Carthagena : Valencia, north-eastward of Murcia ; this has a city and sea-port of the same name, and another port of great trade, called Alicant.

Spain is divided into Fourteen Districts, *viz.*

Asturia,	Leon,	Valencia,	Murcia,
Biscay,	Old Castile,	New Castile,	and
Navarre,	Arragon,	Estramadura,	Granada.
Galicia,	Catalonia,	Andalusia,	

Its chief towns are Madrid, the capital ; Barcelona ; Seville ; Corunna, and Cadiz, sometimes called Cales.

The principal rivers are the Ebro, the Tagus, and the Douro, all of which have their rise in Spain.

On a promontory in the south of Spain stands Gibraltar, which has been in the possession of the English for a century, and is so defended by nature and art as to be considered impregnable. Not far from Spain are the Balearic Isles, called Majorca, Minorca, and Yvica.

Proceeding eastward along the Mediterranean sea is the kingdom of France, which is bounded on the east, by Italy; Switzerland and Germany, on the north by the English channel, on the west by the Bay of Biscay, and on the south by the Pyrenees, which separate it from Spain, and a part of the Mediterranean sea.

France was anciently divided into provinces ; but since the revolution it has, with the Netherlands and various other territories, acquired by the war, been divided into 120 departments, which are as follow :

Ancient Provinces.		Departments.	Chief Towns.
Provence	4	Basses-Alpes, Bouche-du-Rhone, Var, Vauclus.	Digne, Aix, Toulon, Avignon.
Dauphiné	3	Hautes Alpes, Drome, Ifere,	Gap, Valence, Grenoble.
Franche Compté	3	Doubs, Jura, Haute-Saone.	Besançon, Lons-le Saunier, Vesoul.
Alsace	2	Bas Rhin, Haut Rhin.	Colmar, Strasbourg.
Lorraine	4	Meuthe, Meuse, Moselle, Vosges.	Nancy, Bas-sur-Ornain, Metz, Epinal.

Ancient

Ancient Prov.		Departments.	Chief Towns.
Champagne	4	Ardennes, Aube, Marne, Haute-Marne.	Mezieres, Troyes, Chalons-sur Marne, Chaumont
Les deux Flandres	2	Nord, Pas-de-Calais.	Douai, Arras.
Isle de France	6	Aisne, Oise, Seine, Seine et Oise, Somme, Seine et Marne.	Laon, Beauvais, Paris, Versailles, Amiens, Melun.
Normandie	5	Calvados, Eure, Manche, Orne, Seine-Inferieure	Caen, Evreux, Coutances, Alençon, Rouen.
Bretagne	5	Cotes-du Nord, Finisterre, Isle & Vilaine, Loire-Inferieure, Morbihan.	St. Brieux, Quimper, Rennes, Nantes, Vannes.
Haut & Bas Maine	4	Indre et Loire, Mayenne, Mayenne et Loire, Sarthe.	Tours, Leval, Angers, Le Mans.
Poictou	3	Deux Sevres, Vendée, Vienne,	Niort, Fontenoy. le Peuple, Poictiers.
Orleanois	8	Eure et Loir, Loir et Cher, Loiret.	Chartres, Blois Orleans.
Berri	2	Indre, Cher	Chateauroux, Bourges.
Nivernois	1	Nievre.	Nevers.
Valromey	4	Ain, Cote-d'or, Yonne, Saone et Loire.	Bourg, Dijon, Auxerre, Macon,
Bourgogne	2	Loire, Rhone.	Montbrison, Lyons.
Bourbonnois	1	Allier.	Moulins.
Marche	3	Correge, Creuse, Haute Vienne.	Tulle, Gueret, Limoge.
Angoumois	1	Charente	Angouleme.
Aunis	1	Charente-inferieuse.	Saintes.
Piugord	1	Dordogne.	Perigueux.
Bordelois	4	Gironde Landes, Lot en Garonnes, Gers.	Bourdeaux, Mont-de-Marsan, Agen, Auch.
Quercy	1	Lot	Cahors.
Rouvergue	1	Aveyron	Rhodez.
Bearn	1	Basses Pyreneés	Pau.
Bigorre	1	Hautes Pyrenées	Tarbe.
Couserans	1	Arriege	Tarascon.
Rousillon	1	PyrenéesOriental	Perpignan.
Languedoc	7	Ardeche, Ande, Gard, Haute Goronne Herault Lozere Tarn.	Privas Carcassonne, Nimes, Toulouse, Montpelier Mede, Castres.

K

Ancient.

Ancient Prov.	Departments.	Chief Towns.
Velay	3 { Cantal, Haute-Loire, Poy-le-Dome.	{ St. Fleur, Le Puy, Claremont. }
Corse	2 Golo, Liamone,	Bastia, Ajaccio.
Savoy	3 { Mont-Blanc. Alpes Maritimes. Leman.	{ Chambray, Nice, Geneva.
Hainault, Austrian Flanders, Brabant, Liege.	9 { Dyle, Escaut, Forets, Jemapes, Lys, Meuse Inferieure, Deux Nethes, Ourthe, Sambre et Meuse	{ Brussels, Gand, Luxembourg, Mons, Bruges, Maestricht, Angers Liege, Namur.
Countries between ye Meuse and Rhine, the Rhine and Moselle	4 { Roer, Sarre, Rhin et Moselle Mont-Tonnerre,	{ Aix-la-Chapelle, Treves, Coblentz, Mayence.

102

Paris, the capital of France, is, next to London, the largest and most considerable city in Europe. It contains, at this time, immense collections of works of art, ancient and modern. The other principal towns of France are Lyons, Marseilles, Bourdeaux, and Lisle.

The principal mountains in France are the Alps, which ancien ly divided it from Italy; and the Pyrenées, which divide it from Spain.

The principal rivers are the Rhone, the Garonne, the Loire, the Seine, and the Somme. The Rhine forms the boundary between France and Germany.

The canals in France are very numerous; the chief work of this kind is the canal of Languedoc, about one hundred and eighty miles in length.

Near Toulon are the isles of Hyeres, which are the same as Homer's Isle of Calypso. On the western coast is the Isle of Oleron. The Isle of Rhe is opposite Rochelle. Bellisle has been repeatedly attacked by the English. The Isle of Ushant is the most westerly headland in France.

Italy is divided from France on the west by part of the Alps; from Germany on the north, by the same mountains called the Alps; and is every where else surrounded by the Mediterranean Sea, and the Gulph of Venice, which is a branch thereof.

It is divided into the Italian Republic; the kingdom of Etruria; the Roman states; and the kingdom of Naples.

The

The Appenines form a grand chain of mountains, which runs through almost the whole extent of Italy. Mount Vesuvius, near Naples, is a celebrated volcanic mountain. But Vesuvius, compared with Etna in Sicily, is only a small hill; the circuit of Vesuvius is thirty miles, that of Etna is one hundred and eighty. The ashes of Vesuvius are some- times thrown seven miles, but those of Etna are frequently thrown thirty.

Rome was the principal city of the Pope's dominions, and the capital of Italy. Florence is the capital of Etruria, and is now regarded as the Athens of modern Italy. Milan is the capital of the Italian States.

Sicily, the largest of the Italian islands, is separated from the south-west part of Naples by the Strait of Messina. This strait was famous for the Scylla and Charybdis of the ancients, the former being a rock, the latter a whirlpool, both very dangerous to the navigators of that period. The chief towns are Palermo, Messina, and Syracuse. The sovereign was sometimes styled King of Naples, and some- times the King of the Two Sicilies. Sardinia, another large island, is situated almost in the centre of the Medi- terranean; the principal town is Cagliari. Corsica is se- parated from the northern parts of Sardinia by the Strait of Bonifacio; its chief town is Bastia. The island of Malta lies about sixty miles south of the island of Sicily, and is celebrated for the Strength of its fortifications, and is now possessed by the English.

Candia, to the south of Greece, is famous for Mount Ida; and both Malta and Candia are renowned for withstanding sieges by the Turks, who in the former lost thirty thousand men, and in the latter one hundred and eighty thousand.

Rhodes, N.E. of Candia, is famous for its collossal statue, between the legs of which ships sailed into the harbour. In its right hand was a light-house for the direction of mariners. It was destroyed by an earthquake.

The principal rivers are the Po, the Tiber, the Var, and the Adige.

Germany was formerly divided into 9 great divisions, cal- led circles: 3 northern, Westphalia, Lower Saxony, and Upper Saxony: 3 in the middle, Lower Rhine, Upper Rhine, and Franconia: and three southern, Suabia, Bavaria and Austria. These circles were subdivided into principali- ties, duchies, electorates, bishoprics, &c. Besides these there were a number of free cities, which were sovereign

states;

states; some of them styled Imperial towns, and quartered the Imperial Eagle in their arms.

The emperor was elected by ten electors, for life, under the title of Emperor of Germany and King of the Romans. The present emperor is also, in his own right, Archduke of Austria, and king of Bohemia. The ten electors were the king or Elector of Bohemia; the Elector of Bavaria; the Elector of Saxony; the Elector of Brandenburgh (king of Prussia); the Elector of Hanover; the Elector Arch-Chancellor of the Empire, whose residence was Ratisbon; the Elector of Saltzburgh; the Elector of Baden; the Elector of Wurtemburgh, and the Elector of Hesse.

The Electors of Saxony and Hanover were regarded as the principal potentates in the north of Germany: the Elector of Bavaria, and the Elector of Wurtemburgh in the south. Prussia and Austria were considered as independent powers. Almost every prince in Germany, of which there were about 200, was arbitrary in the government of his own estate; but together they formed a great confederacy, governed by political laws. The head of those petty sovereigns was the emperor.

The chief towns are Vienna, the residence of the present emperor; Dresden, the residence of the Elector of Saxony, famous for its gallery of pictures, its various collection in the fine arts, and its porcelain manufactory; Berlin, which is the capital of the Prussian dominions; Hamburgh, situated on the Elbe, and one of the first commercial cities in Europe; Leipsic, and Frankfort, famous for their fairs; Gottingen, Jena, Leipsic, and Halle, celebrated for their universities; besides Hanover, Munich, Manheim, Wurtemberg, Heidelberg, Augsburgh, Constance, and Prague.

The principal rivers of Germany are the Danube, the Rhine, the Maine, and the Elbe.

The Austrian Dominions.

The Austrian dominions comprehended Austria, Bohemia, Hungary, part of Poland, with the Venetian states. By the partition of Poland, Austria acquired one sixth part of that country, and four millions of subjects.

The capital of this empire is Vienna, where the emperor is regarded as the successor to Augustus: in the other provinces he is looked upon as the nominal king of Hungary

and

and Bohemia. The other chief towns are Venice, Prague, Presburgh, Buda, Cracow and Trieste.

The principal Mountains are the Tyrolese, the Alps, and the Carpathian Mountains.

There were in Germany several free cities, which were small commonwealths under the protection of the Germanic body, such as Ratisbon, Frankfort, Hamburg, &c. And among the Alps were several small commonwealths, commonly known by the name of the Swiss Cantons.

Switzerland, remarkable for its mountains, is divided into thirteen cantons, Zurich, Berne, Underwalden, Zug, Schwejtz, Basil, Glaris, Soleure, Uri, Appenzel, Lucerne, Fribourg, and Schaffhausen. The three principal towns are, Basil, Berne, and Zurich.

The sources of the Rhine and the Rhone, two of the grandest rivers in Europe, are to be found in the mountains of Switzerland. The lakes of Constance and Geneva have been long celebrated for their beauty. The Alps, which divide Switzerland from Italy, the mountains of St. Gothard, in the Canton of Uri, and Mont Blanc, on the borders of Savoy, are the highest in Europe.

Denmark and Norway, two kingdoms under the same sovereign, are bounded on the north and west by the ocean, on the south by part of Germany, and the Baltic Sea, and on the east by Sweden : The capital of Denmark is called Copenhagen, and that of Norway, Christiana.

On the coast of Norway is the Maelstrom, a whirlpool of great extent, and very dangerous to ships that approach thereto.

Greenland and the Ferro Islands are subject to Denmark, and so is Iceland, celebrated for the burning Mount Hecla, a volcano one mile in height.

Sweden has Denmark on the west, the Baltic Sea on the south, Russia on the east, and the ocean on the north. It includes the greatest part of ancient Scandinavia, and is divided into Sweden Proper, Gothland, Finland, Swedish Lapland, and the Swedish Islands.

The chief towns are Stockholm, the capital, which stands on seven rocky islands, united by bridges; Upsal, Gothenburg, Tornea, and Abo.

Russia has part of Sweden and the Baltic Sea on the

west

west, Crim Tartary on the south : Great Tartary in Asia on the east, and the ocean on the north.

This vast empire comprehends in fact all the northern parts of Europe, and Asia, but only a small part of its inhabitants are in a state of civilization. By the partition of Poland Russia has acquired two thirds of that country, and six millions of inhabitants.

The principal towns are Petersburgh, the capital ; Moscow ; Archangel ; Cherson ; Astracan, and Tobolsk. The chief rivers, the Wolga, the Don, the Nieper, and Neister.

More to the eastward is Turkey in Europe, which consists of many provinces, and includes ancient Greece, Constantinople in the eastern part thereof, being the residence of the Grand Seignior, sovereign of the empire.

The northern provinces are Moldavia, Bessarabia, Wallachia, Servia, Bosnia, and Dalmatia ; those in the middle are Bulgaria, Romania, Macedonia, Albania, and Epirus ; the southern parts, called Greece, contain Thessally, Achaia, and the Morea. The famous city of Delphos was in the district of Achaia, but it is now reduced to a mean village called Castri.

The metropolis of Turkey, Constantinople, is finely situated between the sea of Marmora and the Black Sea : Adrianople is the second city in the Turkish empire.

The principal rivers are the Danube, the Saave, and the Neister. The chief mountains are Pindus and Olympus, which separate Thessaly from Epirus ; Parnassus in Livadia, Athos, and Hæmus. The islands are very numerous, the chief are Rhodes, and Candia, in the Mediterranean ; there are also Zante, Cephalonia, Corfu, and others lying west of Turkey, forming the republic of the Seven Islands.

The United Kingdom of Great Britain and Ireland.

This being our native country we shall be a little more particular in the description of it.

The island of Great Britain is divided into England, Wales, and Scotland. It is about six hundred miles in length, and half as broad, and is known to contain above twelve millions of inhabitants.

England

England contains forty Counties or Shires, situated in the following order, taken from north to south :

Counties	Chief Towns.	Counties.	Chief Towns.
Northumberland	Newcastle	Buckinghamshire	Aylesbury
Durham	Durham	Northamptonshire	Northampton
Cumberland	Carlisle	Bedfordshire	Bedford
Westmorland	Appleby	Huntingdonshire	Huntingdon
Yorkshire	York	Cambridgeshire	Cambridge
Lancashire	Lancaster	Norfolk	Norwich
Cheshire	Chester	Suffolk	Bury
Derbyshire	Derby	Essex	Chelmsford
Shropshire	Shrewsbury	Hertfordshire	Hertford
Nottinghamshire	Nottingham	Middlesex	London
Lincolnshire	Lincoln	Kent	Canterbury
Rutland	Oakham	Surrey	Guildford
Leicestershire	Leicester	Sussex	Chichester
Staffordshire	Stafford	Berkshire	Reading
Warwickshire	Warwick	Hampshire	Winchester
Worcestershire	Worcester	Wiltshire	Salisbury
Herefordshire	Hereford	Dorsetshire	Dorset
Monmouthshire	Monmouth	Somersetshire	Wells
Gloucestershire	Gloucester	Devonshire	Exeter
Oxfordshire	Oxford	Cornwall	Launceston.

We shall give a brief account of some of the principal cities and towns in England, without any particular regard to the order of arrangement.

London, the metropolis of England, is perhaps the most populous, and richest, city on the face of the earth : including Westminster and Southwark, it may perhaps be deemed three cities.

London, taken in this extent, presents almost every variety which diversifies human existence. Towards the east it is a sea-port, replete with mariners, and with trades connected with that profession. In the centre it is the seat of numerous manufactures, and prodigious commerce, while the western, or fashionable, extremity, presents royal and noble splendour, amidst scenes of luxury and dissipation. This city is supplied with water by the Thames, the water of which is thrown into the houses by machinery erected at London Bridge, and by the New River, which flows from Ware in Hertfordshire. The higher parts of London, towards Mary-le-bone, have their water from a number of large ponds situated on Hampstead Heath.

K 4   York

York is the next city to the capital in dignity, though not in extent, or in opulence : it is regarded as the metropolis of the north of England. The cathedral of this city is greatly celebrated ; the western front being peculiarly rich, the chief spire very lofty, and windows of the finest painted glass.

Liverpool approaches, now, the nearest to London in wealth and commerce. It is only about a century since this immense town was a mere village. In 1699 it was constituted a parish. In 1710 a dock was constructed, and the chief merchants came originally from Ireland. The infamous traffic in slaves was a distinguishing feature of Liverpool, and it was there that from one hundred to one hundred and fifty ships were employed in that trade. In a single year during the American war Liverpool fitted out 170 privateers.

Bristol is still a large and flourishing city, though much of its commerce with the West Indies and America have passed to Liverpool. Bristol is famous for its Hot Wells. In the adjacent rocks are found beautiful crystals, called Bristol Stones. The trade of Bristol is chiefly with Ireland. the West Indies, or North America, Hamburgh, and the Baltic. By the navigation of the two rivers Severn and the Wye, Bristol engrosses most of the trade of Wales. In 1787 Bristol employed one thousand six hundred coasting vessels, and upwards of four hundred ships engaged in foreign commerce.

Manchester is celebrated for its cotton Manufactures, which are known and prized in every part of Europe.

Birmingham was originally a village, but is now a town of immense manufactures in iron ware. The extension of Birmingham originated, in a great degree, from Mr. John Taylor, who introduced the manufacture of gilt buttons, and japanned and enamelled works. The great fabric of the arts, called Soho, belonging to Messrs. Boulton and Watts, is situated about two miles from Birmingham.

Sheffield is famous for its cutlery and plated goods.

Leeds, Bradford, Halifax, and Wakefield, are the chief centres of the manufactories of woollen cloth, &c. Leeds is the principal mart for broad cloths. The cloth-hall appropriated to the sale is a vast edifice, and the whole business

business is transacted within the space of an hour on the market days.

Hull is celebrated for its large Dock : and its trade with America and the south of Europe is very important. The coasting traffic is extensive in coals, corn, wool, and various manufactures.

Newcastle, so named from a fortress erected by Edward the First, is a large and very populous town, in the centre of the grand coal-mines in the counties of Durham and Northumberland, which have for many centuries supplied London, and most of the east and south of England with that species of fuel.

In the west of England, Exeter, the capital of Devonshire, is an ancient and respectable city, the principal commerce of which is in coarse woollen goods, manufactured in Somersetshire, Devonshire, and Cornwall. They are exported to Italy and other parts of the continent to a very great amount, and the East India Company purchase yearly a very large quantity. Some ships from Exeter are engaged in the cod and whale fishery.

Salisbury is famous for its flannels and cutlery, particularly for the manufacture of scissors. Wilton is celebrated for its carpets.

Winchester, the chief city of Hampshire, was for centuries the metropolis of England : it still retains many vestiges of ancient fame and splendor. Besides a cathedral, Winchester has a college founded by William of Wickham, which has sent forth many illustrious characters.

Portsmouth, in the same county, is the grand naval arsenal of England. The harbour is noble and capacious, narrow at the entrance, but spreading into an inland bay, five miles in length, and from two to four miles in breadth.

Canterbury, the chief town in Kent, and the metropolis of the English church, is chiefly remarkable for ecclesiastical antiquities.

Norwich, the capital of Norfolk, from its size and consequence, is justly styled a city. It is a place of great trade, particularly in camblets, crapes, stuffs, and other woollen manufactures. The wool is chiefly from the counties of Lincoln, Leicester, and Northampton, and the principal exports are to Holland, Germany, and the Mediterranean.

K 5　　　　　　　　Cambridge

Cambridge is remarkable for a university, containing 12 colleges and 4 halls, all well endowed ; and are as follow :

COLLEGES. When Founded.	By whom Founded.
1284 *Peter-house,*	Hugh de Bathan, Bp. of Ely.
1346 *Corpus Christi,* or *Bennet.* }	Henry of Monmouth, Duke of Lancaster.
1348 *Gonvil* and *Caius*	So called from its several Founders.
1441 *King's* - - - -	Henry VI.
1448 *Queen's* - · - -	Margaret his Queen.
1497 *Jesus* - - - -	John Alcocke, LL. D. Bishop of Ely.
1506 *Christ's* - - - -	Margaret, Countess of Richmond.
1546 *St. John's* - · -	Ditto.
1542 *Magdalen* - - -	Edward Strafford, Duke of Buckingham.
1546 *Trinity* - - - -	King Henry VIII.
1584 *Emanuel* - - -	Sir Walter Mildmay. [Sussex.
1598 *Sidney Sussex* - -	Frances Sidney, Countess of
1809 *Downing* - - -	Sir George Downing.

HALLS.

1343 *Clare* - - - -	Richard Badew.
1347 *Pembroke* - - -	Mary, Countess of Pembroke.
1353 *Trinity* - - - -	W. Bateman, Bp. of Norwich.
1549 *Catherine* - - '-	Rt. Wood, the Chancellor.

Oxford is famous for having the finest University in the world, which consists of 20 colleges endowed, and five halls not endowed, *viz.*

872 *University* - - -	The Saxon King Alfred.
1262 *Baliol* - - - -	John Baliol, King of Scotland.
1274 *Merton* - - - -	Walter de Merton, Bishop of Rochester.
1316 *Exeter* - - - -	Walter Stapleton, Bishop of Exeter.
1325 *Oriel* - - - -	King Edward II.
1340 *Queen's* - - - -	Robert Egglesford, B. D.
1375 *New* - - - - -	William of Wickham, Bishop of Winchester.
1427 *Lincoln* - - - -	R. Fleming, and T. Rotherham, Bishop of Lincoln.
1437 *All Souls* - - -	H. Chicheley, Abp. of Cant.
	1459

1439 *Magdalen* - - - Wm. of Wainfleet, Bishop of Winchester.
1511 *Brazen Nose* - - Wm. Smith, Bp. of Lincoln, and Sir R. Sutton, Knt,
1516 *Corpus Christi* - - R. Fox, Bp. of Winchester.
1549 *Christ Church* - - King Henry VIII,.
1555 *Trinity* - - - - Sir Thomas Pope.
1557 *St. John's* - - - Sir T. White, Lord Mayor of London.
1571 *Jesus* - - - - - Queen Elizabeth.
1609 *Wadham* - - - Nicholas Wadham, Esq.
1620 *Pembroke* - - - T. Tesdale, Esq. and Rich. Whitwick, B. D.
1700 *Worcester* - - - Sir Thomas Cooke.
1740 *Hartford* - - - Dr. Newton.

St. Edmund's ⎫	HALLS	⎧ Queen's ⎫	
St. Alban's		Merton	
St. Mary's	belonging to ⎨	Oriel	⎬ Colleges.
New Inn		New	
Magdalen ⎭		⎩ Magdalen ⎭	

The PRINCIPALITY of WALES.

WALES was originally independent of England, but in the reign of King Henry the Seventh it was incorporated with it. This country is very mountainous and barren, except in the vallies and intervals, where it yields plenty of grass and corn. The situation is westward, bordering on the Irish Sea. The air bleak and sharp, but wholesome : the cattle are numerous, but very small ; and on the hills are abundance of goats. This country is divided into North and South.

Wales is divided into Twelve Counties, as follow :

Counties.	Chief Towns.	Counties.	Chief Towns.
Flintshire	Flint	Radnorshire	Radnor
Denbighshire	Denbigh	Brecknockshire	Brecknock
Montgomeryshire	Montgomery	Glamorganshire	Cardiff
Anglesey	Beaumaris	Pembrokeshire	Pembroke
Caernarvonshire	Caernarvon	Cardiganshire	Cardigan
Merionethshire	Harlech	Carmarthenshire	Carmarthen.

North Wales contains Anglesey, Carnarvonshire, Denbighshire, Flintshire, Merionethshire, and Montgomeryshire.

Anglesey is an island on the north-west part of the country, about 80 miles in compass. The common passage to Ireland is from Holyhead in this island to Dublin.

South

South Wales contains Brecknockshire, Cardiganshire, Carmarthenshire, Glamorganshire, Pembrokeshire, and Radnorshire.

Pembrokeshire is a very pleasant and plentiful county, for the most part surrounded by the sea. It is famous for a Harbour called *Milford Haven*, which is justly esteemed to be in all respects one of the best in the world.

SCOTLAND.

SCOTLAND is the northern division of *Great Britain*, and is situated to the North of *England*; the capital city is called Edinburgh; it is divided into thirty-three counties, as follow :

Shires.	Chief Towns.	Shires.	Chief Towns.
Edinburgh	Edinburgh	Bute and Caithness	Rothsay
Haddington	Dunbar	Renfrew	Renfrew
Merse	Dunse	Stirling	Stirling
Roxburgh	Jedburgh	Linlithgow	Linlithgow
Selkirk	Selkirk	Argyle	Inverary
Peebles	Peebles	Perth	Perth
Lanerk	Glasgow	Kincardin	Bervie
Dumfries	Dumfries	Aberdeen	Aberdeen
Wigtown	Wigtown	Inverness	Inverness
Kircudbright	Kircudbright	Nairne and Cromartie	Nairne and Cromartie
Air	Air	Fife	St. Andrews
Dumbarton	Dumbarton	Kinross	Kinross
Forfar	Montrose	Ross	Tain
Bamff	Bamff	Elgin	Elgin
Sutherland	Strathy Darnoo	Orkney	Kirkwall.
Clacmannan	Clacmannan		

Berwick upon Tweed lies between England and Scotland, and is distinguished from both, by having its peculiar privileges, and a small territory within its jurisdiction.

The most considerable towns in Scotland next to Edinburgh, are Glasgow and Aberdeen, all of which are famous for their universities; Glasgow is no less so for its extensive commerce.

The Islands belonging to Scotland are the Shetland, the Orkney, and the Hebrides, or Western Islands.

The Hebrides, or Western Isles, are said to be above 300 in number, the most considerable of which are Arran, Sky, and Mull; and the Isles of Orkney, and Shetland, to the northward of each of which, there are many in number.

The principal rivers are the Forth, the Tay, the Dee, and the Don : and the most considerable Lakes, Loch Tay and Loch Lomond, which contains several Islands; and Loch Ness, in Invernesshire.

IRELAND,

IS a large Island to the west of *England* and *Scotland*, the chief city of which is *Dublin;* it is divided into four provinces, viz. *Ulster,* northward; *Leinster,* eastward; *Munster,* southward; and *Connought,* westward. These are again subdivided into the following Counties.

Counties.	Chief Towns.		Counties.	Chief Towns.
Leinster. Dublin	Dublin	**Ulster.**	Antrim	Carrickfergus
Louth	Drogheda		Londonderry	Derry
Wicklow	Wicklow		Tyrone	Omagh
Wexford	Wexford		Fermanagh	Inniskilling
Longford	Longford		Donegal	Lifford
East Meath	Trim	**Connaught.**	Leitrim	Roscommon
West Meath	Mullingar		Roscommon	Ballingrobe
King's County	Phillipstown		Mayo	Carric on Shan.
Queen's County	Maryborough		Sligo	Sligo
Kilkenny	Kilkenny		Galway	Galway
Kildare	Nass & Athy	**Munster.**	Clare	Ennis
Carlow	Carlow		Cork	Cork
Ulster. Down	Downpatrick		Kerry	Tralee
Armagh	Armagh		Limerick	Limerick
Monaghan	Monaghan		Tipperary	Clonmel
Cavan	Cavan		Waterford	Waterford.

The chief towns next to Dublin, the capital, are Cork, Londonderry, and Belfast. Cork is a flourishing, commercial City, and remarkable for its fine harbour. The principal Rivers are the Shannon, the Blackwater, the Boyne, and the Liffy.

In St. Georges's channel, almost equally distant from England, Scotland, and Ireland, is situated the Isle of Man, the Royalty of which, under the Kings of Great Britain, was formerly in the family of the Stanleys, Earls of Derby; but the male issue of that family being extinct, it was enjoyed by the Duke of Athol, descended from the Derby Family by a female branch, till the Session of Parliament 1765, when it was annexed to the crown.

The Britannic Isles above described are separated from France, on the South by the English channel; and from Holland, Germany, Denmark and Norway, by the German Ocean on the east; the northern and western sides being washed by oceans of the same name.

HOLLAND, or, as it is now called, the *Batavian Republic,* has Germany on the East and North, the German ocean to the west, and France to the south. It consists of the seven following provinces.

Pro-

Provinces.	Chief Towns.	Provinces.	Chief Towns.
Groniningen	Groningen	Utrecht	Utrecht
Friesland	Lewarden	Guelderland	Zutphen
Over-yssel	Deventer	Zealand	Middleburgh.
Holland	Amsterdam		

The chief Towns, with regard to commercial purposes, are Amsterdam, Leyden, Rotterdam, and Haarlem.

The Hague is the largest, and was the richest village in the world : it is thirty miles from Amsterdam, and was, before the revolution, the seat of government, and the residence of the principal people.

Amsterdam, the capital, is curiously built upon wooden piles. Leyden is famous for its university. The streets have canals running through them, the borders of which are planted with rows of trees. The principal rivers are the Rhine, the Maese, and the Scheldt. The canals are very numerous, and serve for the same purpose as roads in other countries.

ASIA.

ASIA is separated from Europe towards the north-west; towards the south-west by the eastern part of the Mediterranean Sea, and by the Isthmus of Suez and the Red Sea, which divide it from Africa. It is bounded on the south by the Indian Ocean, on the east by the Pacific, and on the north by the Northern or Frozen Ocean ; its dimensions may be conceived from what follows :

It seems most regular to divide this large country according to its present possessors, the Grand Seignior, or Emperor of the Turks, the King of Persia, the Great Mogul, and the other potentates of India; the Emperor of China, and the potentates of Tartary.

The Turkish possessions in Asia are Anatolia, Syria, Arabia, Armenia, or Turcomania, Georgia, and Mesopotamia, or Diarbeck, of which in their order.

Anatolia, formerly called Asia Minor, is encompassed on the north, west, and south sides, by the Euxine, the Marmorian, the Archipelago, and the Mediterranean Seas ; it is separated from Syria on the south-east by the mountains called Taurus, and from Turcomania on the east by the river Euphrates.

Syria, called by the Turks Suristan, is subdivided into Syria proper, Phœnicia, and Palestine, or Judea, whose chief cities are Aleppo, Damascus, and Jerusalem.

Arabia

Arabia (a country which preserves its ancient name, as do the inhabitants their roaming disposition) is bounded on the west by the Red Sea and the Isthmus of Suez, on the north by Palestine, Syria, and Diarbeck; on the east by the Persian Gulph, and on the south-west by the Arabian Sea, and part of the Indian Ocean.

It is divided into three parts, called the Desert, the Stony, and the Happy; the two first lie to the northward, the other to the south.

There are very few towns in the desert or stony parts of this country; the Arabs living in tents, and removing with their families from place to place, as profit or convenience suggest. But in Arabia the Happy, (one of the finest countries in the world) there are several of note, such as Medina, where the sepulchre of Mahomet, the founder of the Turkish religion, is; Mecca, his birth-place, to which every Turk or Mussulman is obliged by his religion to come in pilgrimage once in his life-time, or to send another in his stead; Aden, a place of traffic; and Mocha, famous for its coffee.

Armenia, or Turcomania, is bounded on the West by Anatolia, on the South by Diarbeck, on the East and North by Georgia and the Euxine Sea.

Georgia, formerly called Iberia, including Mingreli and Gurgistan, is bounded on the North by part of Russia, on the West by the Euxine sea, on the South by Turcomania, and part of Persia, and on the East by part of Persia; the cities of the greatest note are Fasso and Tefflis.

Mesopotamia, or Diarbeck, is bounded on the north by Turcomania, on the west by Syria, on the south by Arabia the Desert, and on the east by Persia; its principal cities are Diarbeker and Bagdat.

Besides these large possessions on the Continent of Asia, the Turks hold several island, in the Archipelago; with Rhodes and Cyprus in the Mediterranean Sea, the last of which is very considerable.

The next division of Asia, proceeding eastwardly, is Persia, which has the Turkish dominions on the west, the Persian Gulph and part of the Indian ocean on the south; the Empire of the Great Mogul on the east, and on the north part of Tatary, the Caspian sea, and part of the Russian Empire. This is a very large country, but at present it is torn to pieces by different competitors for the sovereign power; the capital city is Ispahan; the most considerable of the

the others are Derbent on the Caspian sea, and Gombroon and Bassora on the Persian Gulph.

Proceeding still eastward, the next empire is that of the Great Mogul, which has Persia on the west, the two Indian Peninsulas and the Bay of Bengal on the south, China on the east, and part of Tartary on the north.

This is another large tract, with the inland parts of which the Europeans are not much acquainted.

The principal cities are Agra, Lahor, Delhi, Cabul, and Cassimir; but whether Agra or Lahor is the capital, is difficult to determine, the Mogul hath a magnificent palace at each of these cities.

The maritime parts of the continent of India are divided by the Bay of Bengal, a branch of the Indian ocean, into two Peninsulas anciently called India within, or on this side the Ganges and India, and without, or beyond the Ganges: besides which two Peninsulas there are several large Islands belonging to India, of which in their Order.

The Peninsula on this side the Ganges, contains several distinct Territories or Kingdoms, most of which either are or were subject, or at least tributary, to the Mogul; the western side thereof is called the Coast of Malabar, the eastern the Coast of Coramandel.

The Coast of Malabar contains several European settlements, such as Bombay, an island belonging to the English East-India company, and Goa, to the Portuguese, at each of which they have the sovereignty; and the English trade at least, if they have not forts, at Guzurat, Surat, Calicut, and Cochin.

The Island of Ceylon, by some called Zeloan, is situated a little to the east of Cape Comorin, the most souther point of the Peninsula.

The Coast of Coromandel, which is washed by the Bay of Bengal, tends towards the north and north-east from Cape Comorin, and extends to the mouth of the Ganges; the principal settlements of the English on this coast are, Madras or Fort St. George, and Fort St. David, near which the French had a settlement called Pondicherry; which neighbouring settlements were for several years at war with each other, with various success, the natives, headed by their Princes, called Nabobs, having taken part therein, some on one side, and some on the other; but the English were at last victorious, and have lately had large provinces yielded to them by the Princes of the country.

The

The Peninsula on the other side of the Ganges, consists of the large Kingdoms of Bengal, having a capital of the same name; Pegu, whose chief cities are Pegu and Arracan; Siam, having a capital of the same name; Malacca, situated to the south, is almost encompassed by the sea, and the city, so called, is situate near the southern extremity; Cochin-China, whose chief city is Cambodia, and Tonquin, whose capital is of the same same.

South-west of Malacca is the Island of Sumatra.

South-east of this lies the Island of Java, separated by the Straits of Sunda; the western point of which is called Java Head by English mariners, it being often the first land made by them after they have doubled the Cape of Good Hope; the principal cities are Bantam and Batavia, the latter of which till lately belonged to the Dutch East India Company, who were sovereigns over the greatest part of this large and fruitful Island. It now belongs to England.

Eastward from Malacca and Sumatra is the Island of Borneo, almost round, and near 600 miles in diameter.

The Island of Celebes is to the east of Borneo, but much less than it. Proceeding eastward are the Molucca, or Spice Islands; the Dutch having made themselves masters of these, thereby engrossing the spice trade to themselves.

The Philippine Isles are very numerous, some authors have reckoned 10,000 of them; the most considerabe is Luconia, whose capital is Manilla.

To the north and north-west of these is situated the potent Empire of China, reckoned by some to be as big as all Europe; it hath the Pacific ocean on the east and south-east; Cochin-China and Tonquin on the south-west; the Mogul's Empire on the west, and on the north-west and north a part of Tartary.

There are a great number of cities in this Empire, of which Pekin, situated in the northern part of the country, is the capital; the European trade to this country is chiefly carried on at Canton, a great seaport in one of the southern provinces.

The most considerable Chinese Islands are those which compose the Empire of Japan; which consists of several large Islands, the largest of these is Niphon; and the towns are Jeddo, Miaco and Nagasaki.

Thus we have taken a cursory survey of all the southern parts of Asia; the northern hath one general name, viz. Tartary, which has Persia, India, and China, on the south;

the Pacific ocean on the east, the northern or frozen ocean
on the north, and Russia on the west; this large tract is
subject to divers Potentates, of whom little is known.

AFRICA.

AFRICA is a large Peninsula, which is joined to the Continent of Asia by the Isthmus of Suez, a narrow desert between the Mediterranean and the Red Seas.   The inland
parts of this Continent are not much known to the Europeans ; so that only the sea coasts will be mentioned here,
beginning at the Isthmus of Suez, and coasting first along
the Mediterranean Sea.

Egypt is under the dominion of the Turks ; its present capital is called Cairo ; the piratical States of Tripoly, Tunis,
and Algiers, have capitals of the same name, and the capital of the Empire of Morocco is the city of Fez.

Along the coasts of the Atlantic Ocean there are no extensive dominions, the inhabitants being mostly subject to
petty Princes of their own, who being almost continually at
war with one another, sell their prisoners for slaves; the
European nations have been induced, for the protection of
their trade therein, and other commodities, to erect several
small forts in different places, to enumerate which would be
tedious : the Madeiras, the Canaries, and the Cape Verd
Islands are the most considerable on this coast ; the only
one possessed by the English is a very small one, called St.
Helena, frequented by the East-India ships.

At the southern extremity of the Continent is situated the
Cape of Good Hope, where there is a tolerable town for the
convenience of shipping, built by the Dutch East-India
Company ; from hence along the eastern coast, both on the
ocean and in the Red Sea, very little remarkable offers itself to notice.   At some distance, however, from the part
of this coast is situated one of the largest islands in the
world, called Madagascar, which has been at different
times the Asylum of European Pirates.

AMERICA.

AMERICA, by some called the New World, because discovered about 318 years ago, being, before that time unknown to the inhabitants of Europe, Asia, and Africa, is divided into two remarkable divisions, called North and South
America, which are joined together by the Isthmus of Da-
rien or Panama.

North

North America includes the United States, Spanish and British America, and the independent Indian nations.

The inland seas of North America are the Gulphs of Mexico, California, and St. Lawrence, with Hudson's Bay, and Davis's Straits. The Gulph of St. Lawrence is closed by the Island of Newfoundland, and the great Sand Bank, about four hundred miles in length, celebrated for the Cod-fishery.

The Lakes Superior, Michigan, Huron, Winnipeg, and Slave Lake, are the greatest in the world, and may with propriety be denominated Seas. The rivers are also grand features of North America. Of these, the principal are the Missouri or Mississipi, the Ohio, and the St. Lawrence : and the most celebrated mountains are the Apalachian, passing through the territory of the United States. Among these the Ohio has its rise.

The UNITED STATES are divided into northern, middle and southern.

The northern States are Vermont, New Hampshire, Massachusetts, Connecticut, and Rhode Island. The mid-dle States are New York, New Jersey, Pennsylvania, De-laware, and the Territory on the northward of the Ohio. The southern States are Maryland, Virginia, Kentucky, North Carolina, Georgia, and the country south of Ken-tucky. The chief cities and towns are Washington the capital, Philidelphia, New York, Boston, Baltimore, and Charlestown.

The Spanish dominions were Loiusiana, (which have been lately ceded to the United States for a certain sum of mo-ney.) East and West Florida, New Mexico, and Old Mex-ico, or New Spain. Mexico is the capital of all Spanish America. The chief river in Spanish America is Rio Bravo, and the principal Lake is Nicaragua.

The British dominions are amazingly extensive, and in-clude Upper and Lower Canada, Nova Scotia, New Brunss-wick, the Island of Cape Bieton, Newfoundland, the Ber-mudas, or Summer Islands.

The Native Tribes and Independent Countries. These are Greenland, Labrador, the Regions around Hudson's Bay, those Nations lately discovered by Sir A. Mackenzie, and those on the western coast.

Of the West Indias. The most important of these Islands are Cuba, and Porto-Rico, Spanish ; St. Domingo, and Jamaica, English. North of St. Domingo and Cuba are the

the Bahama's, the principal of which is Providence Island. The Caribbee Islands extend from Tobago in the south, to the Virgin Islands in the north. Those belonging to England are Barbadoes, Antigua, St. Christopher's, St. Vincent, Dominica, Grenada, Trinidad, Montserrat, Nevis, and the Virgin Isles, Guadaloupe, St. Lucie, and Tobago. The Danes formerly possessed St. Croix, and St. Thomas. St. Bartholomew belongs to the Swedes, and Eustatia to the English.

From these Islands are procured sugar, rum, cotton, indigo, spices, cocoa, and coffee : in time of war the smaller and inferior islands are often changing their masters.

South America comprehends Terra Firma, Guiana, Amazonia, Peru, Brazil, Paraguay, Chili, and Patagonia.

Amazonia and Patagonia are not under the yoke of any European power; they are divided into several kingdoms, each of which has its chief. The inhabitants have no temples or priests, but worship images of their departed heroes.

South America has no inland sea, but the river Amazons, and that of La Plata are celebrated as the largest in the world. They both have their rise among the Andes. The mountains of South America are the loftiest on the whole face of the globe, and are intermixed with Volcanos of the most sublime and terrific description. The Andes follow the windings of the coast, and extend four thousand six hundred miles. The highest are near the Equator, and are covered with perpetual snow. The Spanish dominions in South America are Buenos Ayres, Peru, Chili, and New Grenada. Peru and Chili are famous for their gold and silver mines. In Chili it never rains, the sky is seldom cloudy, but the night dews supply the want of rain.

The Portuguese territory of Brazil is perhaps equal in extent to the Spanish, compensating by its breadth for its deficiency in length. Guiana belongs partly to the French and partly to the Dutch. Cayenne consists of an extensive territory on the Continent, and of an island of that name.

The southern extremity of South America is Patagonia, a desolate country, inhabited by a savage race, some of whom are of collossal stature. The islands contiguous to South America are Trinidad, the Falkland Islands, Terra del Fuego, Chiloe, and Juan Fernandez. The Gallipago Islands are near the equator, and the Pearl Islands lie in the Bay of Panama.

ASTRONOMY.

ASTRONOMY.

ASTRONOMY is a Science which treats of the motions and distances of the heavenly bodies, and of the appearances arising from them.

There have been a great variety of opinions, among philosophers, concerning the disposition of the great bodies of the universe, or the position of the bodies which appear in the Heavens : but the notion now embraced by the most judicious astronomers is, that the Universe is composed of a vast number of Systems or Worlds ; that in every system there are certain bodies moving in free space, and revolving at different distances around a Sun, placed in or near the centre of the system, and that these Suns, or the other bodies, are the Stars which are seen in the Heavens.

That sytem to which our Earth belongs, is by astronomers called the *Solar System ;* and the opinion, which supposes the Sun to be fixed, in or near the centre, with several bodies revolving round him, at different distances, is confirmed by all the observations hitherto made.

This opinion is called the *Copernican System :* from Nicholas Copernicus, a Polish Philosopher, who, about the year 1473, revived this notion from the oblivion it had been buried in for many ages.

The Sun is therefore is placed in the midst of an immense Space, wherein ten opaque spherical bodies revolve about him as their centre. Seven of these wandering globes are called the planets, who, at different distances, and in different periods, perform their revolutions, from west to east, in the following order.

1. ☿ *Mercury* * is nearest to the Sun of all the planets, and performs its course in about three months or 87 d. 23h. II. ♀ *Venus,* in about seven months and a half, or 224d. 17h. III. ● The *Earth,* in a year, 365d. 6h. IV. ♂ *Mars,* in about two years, or 686d. 23h. V. ♃ *Jupiter,* in twelve years, or 4232d. 12h. VI. ♄ *Saturn,* spends almost thirty years, that is 10759d. 8h. in one Revolution round the Sun. And the ♅ *Herschel* Planet, whose year is equal to almost eighty-two of ours. The distances of the planets from the Sun are nearly in the following proportion,

* *The Characters placed before the Names of the Planets are, for brevity's sake, commonly made use of by Astronomers instead of the words at lengh, as ♀ for Venus.*

viz.

viz. supposing the distance of the Earth from the Sun to be divided into 100 equal Parts ; that of *Mercury* will be about 37 of those Parts : of *Venus* 66 ; of *Mars* 155 ; of *Jupiter* 493 ; of *Saturn* 903 ; and that of the *Herschel* 1813.

The Orbits* of the planets are not all in the same plane, but variously inclined to one another : so that, supposing the orbit of the earth to be the standard, the others will have one half above, and the other half below it ; intersecting one another in a line passing through the Sun.

Besides these seven large planets, three smaller bodies have been discovered revolving about the Sun between the Orbits of *Mars* and *Jupiter.*

The plane of the Earth's Orbit is called the Ecliptic ; and this the Astronomers make the standard, to which the planes of the other orbits are judged to incline.

The right line passing through the Sun, and the common intersection of the plane of the Orbit of any planet with the eliptic, is called the Line of the Nodes of that planet, and the points themselves, wherein the orbits cut the ecliptic, are called the nodes. The orbits of the planets are not circles, but ellipsis or ovals.

What an Ellipsis is may be easily understood from the following description : imagine two small pegs or pins fixed upright on any plane, as a table, and suppose them tied with the ends of a thread, somewhat longer than their distance from one another ; now if a pin be placed in the double of the thread and turned quite round (always stretching the thread with the same force) the curve described by the motion will be an Ellipsis. The two points where the pegs stood, (about which the thread was turned) are called the foci of that ellipsis ; and if without changing the length of the thread, we alter the position of the pegs, we shall then have an ellipsis of a different kind from the former ; and the nearer the Foci are together, the nearer will the curve described be to the circle, until at last the two Foci coincide, and then the pin in the doubling of the thread will describe a perfect circle.

The orbits of all the planets have the Sun in one of their Foci, and half the distance between the two Foci is called the eccentricity of the orbits. This eccentricity is

* By the orbit of a Planet is understood the Track or Ring, described by its circuit round the Sun, but by the plane of the Orbit is meant a flat surface, extended every way through the Orbit infinitely.

different

different in all the planets, but in the most of them it is in little schemes or instruments made to represent the planetary orbit, and need not here be noticed.

The ten planets above mentioned are called primaries, or primary planets, but beside these there are 18 other lesser planets, which are called Secondaries, Moons, or Satellites. These moons always accompany their respective primaries, and perform their revolutions round them, whilst both together are also carried round the Sun.

Of the Primary Planets there are but four, as far as observation can assure us, that have these attendants, *viz.* the *Earth, Jupiter, Saturn,* and the *Herschel.*

The *Earth* is attended by the *Moon,* who performs her revolution in about $29\frac{1}{2}$ Days, at the distance of about 30 diameters of the *Earth* from it ; and once a year is carried round the Sun along with the *Earth.*

Jupiter has four Moons or Satellites ; the first or innermost performs its Revolution in about one day and $18\frac{1}{2}$ hours, at the distance of $5\frac{1}{2}$ Semidiameters of *Jupiter* from his centre ; the second revolves about *Jupiter* in 3 days and 18 hours, at the distance of 9 of his Semi-Diameters ; the third in 7 days and 3 hours, at the distance of $14\frac{1}{2}$ Semi-Diameters ; the fourth and outermost performs its course in the space of 16 days 18 hours, and its distance from *Jupiter's* centre is 25 of his Semi-Diameters.

Saturn has no less than seven Satellites ; the first or innermost revolves about him in 1 day, and 21 hours, at the distance of $4\frac{1}{8}$ diameters of *Saturn* from his centre ; the second completes his period in $2\frac{3}{4}$ days, at the distance of $5\frac{3}{4}$ diameters ; the third, in about $4\frac{1}{2}$ days, at the distance of 8 diameters ; the fourth performs his course in about 16 days, at the distance of 8 diameters ; the fifth takes $79\frac{1}{2}$ days to finish his course, and is 54 diameters of *Saturn* distant from his centre. The sixth performs its revolution in 1 Day ; and the seventh in little more than 22 hours; these two are nearest to the planet, but being discovered last are called the sixth and seventh instead of the first and second. The Satellites, as well as the primaries, perform their Revolutions from West to East ; the planes of the Orbits of the Satellites of the same Plane are variously inclined to one another, and consequently are inclined to the Planes of the Orbits or their primary.

Besides these attendants, *Saturn* is encompassed with a thin ring that does no where touch his body ; the Diameter

ter

ter of this ring is to the Diameter of *Saturn*, as 6 to 4 ; and the void space between the ring and the body of *Saturn* is equal to the breadth of the ring itself; so that in some situations the Heavens may be seen between the ring and his body.

This surprising phenomenon of *Saturn's* Ring is a Modern discovery ; neither were the Satellites of *Jupiter* and *Saturn* known to the Ancients ; the former were first discovered by the famous Italian Philosopher Gallico, by a Telescope, which he first invented ; and the celebrated Cassini, the French King's Astronomer, was the first that saw the five Satellites of Saturn ; which by reason of their great distances from the Sun, and the smallness of their own bodies, cannot be seen by us, but by the help of very good glasses.

The six Satellites of *Herschel* revolve about the Planet in the following times : The first in 5 d. 21 h. the second in 10 d. 17 h. the third in 11 Days, the fourth in 18 d. 11 h. the fifth in 38 Days ; and the sixth in 107 d. 18 h.

The motion of the primary planets round the Sun, (as also of the Satellites round their respective primaries) is called their annual motion ; because they have a year, or the alteration of the seasons, to complete in one of those revolutions. Besides their annual motion, four of the planets, *Venus*, the *Earth*, *Mars*, *Jupiter*, and *Saturn*, are known to revolve about their own Axis, from West to East ; and this is called their diurnal motion. For, by this rotation each point of their surface is carried successively towards, and from the Sun, who always illuminates the hemisphere which is next to him, the other remainining obscure : And, while any place is in the hemisphere illuminated by the Sun, it is day ; but when it is carried to the obscure hemisphere, it becomes night ; and so continues until, by this rotation, the said place is again enlightened by the Sun.

The *Earth* performs its revolutions round its axis in 23 hours 59 minutes ; *Venus* in 28 hours ; *Mars* in about 24 hours and 58 minutes ; and *Jupiter* moves round his own axis in 9 hours and 56 minutes.

The Sun is also found to turn round his axis from West to East in 25 days ; and the Moon which is nearest to us of all the planets, revolves about her axis in a month, or in the space of time that she turns round the earth ; so that the Lunarians have but one day throughout their year.

The

The planets are all opaque bodies, having no light but what they borrow from the Sun; for that side of them which is next towards the Sun has always been observed to be illuminated in whatever position they be; but the opposite side, which the solar rays do not reach, remains dark and obscure; whence it is evident that they have no light but what proceeds from the Sun, for if they had, all parts of them would be lucid, without any darkness or shadow. The planets are likewise proved to be globular, because let what part soever of them be turned towards the Sun, its boundary, or the line separating that part from the opposite, always appears to be circular; which could not happen if they were not globular.

The *Earth* is placed betwixt the Orbs of *Mars*, and *Venus*. *Mercury*, *Venus*, *Mars*, *Jupiter*, *Saturn*, and the *Herschel*, all move round the Sun; both which may be proved from observations, as follow:

1. Whenever *Venus* is in conjunction with the Sun, that is, when she is in the same direction from the *Earth*, or towards the same part of the heavens the Sun is in, she either appears with a bright and round face, like a full Moon, or else disappears; or, if she is visible, she appears horned like a new Moon; which Phenomenon could never happen, if *Venus* did not turn round the Sun, and was not betwixt her and the *Earth*; for since all planets borrow their light from the Sun, it is necessary that *Venus*'s lucid face should be towards the Sun; and when she appears fully illuminated, she shows the same face to the Sun and the Earth; whence, at that time, she must be beyond the Sun, for in no other position could her illuminated face be wholly seen from the Earth. Further, when she disappears, or, if visible, appears horned; that face of hers, which is towards the Sun is either wholly turned from the Earth, or only a small part of it can be seen by the Earth; and in this case she must of necessity be betwixt us and the Sun. These observations must be made with a telescope.

Besides the foregoing there is another argument to prove that *Venus* moves round the *Sun* in an Orbit that is within the Earth; because she is always observed to keep near the *Sun*, and in the same quarter of the Heavens that he is in, never receding from him more than about $\frac{1}{8}$ of a whole circle; and therefore she can never come in opposition to him, that is, the Earth never can be between the Sun and Venus, which would necessarily happen, did she perform her course round the Earth either in a longer or shorter time than a year.   I.   And

And this is the reason why *Venus* is never to be seen near midnight, but always either in the morning or evening, and at most not above three or four hours before Sun-rising, and after Sun-setting from the time of *Venus's* superior conjunction, or when she is beyond the *Sun*, she is more easterly than the Sun, and therefore sets later, and is seen after Sun-setting; and then she is commonly called the *Evening-Star*: but from the time of her inferior conjunction, till she comes again to the superior, she then appears more westerly than the Sun, and is only to be seen in the morning before Sun rising; and is then called the *Morning-Star*.

After the same manner we prove that *Mercury* turns round the Sun, for he always keeps in the Sun's neighbourhood, and never recedes from him so far as *Venus* does; and therefore the Orbit of Mercury must lie within that of *Venus*, and on account of his nearness to the Sun he can seldom be seen without a Telescope.

Mars is observed to come in opposition, that is, the Earth is sometimes between the Sun and Mars; he always preserves a round, full, and bright face, except when he is near his quarters, when he appears somewhat gibbous, like the moon, three or four days before or after the full : Therefore the Orbit of *Mars* must include the Earth within it, and also the Sun ; for if he were betwixt the Sun and us at the time of his inferior conjunction, he would either quite disappear, or appear horned, as *Venus* and the Moon do in that position.

Mars, when he is in opposition to the Sun, appears to us almost seven times larger in diameter than when he is in conjunction with him; and therefore must needs be almost seven times nearer to us in one position than in the other : For the apparent magnitudes of distant objects increase or decrease in proportion to their distances from us ; but *Mars* keeps always, nearly, at the same distance from the Sun, therefore it is plain that it is not the Earth but the Sun that is the centre of his motion.

It is proved, in the same way, that *Jupiter, Saturn,* and the *Herschel,* have both the Sun and Earth within their Orbits ; and that the Sun, and not the Earth, is the centre of their motions ; although the disproportion of the distances from the Earth is not so great in *Jupiter* as in *Mars*, nor so great in *Saturn* as it is in *Jupiter*, because they are at a much greater distance from the Sun.

We

We have now shown that all the planets turn round the *Sun*, and that *Mercury* and *Venus* are included between him and the Earth, whence they are called the inferior planets, and that the Earth is placed between the Orbits of *Mars* and *Venus*, and therefore included within the Orbits of *Mars*, *Jupiter*, *Saturn*, and the *Herschel* Planet, whence they are called the superior Planets : and since the Earth is in the middle of these moveable bodies, and is of the same nature with them, we may conclude, that she has the same sort of motions :—but that she turns round the *Sun* is proved thus :.

All the planets seen from the Earth appear to move very unequally ; as sometimes to go faster, at other times slower, and sometimes to be stationary, or not to move at all ; which could not happen if the Earth stood still*.

The annual periods of the planets round the Sun are determined by carefully observing the length of time from their departure from a certain point to the Heavens (or from a fixed Star) until they arrive at the same again. By these kinds of observations the ancients determined the periodical revolutions of the planets round the Sun ; and were so exact in their computations as to be capable of predicting eclipses of the Sun and Moon : But since the invention of telescopes astronomical observations are made with greater accuracy, and consequently our tables are far more perfect than those of the ancients.

And, in order to be as exact as possible, Astronomers compare observations made at a great distance of time from one another, including several periods ; by which means the error that might be in the whole, is in each period subdivided into such little parts, as to be very inconsiderable. Thus the mean length of a solar year is known even to seconds.

The diurnal rotation of the planets round their Axis was discovered by certain spots which appear on their surfaces : these spots appear first on the margin of the planets disks, or the edge of their surfaces, and seem by degrees to creep towards their middle: and so on, going still forward, till they come to the opposite side or edge of the Disk, where they set or disappear; and after they have been hid for the same space of time that they were visible, they again appear to rise in or near the same place

* This subject, and whatever relates to the Science of Astronomy is made very intelligible in the 2nd. vol. of Scientific Dialogues.

as they did at first; then to creep on progressively, taking the same course as they did before. Spots of this kind have been observed on the surfaces of the *Sun*, *Venus*, *Mars*, *Jupiter*, and *Saturn*, by which means it has been found that these bodies turn round their own axis in the times before mentioned.

It is very probable, that *Mercury* and the *Hershel* have likewise a motion round their axis, that all the parts of their surface may alternately enjoy the light and heat of the Sun, and receive such changes as are proper and convenient for their nature: but by reason of the nearness of *Mercury* to the *Sun*, and of the immense distance of the *Herschel*, from him, no observation has hitherto been made, by which their spots (if they have any) could be discovered, and therefore their diurnal motions have not been determined. The diurnal motion of the earth is concluded to exist from the apparent revolution of the Heavens, and of all the Stars round it, in the space of a natural day. For it is much easier to conceive that this comparatively small Globe should turn round its own axis, once in 24 hours, than that such a great number of much larger bodies, some of them so immensely distant, should revolve round it in so short a space of time. The solar spots do not always remain the same, but sometimes old ones vanish, and afterwards others succeed in their room; sometimes several small ones gather together and make one large spot, and sometimes a large spot is seen to be divided into many small ones. But notwithstanding these changes, they all turn round with the Sun in the same time.

Each Planet is observed always to pass through the constellations *Aries*, *Taurus*, *Gemini*, *Cancer*, *Leo*, *Virgo*, *Libra*, *Scorpio*, *Sagittarius*, *Capricornus*, *Aquarius*, *Pisces*, and it also appears that every one has a track peculiar to itself; by which the paths of the six Planets form among the Stars a kind of road, which is called the Zodiac ; the middle part whereof, called the ecliptic, is the orbit described by the earth, with which the orbits of the other Planets are compared.

As the ecliptic runs through twelve constellations it is supposed to be divided into twelve equal parts, of 30 degrees each, called Signs, having the same names with the twelve constellations they run through.

The plane of the ecliptic is supposed to divide the celestial sphere in two equal parts, called the northern and
                                                            southern

southern hemispheres : and a body situated in either of these hemispheres is said to have north or south latitude, according to the hemisphere it is in : thus the latitude of a celestial object is its distance from the ecliptic.

The planes of the other five orbits are observed to lie partly in the northern and partly in the southern hemisphere; so that every one cuts the ecliptic in two opposite points called nodes ; one, called the ascending node, is that through which the Planet passes, when it moves out of the southern into the northern hemisphere; and the other called the descending node, is that through which the Planet must pass in going out of the northern into the southern hemisphere. The right line joining the two nodes of any Planet is called the line of the nodes.

The names of most of the constellations were given by the ancient astronomers, who reckoned that star in *Aries*, now marked ♈ (according to *Bayer*) to be the first point in the ecliptic, this for being next the Sun when he entered the vernal equinox ; at that time each constellation was in the sign by which it was called: but observations show, that the point marked in the Heavens by the vernal equinox has been constantly going backwards by a small quantity every year ; whereby the Stars appear to have advanced as much forwards, so that the constellation *Aries* is now almost removed into the sign *Taurus;* the said first star in *Aries* being got almost 30 degrees forward from the equinox ; which difference is called the *Procession of the Equinox,* whereof the yearly alteration is about 50 seconds of a degree or about a degree in 72 years.

All the Planets have one common focus, in which the Sun is placed ; for as no other supposition can solve the appearances that are observed in the motion of the Planets, and as it also agrees with the strictest physical and mathematical reason ; therefore it is now received as an elementary principle.

The line of the nodes of every Planet passes through the Sun; for as the motion of every Planet is in a plane passing through the Sun, consequently the intersections of these planes, that is, in the lines of the nodes, must also pass through the Sun.

All the Planets in their revolutions are sometimes nearer, sometimes farther from the Sun; this is a consequence of the Sun not being placed in the centre of each orbit, the orbits being ellipses.

L 3

The

The Aphelion, or superior Apsis, is that point of the orbit which is farthest distant from the Sun: and the perihelion, or inferior apsis, is that point which is nearest the Sun : And the transverse diameter of the orbit, or the line joining the two apses, is called the line of the apses.

The Planets move faster as they approach the Sun, or come nearer to the perihelion, and slower as they recede from the Sun, or come nearer the aphelion. This is not only a consequence from the nature of the Planets motions about the Sun, but it is confirmed by all good observations.

If a right line be drawn from the Sun, through any Planet, (which line is called by some the *Vector Radius*) and be supposed to revolve round the Sun with the Planet, then this line will describe, or pass through, every part of the plane of the orbit, so that the Vector Radius may be said to describe the area of the orbit.

There are two chief laws observed in the Solar System, which regulate the motions of all the planets ; namely.

I. The Planets describe equal areas in equal times ; that is, in equal portions of time the Vector Radius describes equal areas or portions of the space contained within the Planet's orbit.

II. The squares of the periodical times of the Planets are as the cubes of the mean distances from the Sun : That is, as the square of the time which the Planet *A* takes to revolve in its orbit, is to the square of the time taken by any other Planet *B*, to run through its orbit, so is the cube of the mean distance of *A* from the Sun, to the cube of the mean distance of *B* from the Sun.

The mean distance of a Planet from the Sun is its distance from him when the Planet is at either extremity of the conjugate diameter, and is equal to half of the transverse diam ter.

The foregoing are the two famous laws of *Kepler*, a great astronomer, who flourished in *Germany* about the beginning of the 17th century, and who deduced them from a multitude of observations : but the first who demonstrated these laws, was the incomparable Sir *Isaac Newton*.

By the second law, the relative distances of the Planets from the Sun are known ; and if the real distance of any one be known, the absolute distances of all the others may thereby be obtained.

Besides the Planets already mentioned, there are other great bodies that sometimes visit our System, which are

a sort

a sort of temporary Planets; for they come and abide with us for a while, and afterwards withdraw from us for a certain space of time, after which they again return. These wandering bodies are called Comets.

The motions of the Comets in the heavens, according to the best observations hitherto made, seems to be regulated by the same immutable law with the Planets: for their orbits are elliptical, like those of the Planets; but vastly narrower or more eccentric. Their orbits have different inclinations to the Earth's orbit; some inclining north-wardly, others southwardly, much more than any of the planetary orbits do.

Although both the Comets and the Planets move in elliptic orbits, yet their motions seem to be vastly different, for the eccentricities of the Planets orbits are so small that they differ but little from circles; but the eccentricities of the Comets are so very great that the motions of some of them seem to be almost in a right line, tending directly towards the Sun. Now, since the orbits of the Comets are so extremely eccentric, their motions, when they are in their perihelia, or nearest distance from the Sun, must be much swifter than when they are in their aphelia, or farthest distance from him; which is the reason why the Comets make so short a stay in our System, and, when they disappear, are so long in returning.

The figures of the Comets are observed to be very different; some of them send forth small beams, like hair, every way round them; others are seen with a long fiery tail, which is always opposite to the Sun. Their magnitudes are also very different, but in what proportion they exceed each other, is as yet uncertain. Nor is it probable that their numbers are yet known, for they have not been observed with due care, nor their theories discovered, but of late years. The ancients were divided in their opinions concerning them: some imagined that they were only a kind of Meteors, kindled in our atmosphere, and were there again dissipated; others took them to be some ominous prodigies; but modern discoveries prove that they are worlds, subject to the same laws of motion as the Planets are; and they must be very hard and durable bodies, else they could not bear the vast heat which some of them, when in their perihelia, receive from the Sun, without being utterly consumed. The great Comet which appeared in the Year 1680, was within ¼ part of the Sun's

diameter

diameter from his surface ; and therefore its heat must be intense beyond imagination, and when it is at its greatest distance from the Sun, the cold must be as rigid.

The fixed Stars are those bright and shining bodies which in a clear night, appear to us every where dispersed through the boundless regions of space. They are termed fixed, because they are found to keep the same immutable distance from each other in all ages, without having the motions observed in the Planets. The fixed Stars are all placed at such immense distances from us, that the best of telescopes represent them no bigger than points, without having any apparent diameter.

It is evident from hence, that all the Stars are luminous bodies, and shine with their own proper and native light, else they could not be seen at such a great distance. For the satellites of *Jupiter*, *Saturn*, and the *Herschel*, though they appear under considerable angles through good telescopes, yet are altogether invisible to the naked eye.

Although the dista. ce betwixt us and the Sun. is vastly great, when compared to the diameter of the Earth, yet it is nothing when compared with the prodigious distance of the fixed Stars ; for the whole diameter of the Earth's annual orbit appears / from the nearest fixed Star no larger than a point, and the fixed Stars are at least 100,000 times f.rther from us than we are fro.n the Sun ; as may be de--monstrated from the observations of those who have endeavoured to find the parallax of the Earth's annual orbit, or the angle under which the Earth's orbit appears from the fixed Stars.

Hence it follows, that though we approach nearer to a fixed Star at one time of the year than we do at the opposite, and that by the whole length of the diameter of the Earth's orbit, or 190 millions of miles, yet this distance, being so small in comparison with the distance of the fixed Stars, their magnitudes or positions cannot thereby be sensibly altered. Therefore we may always without error suppose ourselves to be in the same centre of the heavens, since we have always the same visib e prospect of the Stars without any alteration.

If a spectator were, placed as near to any fixed Star as we are to the *Sun*, he would there observe a body as large as the Sun appears to us ; and our Sun would appear to him no bigger than a fixed Star, and undoubtedly he would reckon the Sun as one of them, in numbering the Stars.

. Wherefore

Wherefore since the Sun differeth in nothing from a fixed Star, the fixed Stars may be reckoned as so many Suns.

It is not reasonable to suppose that all the fixed Stars are placed at the same distance from us; but it is more probable that they are every where interspersed through the vast indefinite space of the universe; and that there may be as great a distance betwixt any two of them as there is betwixt our Sun and the nearest fixed Star. Hence it follows, why they appear to us of different magnitudes, not because they really are so, but because they are at diffe.ent distances from us; those that are nearest excelling in brightness and lustre those that are more remote, which give a fainter light, and appear smaller to the eye.

Astronomers distribute the Stars into several orders or classes; those that are nearest to us, and appear brightest to the eye, are called Stars of the first magnitude; those that are nearest to them in brightness and lustre are called Stars of the second magnitude; those of the third class are styled Stars of the third magnitude; and so on until we come to the Stars of the sixth magnitude, which are the smallest that can be discerned by the naked eye. There are infinite numbers of smaller Stars that can be seen through telescopes; but these are not reduced to any of the six orders, and are only called telescopic Stars. It may be here observed, that though astronomers have reduced all the Stars that are visible to the naked eye into some one or other of these classes, yet we are not thence to conclude that all the Stars answer exactly to some or other of these orders; but there may be in reality as many orders of the Stars as there are numbers, few of them appearing of the same size and lustre.

The ancient astronomers, that they might distinguish the Stars in regard to their situation and position to each other, divided the whole starry firmament into several asterisms, or systems of Stars, consisting of those that are near to one another. These asterisms are called constellations. and are digested into the forms of some animals, as men, lions, bears, serpents, &c. or to the images of some known things, as a crown, a harp, a triangle, &c.

The starry firmament was divided by the ancients into 48 images or constellations; twelve of these they placed in that part of the heavens in which the planes of the planetary orbits are; this part is called the Zodiac, because the constellations placed therein resemble some living creature. The two regions of the Heavens on each side of the Zodiac are called the north and south parts of the heavens.

The

The constellations within the Zodiac are, 1. *Aries* ♈.
the Ram; 2. *Taurus* 8, the Bull; 8. *Gemini* ♊, the
Twins; 4. *Cancer* ♋, the Crab; 5. *Leo.* ♌, the Lion;
6. *Virgo,* ♍, the Virgin; 7. *Libra* ♎, the Balance; 8.
Scorpio ♏, the Scorpion; 9. *Sagittarius* ♐, the Archer;
10, *Capricornus* ♑, the Goat, 11. *Aquarius* ♒, the
Water-bearer; and 12, *Pisces,* ♓ the Fishes.

The con tellations on the north side of the Zodiac are
thirty-six, *viz.* the *Little Bear,* the *Great Bear,* the *Dragon, Cepheus,* a king of *Ethiopia ;* the *Greyhounds ; Bootes,*
the keeper of the Bear; *Mans Menelaus ; Berenice's Hair;
Charles's Heart ;* the *Northern Brown ; Hercules* with his
club watching the Dragon; *Cerberus;* the *Harp ;* the
Swan ; the *Fox ;* the *Goose ;* the *Lizard ; Cassiopeia ; Per-
seus ; Andromeda;* the *Great Triangle ;* the *Little Triangle;
Auriga ; Pegasus,* or the *Flying Horse ;* the *Dolphin ;* the
Arrow; the *Eagle; Serpentarius,* the *Serpent ; Sobieski's
Shield ; Camelopardus ; Antinous ;* the *Colt;* the *Lynx;*
the *Little Lion ;* and *Musca.*

The constellations noted by the ancients on the south
side of the Zodiac, were the *Whales,* the *River Eridanus,*
the *Hare, Orion,* the *Great Dog, Little Dog,* the *Ship
Argo, Hydra,* the *Centaur,* the *Cup,* the *Crow,* the *Wolf,*
the *Altar,* the *Southern Crow* and the *Southern Fish.* To
these have been lately added the following, *viz.* The *Phœ-
nix,* the *Crane,* the *Peacock, Noah's Dove,* the *Indian,* the
Bird of Paradise, Charles's Oak, the *Southern Triangle,*
t ie *Fly* or *Bee,* the *Swallow,* the *Camelion,* the *Flying
Fish, Teucan,* or the *American Goose,* the *Water Serpent,*
and the *Sword Fish.*

The ancients feigned these particular constellations or
figures in the heavens, either to commemorate the deeds of
some great man, or some notable exploit or action ; or else
took them from the fables of their religion, &c. And
modern astronomers still retain them, to avoid the con-
fusion that would arise by making new ones, when they
compare the modern observations with the old ones.

Some of the principal Stars have particular names given
them, as *Syrius Arcturus,* &c. There are also several Stars
that are not reduced into constellations, and these are called
unformed Stars.

Besides the Stars visible to the naked eye, there is a very
remarkable space in the heavens, called the *Galaxy,* or
Milky Way. This is a broad circle of a whitish hue, like
milk,

milk, going quite round the whole Heavens, and consisting of an infinite number of small Stars, visible through a telescope, though not discernible by the naked eye, by reason of their exceeding faintness; yet, with their light they combine to illumine that part of the Heavens where they are, and to cause that shining whiteness.

The places of the fixed Stars, or their relative situations one from another, have been carefully observed by astronomers, and digested into catalogues. The first among the *Greeks*, who reduced the Stars into a catalogue, was *Hipparchus*, who from his own observations and of those who lived before him, inserted 1022 Stars, has catalogued 120 years before the Christian Æra, this catalogue has been since enlarged and improved by several astronomers, to the number of 3000, of which there are a great many telescopial, and not to be discerned by the naked eye; and these are all ranked in the catalogues from the seventh magnitude.

It may seem strange to some, that there are no more than this number of Stars visible to the naked eye, for sometimes, in a clear night, they seem to be innumerable. But this is only a deception of our sight, arising from their vehement sparkling, while we look upon them confusedly, without reducing them into any order; for there can seldom be seen above 1000 stars in the whole Heavens with the naked eye at the same time; and if we would distinctly view them, we shall not find many but what are inserted upon a good celestial Globe.

Although the number of stars that can be discerned by the naked eye are so few, yet it is probable there are many more which are beyond the reach of our optics; for through telescopes they appear in vast multitudes, every where dispersed, throughout the whole Heavens; and the better our glasses are, the more of them we shall discover. The ingenious Dr. *Hook* has observed 74 stars in the *Pleiades*, of which the naked eye is never able to discern above 7; and in the *Orion*, which has but 84 stars in the *British* catalogue (and some of them telescopial) there has been numbered 2000 stars.

Those who think that all these glorious bodies were created for no other purpose than to give us a little dim light must entertain a very slight idea of the Divine Wisdom; for we receive more light from the Moon itself than from all the stars put together

And

And since the Planets are subject to the same laws of motion with our Earth, and some of them not only equal to, but vastly exceed it in, magnitude, it is not unreasonable to suppose that they are all habitable worlds. And since the fixed stars are no way behind our sun, either in size or lustre, is it not probable that each of them have a System of Planetary Worlds turning round them, as we revolve about the sun ? And if we ascend as far as the smallest star we can see, shall we not then discover innumerably more of these glorious bodies, which are now altogether invisible to us; ‧ ‧ ‧ ‧ ‧ ‧ ‧ ‧ ‧ ‧ through the boundless space of the Uni‧ ‧ ‧ ‧ ‧ Wi‧ ‧ ‧ ‧ ‧ ‧ ‧ ‧ ‧ nt idea must this raise in us of the]‧ ‧ ‧ ‧ P‧ ‧ ‧ ‧ ‧ ‧ ‧ ‧ ‧ ‧ ‧ ‧ where, and at all times present ‧ ‧ ‧ ‧ ‧ ‧ ‧ ‧ ‧ ‧ Power, Wisdom, and Goodness, to ‧ ‧ ‧ ‧ ‧ ‧ ‧ ‧ ‧ ‧ ‧

‧ ‧ ‧ ‧ ‧ ‧ ‧ ‧ ‧ shall proceed to is to say something in ‧ ‧ ‧ ‧ ‧ ‧ ‧ ‧ ‧ king Dials : but first it may be pro‧ ‧ ‧ ‧ ‧ ‧ ‧ ‧ ‧ ‧ speak of the use of a very necessary in‧ ‧ ‧ ‧ ‧ called a ‧ ‧ ‧ rant, the shape of which is here re‧ ‧ ‧ ‧ ‧ ‧ ed.

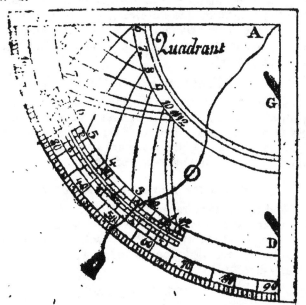

This Quadrant, or quarter of a circle, is useful for various purposes, viz. to take heights and distances, whether accessible or inaccessible : To find the hour of the day, &c.

Description

Description of the Quadrant.

The outward Arc is divided into 90 parts or degrees(being the fourth part of the circle of the sphere) and, figured from 10, 20, &c. to 90; above these figures are letters signifying the 12 calendar months in the year; as *J.* for *January*, *F*, for *February*, &c. And again over those letters for the months are lines to know the hour of the day: and upon the line *G D*, are sights of thin brass to be looked through, or for the sun to shine through. Lastly, in the middle or point of the Quadrant, *viz.* at *A*, is a line or thread of silk, fixed through a hole with a plummet of lead at the end of it, and also a small bead in the middle.—Some of the many uses of this instrument are as follow:

Of Heights.

Suppose you would know the height of a steeple, tower, or tree; hold up the Quadrant, and view through the sights the top of the steeple, tower, or tree, and then step forward or backward, till you find the plummet hang at liberty just at 45 degrees, that is just in the middle of the Quadrant; then the height of the steeple, tower, or tree, is equal to the distance of your standing-place from the bottom of the steeple, adding for the height that you hold the Quadrant from the ground.

To find the Hour of the Day.

Lay the thread just upon the day of the month, then hold it till you slip the small bead or pin's head to rest on one of the 12 o'clock lines; then let the sun shine from the sight at *G* to the other at *D*, the plummet hanging at liberty, the bead will rest on the hour-line of the day.

To find the Latitude of a Place nearly.

Hold up the Quadrant, and through the sights observe, in a clear star-light-night the North-Pole Star; the plummet hanging at liberty, the thread will rest on the degrees of latitude of the place you are in, or where you take your observation.

OF DIALLING.

DIALLING is a very ancient art, even as old as the time of King *Hezekiah*, where mention is made of the Dial of *Ahaz*, in the 2d Book of *Kings*, Chap. xx. ver. 11.

The

The Gnomon, or Sub-stile of a Post or Horizontal Dial should point directly south, and its back will be then directly north, the south may be truly known by a good watch or clock, just at noon; for then the sun is always at the meridian, and makes just 12 o'clock; so that knowing the south, the north is then found, it being its opposite.

To fix a Dial North and South.

Fasten your board on the top of a post, and then with your compass make 4, or 5, or 6 circles, one within the other from the centre or middle, where place a large pin perpendicular or upright, and nicely observe when the sun shines in the forenoon, on which circle the head of the pin shadoweth; then make there a mark; and do the same in the afternoon, when the shade of the pin's-head comes on the same circle; and from the midway of the two marks draw a line to the centre, on which place your meridian or 12 o'clock line; so will the post dial point north and south.

By a meridian line you may also know when the moon, or a star of magnitude, comes to the south; which when they do, they are always at the highest, whether by night or day.

The following Figure represents a Horizontal Dial.

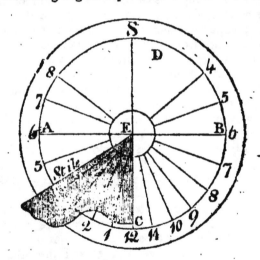

First with a ruler draw the line *A B*, then cross it in the centre with another line, as the line *C D*, which is the meridian, or 12 o'Clock line: and the first line drawn,
viz.

viz. A B is the six o'Clock line : then open your compasses,
and place one foot at the beginning of the degrees, or the arc
edge of your Quadrant ; and extend the other foot to 60
degrees, and with that extent place one foot in the centre
of the Dial at *E*, where the two first liness cross one another
and draw the semicircle *A C B*.

Next, having the 12 o'clock line *E C*, to know what distance must be set off from it, for 1 o'clock and 11 o'clock,
being all one ; be directed by the following small table, *viz.*

52o		Lat.	
D.	M.	Hour.	
11	55	1	11
24	26	2	10
38	13	3	9
53	44	4	8
71	9	5	7

In the first column against 1 hour and 11, you find 11
degrees and 55 minutes; which take off the edge of the
Quadrant, by setting one foot of the compasses at the beginning of the division under *B*, and the other foot to 11 degrees 55 minutes; the compasses so opened, set one foot in
the circle at the bottom of the 12 o'clock line, and with the
other foot of the compasses make a mark in the circle both
towards *A* and *B*, and from those two marks draw lines
towards the centre, which you may afterwards go over with
ink. Then to make the hour lines from 2 and 10 o'clock,
look on the table for 2 and 10 hours, where you will find
24 degrees and 26 minutes, which take off the degrees of
your Quadrant, and mark as the other from the 12 o'clock
line both ways in the circle.

The same is to be done for 3 and 9 o'clock, and also for
4 and 8 o'clock ; and the like for 5 and 7 o'clock ; and for
5 and 7, 4 and 8, above the 6 o'clock line, set off the same
distances as below it.

Then for the height of the Gnomon, or Stile, admit 52
degrees, take it off the edge of the Quadrant with the compasses as before, and with that extent set one foot at bottom of the 12 o'clock line as before, and extend the other
foot in the circle, and make a mark, and then draw a line
from thence to *E* the centre, for the upper edge of the
stile, and so raise it directly over the meridian of the 12
o'clock line. *Of*

Of upright Planes.

Those Planes are said to be erect or upright which stand perpendicular to the Horizon of the place, whose upper part points to the Zenith, and their lower part to the Nadir : and such are the walls of houses, churches, steeples, &c. against which Dials are commonly made.

To draw the hour lines on a direct south plane, in the latitude of 51 deg. 32 min. as described by the following Figure.

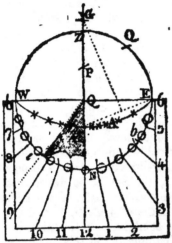

First, draw the circle *ZEWN*, representing an upright direct south plane; next cross it with the diameters *ZQN* for the meridian or, 12 o'clock line ; and *WQE* for the prime vertical circle, or hour-line of six.

Secondly, out of your line of chords take 38 degrees 28 minutes (the complement* of the latitude of the place) and set that distance on the Dial Plane from *Z* to *Q*, and from *E* to *b*, and from *N* to *e*.

Thirdly, lay a ruler from *W* to *Q*, and it will cut the meridian *Z N* in the point *P*, the pole of the world; and a ruler also laid from *W* to *b* will cut the meridian in *Æ*, which is the point through which the Equinoctial must pass ; for the drawing of which you have three points given viz *E Æ* and *W*, and the centre will always be in the meridian line *Z N*.

Fourthly, divide the semicircle *ENW* into 12 equal parts, as the points *O O O*, &c.

* The Complement of any Arc is what that Arc wants of 90° Thus the Complement of 51° 32′ is 38° 26′.

Fifthly,

Fifthly, lay a ruler to Q in the centre, at each of those points OOO, and the ruler will cross the equinoctial circle in the points *** &c. dividing them into 12 unequal parts.

Sixthly, lay a ruler to P (the pole of the World) and every one of the marks *** &c. and the ruler will cross the circle of the plane in the points | | | &c.

Lastly, if through the centre Q and the respective points | | | &c. you draw right lines, they will be true Hour-lines on an erect south-plane. For the Gnomon or Stile, take 38 deg. 28 min. out of the line of chords, and set them from N to e, drawing the line $Q e$ for the axis of the Stile, which must hang directly over the meridian or hour-line of 12, and point downwards to the south pole, because the plane beholds the south part of the meridian.

In making this Dial you make two Dials; for the erect direct North Dial is but the back-side of the south, for as this beholds the south part of the meridian, so the other faces the north part of the meridian; and as the meridian line in the South Dial shows when it is 12 o'clock at noon, so the back-side thereof, viz. the north side, represents the hour-line of 12 o'clock at midnight, and therefore not expressed, nor the hour-lines of 9, 10, 11 at night, or of 1, 2, or 3 in the morning, the Sun being never seen by us above the horizon at those hours: So the North Dial is capable of only receiving the hours of 4, 5, 6, 7, and 8 in the morning, and the same at night, and (in this latitude) not all of them neither; for it shines not in this plane at 8 in the morning, nor at 4 in the afternoon; but it is best to put them down as in the following figure, to know how much it is past in the morning and what it wants of 5 in the afternoon.

An erect North Dial.

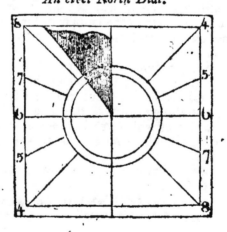

To draw the hour-lines on an erect direct east or west plane. —— Hour-lines in these Dials must he parallel to one another, and the Dial not to have any centre, but drawn as follows :

East·Direct Dial in the Latitude of 51 Deg. 32 Min.

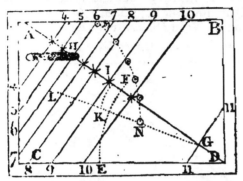

Let *A B C D* be the Dial Plane, on which is to be drawn a direct East Dial: upon the point *D*, if an East Dial, and on the point *C*, if a West, with the Radius (or Chord of 60 degrees) describe the obscure arc *EF*; then from your Chords take 38 deg. 28 min. the complement of the latitude of the place ; and set them from *E* to *F*; and draw the line *D F* quite through the Plane; then that you may proportion the Stile to the Plane, so that you may bring on all the hours from Sun-rising to 11 o'clock, assume two points in the line *F D*, one towards the end *D*, (as the point *G*) for the hour-line of 11, and another at *H*, for the hour line of six ; and through the point *G* and *H*, draw the lines 11 *G* 11, and 6 *H* 6 on the point *G*, with the Chord of 60 degrees, describe the obscure arc *I K*, and taking 15 degrees from the scale of Chords, in the compasses, set one foot in *I*, and with the other cut the arc *I K* and *E* ; through *G* and *K* draw the line *G K L*, cutting the line 6 *H* 6 in the point *L* ; so shall *L H* be the height of a perpendicular stile proportioned to this plane.

For the drawing of the hour-lines, set one foot of the compasses (opened to 60 degrees of the Chords) in *L*, and with the other describe the arc *M N*. between the hour-line of 6, and the line *G L* ; which divide five equal parts in the points ⊙ ⊙ ⊙ ⊙ ⊙ and a ruler laid from the point *L* to each of these points ⊙ ⊙ ⊙ &c. will cut the Equinoctial Line *H D* in the points ***** ; through which points draw lines parallel to 6 *H* 6, as the lines 7*7, 8*7, &c. as may be seen in the figure.   – And

And thus you have made the Dials, *viz.* a West Dial as well as an East ; only the arc *E F*, through which the Equinoctial passes in the East Dial, is drawn on the right hand of the Plane ; but in the West it must be drawn on the left ; and the hour-lines 4, 5, 6, 7, 8, 9, 10, and 11 in the forenoon, on the East Dial, must be 8, 7, 6, 5, 4, 3, 2, and 1, in the afternoon, upon the West Dial, as in the figure.

An Erect and Direct West Dial.

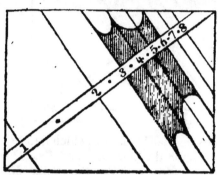

The Stile of the East or West Dials may be either a straight pin of the just length of the line *H O* in the other figure, which is equal to *H L* fixt in the point *H*, on the hour-line of 6, and exactly perpendicular on the Plane, showing the hours by the shadow of the Apex, or very near the top thereof ; or it may be a plate of brass of the same breadth with the distance of the hour-lines of 6 and 3 ; which plate must be set perpendicular upon the hour-line of 6, and so it will show the hour by the shadow of the upper edge thereof, as in the last figure.

Of beautifying and colouring Dials.

First, the boards are to be brushed over with Linseed Oil, thinly ground with *Spanish* brown, done over three or four times (drying between each time) a little thicker each time with the colour ; and this is called *Priming*.

To make the fat Oil for Dials.

Boil Red-lead, and Linseed Oil, and a little litharge of Gold, (about a penny worth) together, till almost as thick as syrup ; and when cold, and well settled, pour the clearest into a bottle or bladder for use.

The Gold Size for Dials.

Mix fine ground yellow Ochre with the aforesaid fat Oil, to such a consistency as when used it may settle smooth of itself. A mixture

A Mixture for Hour Lines.

G,ind Vermilion or Lamp-black with the fat Oil.

To draw Golden Letters or Figures for the Hours.

First draw them with a Pencil dipt in the Gold Size before mentioned; and when so dry as just to stick to your fingers, then with a smooth-edged penknife shape your leaf-gold to your mind; take it up with a piece of cotton cloth fixed to the end of a stick, and lay it on the size, pressing it down with the same cotton, and when dry brush off the loose gold with a feather, and smooth the rough edges of the letters with a pencil dipped in red or black colour.

Of the Dial Plane.

Let the board be of the best seasoned, firmest, clearest oak, one, two, or more feet square, and about three inches thick. Take two boards, and get them planed on both sides, and then laid in the sun-shine, or near a moderate fire, two or three days together, then plane them again, and fix them with good joints, and fasten them in gluing with wooden pegs, as you may have seen coopers fix their pieces of heading to their casks; and when thus glued and dried, plane them again, and then fasten them, by nailing two small plates of iron or tin on the back. If you cannot get seasoned wood; but green, then boil it about an hour in water to make it tough, and keep it from warping. In the general, wood is accounted better than stone, because it keeps the colouring more staunch or firm.

Before you colour your Dial-plate or board, fix your iron stile of 38 degrees (which indifferently serves for all *England)* and having marked your hour-lines with ink, fasten a nail at the end of each hour-line, that the head of each nail may shadow or direct you to the centre when it is coloured. And as it may happen that golden letters or figures may decay in a few years, you may on that account make them with a white-lead paint painted with red in a black margin. When your Dial is finished, nd dry, dip a feather in your oil, and ano nt it thinly; for the finer you mix or grind the colouring with the oil, the more beautiful it appears, though not so lasting.

These hints of colouring Dials, and other very necessary remarks relating to mixtures of colours, dying of stuffs, &c. are collected from Mr. *Salmon's Polygraphice.*

Of

Of Colours.

Whites, are Ceruse, Flake White, and White-lead.

Blacks, are Lampblack, burnt Cherry-stones, and old Ivory burnt.

Reds, are Red-lead, Vermilion, Red-Ochre and Indian Lake.

Greens, are Verdigrise, Verditure, and Sap-green, made of the Juice of Buck-thorn Berries.

Yellows, are Saffron, Yellow-pink, Gamboge.

Brown, is Umber burnt.

Gold Colour is Orpiment.

Again *Verdigrise* with a little Sap-green, makes a good and bright green.

Blues, are Ultramarine, Smalt, Indigo, and blue Brice.

Of mixing Colours.

Colours are mixed by being ground on a stone with clear water, severally, and dried and kept in paper bags for use : except Lampblack, Saffron, Smalt, Gamboge, and Sap-green.

Blue, to compound, temper a little Indigo and Smalt with oil.

A light Blue, mix Smalt and White-lead together.

Lead Colour, mix Lampblack and White-lead together on a Marble.

A Fox Colour, is Umber burnt

Gold Colour, is Orpiment mixt with fat Oil, by a knife on an earthen plate, or gally-tile rather.

To hinder colours from cracking put Oil of Walnuts to them.

Yellow Colour, beat Saffron to powder, and steep it in Vinegar. Or take the yellow Chives in White Lilies and Gum-water mixt for writing.

Red, Vermilion with Gum-Water mixt for writing.

Golden Letters, to write ; mix Vermilion and Gum Ammoniac with yolks of eggs.

Of dying Woods, Stuffs, &c.

To dye *Blue*, take woad one pound, and mix it with four-pints of boiling water, and steep whites in it 24 hours.

To dye red of a clear colour, take 60 pints of water wherein bran has been steeped 14 hours, and when strained dissolve two pounds of alum, and one pound of tartar ;

in

in which water boil what you have to dye for two hours; then take it out, and boil it in half as much fresh water with bran; *viz.* 30 pints; to which add madder 3 pounds, and so perfect the colour with moderate warmth without boiling.

To dye *Green*, First make a yellow by the direction underneath; then take 60 pints of water wherein bran hath been soaked, aforesaid; then strain it; let 3 pounds of alum be dissolved in it, and then boil what you have to dye in it for two hours.

To dye *Yellow*, take woad, two pounds of the said water of bran, and boil till the colour is good.

And if you would turn the said *Yellow* to *Green*, put the stuff into the aforesaid *Blue Dye*.

To dye a *Sand Colour*, add Log-wood to the *Black Dye* before mentioned.

To dye linen or thread, &c. light red: Take powder of Brazil and Vermilion, of each one ounce, boiled in alum-water.

To dye linen or thread yellow, dissolve gamboge in alum-water, &c.

To stain skins blue, boil elder-berries, and with the liquor brush over the skins, and wring them; then boil the berries in alum-water, and wet them twice over.

Of Money.

The current coin of this nation is either made of Copper, Silver, or Gold. Of *Copper* is made the Farthings, Half-pence, Pence, and Two-pences. Of *Silver* the Pennies, Two-pences; Three-pences, Groats, Sixpences, Shillings, Half-crowns, and Crowns. But there is very little Silver coined below the Six-pence. Of *Gold* is made the Quar-ter-Guinea, the third of a Guinea, or Seven Shilling Piece, the Half-Guinea, the Guinea and Five Guinea Pie-ces. There are also some few ancients pieces of Gold of a pale colour, as being alloyed with Silver, and therefore may be reckoned the best, and sometimes called Angel or Crown Gold; but the Old Gold, or broad Pieces, are mostly alloyed with Copper, which makes them of a reddish colour.

Imaginary Money.

We appropriate several names to money of which there are no coin; as

The

The Pound   — — — — — —of 20s. 0d.
The Mark   — — — — — — 13 4
The Noble, or Half-Mark — — — — 6 8
The Angel   — — — — — — 10 0

In *England* accounts are kept in Pounds, Shillings, and Pence *Sterling* ; and their marks are derived from their names in Latin, viz. *l.* for *Libræ*, or Pounds, *s.* for *Solidi*, or Shillings, *d.* for *Denarii*, or Pence, *qr.* for *Quadrantes*, or Farthings, four making a Penny ; and expressed or set down thus

     l.   *s.* · *d.*   *qr.*
     4   16   8   2

but better thus   *l.* 4—16—8 $\frac{1}{2}$:   The Mark for pounds standing before the sum denominates the first number, and the others are known of course ; for after pounds follow shillings, and after shillings succeed pence, &c. When the price of any thing is shillings and pence, it is set down thus :

     — *s.*   *d.*
     4   6

or thus 4s. 6 : and when shillings and pence, and parts of a penny, expressed thus,   *s.*   *d.*

     4   6$\frac{1}{2}$

or thus 4s. 6$\frac{1}{2}$. The latter way by some is accounted the neater, and the best method to express parts of a penny, or farthings : thus,

$\frac{1}{4}$ a farthing, or one fourth part of what it follows.
$\frac{1}{2}$ a half-penny, or one half of what it follows.
$\frac{3}{4}$ three farthings, or 3-4ths or qrs. of what it follows.

And being thus set fraction-wise, the under figure shows how many parts of the quantity before it is divided into, and the upper figure shows how many of those under parts the fraction stands for ; as thus, $\frac{1}{2}$ an ell, $\frac{3}{4}$ of a foot, or 9 inches ; and the same of a shilling is 9 pence ; of a pound is 15s.

If you are to set down 6 yards and a half, write thus,   Yds. 6$\frac{1}{2}$

C.
Nineteen Hundred three Quarters thus,   19$\frac{3}{4}$

lb.
Sixteen Pounds and a Quarter thus,   16$\frac{1}{4}$

or else thus, 19C$\frac{3}{4}$, 16 lb. $\frac{1}{4}$, 5 feet $\frac{1}{2}$, 14 days $\frac{3}{4}$. Here the name is put between the whole number and the fraction, which I think is the plainer and better way : for example, 6$\frac{1}{2}$ Hhds. may, through ignorance or wilfulness, be read 6 half Hhds. as well as 6 Hhds. and half.

INTEREST

INTEREST at Three per Cent. | INTEREST at Four per Cent. | INTEREST at Five per Cent.

	INTEREST at Three per Cent. for							
	One Day.		Thirty Days.			A Year.		Princi-pal.
	l. s. d. f.		l. s. d. f.			l. s. d. f.		
	0 0 0		0 0 0 2			0 0 7		£.1
	0 0 0		0 0 1			0 1 2 1		2
	0 0 0		0 0 1 3			0 1 9 2		3
	0 0 0 1		0 0 2 1			0 2 4 3		4
	0 0 0 1		0 0 3 0			0 3 0		5
	0 0 0 1		0 0 3 2			0 3 7		6
	0 0 0 2		0 0 4			0 4 2		7
	0 0 0 2		0 0 4 3			0 4 9		8
	0 0 0 3		0 0 5 1			0 5 3		9
	0 0 0 3		0 0 5 3			0 6 0		10
	0 0 1		0 0 11 3			0 12 0		20
	0 0 1 2		0 1 5 3			0 18 0		30
	0 0 2		0 1 11 2			1 4 0		40
	0 0 2 2		0 2 5 2			1 10 0		50
	0 0 3		0 2 11 1			1 16 0		60
	0 0 3 3		0 3 5 1			2 2 0		70
	0 0 4 1		0 3 11			2 8 0		80
	0 0 4 3		0 4 5			2 14 0		90
	0 0 5 3		0 4 11			3 0 0		100
	0 0 11 3		0 9 10 1			6 0 0		200
	0 1 1 3		0 14 9 2			9 0 0		300
	0 1 4 3		0 19 8 2			12 0 0		400
	0 1 7 3		1 4 7 3			15 0 0		500
	0 1 9 3		1 9 7			18 0 0		600
	1 1 14 3		1 14 6 3			21 0 0		700
	1 1 19 4		1 19 5 3			24 0 0		800
	1 2 3 3		2 4 4 2			27 0 0		900

	INTEREST at Four per Cent. for							
	One Day.		Thirty Days.			A Year.		Princi-pal.
	l. s. d. f.		l. s. d. f.			l. s. d. f.		
			0 0 0 3			0 0 9 2		£.1
			0 0 1 2			0 1 7		2
			0 0 2 1			0 2 4 2		3
			0 0 3 0			0 3 2 1		4
			0 0 3 3			0 4 0		5
			0 0 4 2			0 4 9 2		6
			0 0 5 1			0 5 7		7
	0 0 1 0		0 0 6 1			0 6 4 3		8
	0 0 1 0		0 0 7 3			0 7 2 1		9
	0 0 1 1		0 1 3 3			0 8 0		10
	0 0 1 2		0 1 1 3			0 16 0		20
	0 0 1 3		0 1 11 2			1 4 0		30
	0 0 2 2		0 2 7 1			1 12 0		40
	0 2 2 3		0 3 3 1			2 0 0		50
	0 0 3 3		0 3 11			2 8 0		60
	0 0 4 2		0 4 7			2 16 0		70
	0 0 5 1		0 5 3			3 4 0		80
	0 0 7 3		0 5 11			3 12 0		90
	0 0 7 2		0 6 6 3			4 0 0		100
	0 0 10 2		0 13 1 3			8 0 0		200
	0 1 5 1		0 19 8 2			12 0 0		300
	0 1 7 3		1 6 3 2			16 0 0		400
	0 1 11 3		1 12 10 1			20 0 0		500
	0 1 6 1		1 19 5 1			24 0 0		600
	0 1 9 1		2 6 0 1			28 0 0		700
	0 9 11 1		2 12 7			32 0 0		800
	0 3 11 2		2 19 2			36 0 0		900

INTEREST at Five per Cent. for								
	One Day.		Thirty Days.			A Year.		Princi-pal.
	l. s. d. f.		l. s. d. f.			l. s. d.		
			0 0 0 3			0 1 0		£.1
			0 0 1 1			0 2 0		2
			0 0 3 3			0 3 0		3
			0 0 3 3			0 4 0		4
			0 0 4 3			0 5 0		5
			0 0 5 3			0 6 0		6
			0 0 6 3			0 7 0		7
			0 0 7 3			0 8 0		8
			0 0 8 3			0 9 0		9
	0 0 0 1		0 0 9 3			0 10 0		10
	0 0 0 2		0 1 7 2			0 1 0		20
	0 0 0 3		0 2 5 1			0 1 10		30
	0 0 1		0 3 3 1			0 2 0		40
	0 0 1 1		0 4 1 1			0 2 10		50
	0 0 1 2		0 4 11 2			0 3 0		60
	0 0 1 3		0 5 9 3			0 3 10		70
	0 0 2 1		0 6 7 4			0 4 0		80
	0 0 2 2		0 7 5 4			0 4 10		90
	0 0 3 1		0 8 3 5			0 5 0		100
	0 0 6 1		0 16 5 10			0 10 0		200
	0 0 9 2		1 4 7 15			0 15 0		300
	0 1 0 2		1 12 10 20			1 0 0		400
	0 1 4		2 1 1 25			1 5 0		500
	0 1 7 1		2 9 3 30			1 30 0		600
	0 1 11		2 17 6 135			1 35 0		700
	0 2 2 1		3 5 9 40			1 40 0		800
	0 2 5 2		3 13 11 245			1 45 0		900

Table of the Value of Gold and Silver.

		l. s. d.
Gold,	1 Pound is worth - -	£48 0 0
	1 Ounce - - - -	4 0 0
	1 Pennyweight - - -	0 4 0
	1 Grain - - - -	0 0 2
Silver,	1 Pound is worth - -	3 0 0
	1 Ounce - - - -	0 5 0
	1 Pennyweight - - -	0 0 3
	1 Grain - - - -	0 0 1/8

N.B. The Prices of the Precious Metals varies continually.

A TABLE for buying or selling any Commodity by the Great Hundred, which is 112 Pounds.

d. q.	l. s. d.	d. q.	l. s. d.	d. q.	l. s. d.	d. q.	l. s. d.
0 1	0 2 4	1	2 18 4	1	5 14 4	1	8 10 4
2	0 4 8	2	3 0 8	2	5 16 8	2	8 12 8
3	0 7 0	3	3 3 0	3	5 19 0	3	8 15 0
1 0	0 9 4	7 0	3 5 4	13 0	6 1 4	19 0	8 17 4
1	0 11 8	1	3 7 8	1	6 3 8	1	8 19 8
2	0 14 0	2	3 10 0	2	6 6 0	2	9 2 0
3	0 16 4	3	3 12 4	3	6 8 4	3	9 4 4
2 0	0 18 8	8 0	3 14 8	14 0	6 10 8	20 0	9 6 8
1	1 1 0	1	3 17 0	1	6 13 0	1	9 9 0
2	1 3 4	2	3 19 4	2	6 15 4	2	9 11 4
3	1 5 8	3	4 1 8	3	6 17 8	3	9 13 8
3 0	1 8 0	9 0	4 4 0	15 0	7 0 0	21 0	9 16 0
1	1 10 4	1	4 6 4	1	7 2 4	1	9 18 4
2	1 12 8	2	4 8 8	2	7 4 8	2	10 0 8
3	1 15 0	3	4 11 0	3	7 7 0	3	10 3 0
4 0	1 17 4	10 0	4 13 4	16 0	7 9 4	22 0	10 5 4
1	1 19 8	1	4 15 8	1	7 11 8	1	10 7 8
2	2 2 0	2	4 18 0	2	7 14 0	2	10 10 0
3	2 4 4	3	5 0 4	3	7 16 4	3	10 12 4
5 0	2 6 8	11 0	5 2 8	17 0	7 18 8	23 0	10 14 8
1	2 9 0	1	5 5 0	1	8 1 0	1	10 17 0
2	2 11 4	2	5 7 4	2	8 3 4	2	10 19 4
3	2 13 8	3	5 9 8	3	8 5 8	3	11 1 8
6 0	2 16 0	12 0	5 12 0	18 0	8 8 0	24 0	11 4 0

EXAMPLE.

First, at 5d. 3q. the pound, what is the Great Hundred? Look in the Table for 5d. 3q. in the first column, and against it in the second you shall find 2l. 13s. 8d. and so much will 112 pounds cost. Again, if a hundred weight cost 4l. 8s. 8d. find 4l. 8s. 8d. and against it, in the Column towards the left hand, you will find 9d. 2q. and so much it is by the pound.

Note. For every farthing that one pound doth cost, reckon two shillings and four pence, and that is the price of the great hundred.

M

Things

A *Ream of Paper*, 20 *Quires*.

A *Quire of Paper*, 24 *Sheets*.

A *Ditto for Printers*, 25 *Sheets*.

A *Bale of Paper*, 10 *Reams*. A *Bundle Ditto*, 2 *Reams*.

A *Roll of Parchment*, 5 *Dozen*, or 60 *Skins*.

A *Dicker of Hides*, 10 *Skins*.

Ditto of Gloves, 10 *Dozen Pair*.

A *Last of Hides*, 20 *Dickers*.

A *Load of Timber unhewn*, 40 *Feet*.

———————————*hewn*, 50 *Feet*.

A *Chaldron of Coals*, 36 *Bushels*.

A *Hogshead of Wine*, 63 *Gallons*.

Ditto of Beer, 54 *Gallons*.

A *Barrel of Beer*, 36 *Gallons*.

Ditto of Ale, 32 *Gallons*.

A *Gross* 144, or 12 *Dozen*.

A *Weigh of Cheese*, 256 *Pounds*.

Days in the Year, 365 ; *Weeks*, 52, *and Hours* 8766.

Pence in the Pound, 240 ; *Farthings*, 960.

An Acre of Land, 160 *square Poles*, or *Perches*.

A *Load*, or *Comb* 40 *Bushels*.

A *Market Load*, 5 *Bushels*.

A *Last of Corn* or *Rape-seed*, 2 *Load*, or 10 *Quarters*.

Ditto of Pot-Ashes, *Codfish*, *White-herrings*, *Meal*, *Pitch*, *and Tar*, 12 *Barrels*.

Ditto of Flax and Feathers, 17 *Cwt of Gunpowder*, 24, *Barrels*, or 2400*lb.* of 4368*lb.*

A *Ton of Wine*, 252 *Gallons* : *Oil of Greenland*, 252 *Gallons* ; *and Sweet Oil of Genoa*, 236 *Gallons*.

A *Ton in Weight*, 20 *C.* of *Iron*, &c. *but of Lead there is but* 19*C.* *and a Half*, *called a Fother*.

A *Tod of Wool*, 28 *Pounds*.

A *Pack of Ditto*, 364 *Pounds*.

A *Load of Bricks*, 500 ; *and of plain Tiles* 1000.

A *Stone of Fish*, 8*lb.* *and of Wool* 14*lb.* *The same for Horseman's Weight*, *and also Hay*; *but Pepper*, *Cinnamon*, *and Alum*, *have but* 13*lb.* ¼ *to the Stone*.

A *Stone of Glass*, 5 *Pounds*; *and a Seam of ditto* 24 *Stone*.

A *Truss of Hay*, 56 *Pounds*, *and a Load of ditto*, 9 *Trusses*. *But New Hay in June and August*, *ought to be* 60 *Pounds to the Truss*;

A *Cade of Red-herrings*, 500 ; *and of Sprats*, 1000. *Iron and Shot* 14*lb.* *to the Stone*.

Barrels of sundry Commodities.

Anchovies, 30 *lb.*	*Raisins*, 1 *Cwt.*
A double Barrel, 60 *lb.*	*Oil* 31 *Gallons, and a Half.*
Nuts or Apples, 3 *Bushels.*	*Spanish Tobacco*, 2 *Cwt. to*
Pot-ash or Barilla, 200 *lb.*	3 *Cwt.*
White or Black Plates, 300.	*Gunpowder,* 1 *Cwt.*
Candles, 10 *doz. lb.*	*Soap*, 240 *lb.*
Salmon or Eels, 42 *Gall.*	*Butter*, 224 *lb.*
Figs, 3 *qrs.* 14 *lb. to* 2 C ¼	*Herrings*, 32 *Gallons.*

Things in wholesale Trade, bought and sold by the Thousand

Cuttle Bones	*Bricks*
Oranges and Lemons	*Clinkers or Flanders Tiles*
Chair Nails	*Billets and Leaves of Horn*
Tacks and Tenter Hooks	*Barrel Hoops*
Pomegranates and Tazels	*Squirrel Skins*
Goose Quills and Thimbles	*Slate and Hilling Stones.*

Pins and small Needles by the 1000 Dozen.

Things sold and bought at Six Score to the Hundred.

Banks and Barlings	*Cole, Ling and Newfound-*
Barrel and Pipe Boards	*land Fish, Stockfish of*
Boomspars and Bow-staves	*all Sorts.*
Canspars and Caprevans.	*Ells of Canvass, and most*
Herrings and Deal Boards	*Foreign Linens*
Nails, Eggs and Cod-fish	*Hogshead Staves.*

Of Bonds, Bills, Indentures, Letters of Attorney, Wills, and other useful Writings.

Precedents of these are very necessary, not only for the understanding of them, but to know how to make them properly on Occasion.

A Bond from One to Another.

KNOW all Men by these Presents, that I Abraham Darnel, *of the Parish of* St. Sepulchre, *in the City of* London, Gentleman, *am held and firmly bound to* John Melvil, *of the said City of* London, *Esq. in the Sum of Fifty Pounds of good and lawful Money of Great Britain, to be paid to the said* John Melvil, *or his certain Attorney, his Executors, Administrators or Assigns; for the true Payment whereof, I bind myself, my Heirs, Executors and Administrators, firmly by these Presents, sealed in*

N 2   *the*

Notes payable on Demand.

	£	s.		£	s.			£	s.	d.
For	2	0	and not exceeding	5	5	.	.	0	0	5
Above	5	5	ditto .	30	0	.	–	0	1	6
Above	30	0	ditto .	50	0	.	.	0	2	0
Above	50	0	ditto .	100	0	.	.	0	3	0
Above	100	0	ditto .	200	0	.	.	0	4	0
Above	200	0	ditto .	500	0	.	.	0	5	0
Above	500	0	ditto .	1000	0	.	.	0	7	6

Bills, or Notes, payable after Date, or Sight.

	£	s.		£	s.			£	s.	d.
For	2	0	and not exceeding	5	5	.	.	0	1	0
Above	5	5	ditto .	30	0	.	.	0	1	0
Above	30	0	ditto .	50	0	.	.	0	2	6
Above	50	0	ditto .	100	0	.	.	0	3	0
Above	100	0	ditto .	200	0	.	.	0	4	0
Above	200	0	ditto .	500	0	.	.	0	5	0
Above	500	0	ditto .	1000	0	.	.	0	7	6

Notes payable on Demand, and re-issuable after Payment.

	£	s.		£	s.			£	s.	d.
For	1	1	and not exceeding			.	.	0	0	3
Above	1	1	ditto .	2	2	.	.	0	0	6
Above	2	2	ditto .	5	5	.	.	0	0	9
Above	5	5	ditto .	20	0	.	.	0	1	0

Foreign Bills of Exchange.

		£	s.		£	s.			£	s.	d.
Where the Sum shall not exceed				100	0	.	.	0	1	0
Above	100	0	ditto .	200	0	.	.	0	2	0
Above	200	0	ditto .	500	0	.	.	0	3	0
Above	500	0	ditto .	1000	0	.	.	0	4	0

RECEIPTS, if in full of all Demands,

	£	s.		£	s.			£	s.	d.
						.	.	0	5	0
For	2	0	and under	10	0	.	.	0	0	2
.	10	0	ditto .	20	0	.	.	0	0	4
.	20	0	ditto .	50	0	.	.	0	0	8
.	50	0	ditto .	100	0	.	.	0	1	0
.	100	0	ditto .	200	0	.	.	0	2	0
.	200	0	ditto .	500	0	.	.	0	3	0
.	500	0	and upwards			.	.	0	5	0

Bonds.

	£	s.		£	s.			£	s.	d.
For any Sum not exceeding			100	0	.	.	1	0	0
Above	100	0	and under	300	0	.	.	1	10	0
.	500	0	ditto .	1000	0	.	.	3	0	0
.	1000	0	ditto .	2000	0	.	.	4	0	0
.	2000	0	ditto .	3000	0	.	.	5	0	0
.	3000	0	ditto .	4000	0	.	.	6	0	0
.	4000	0	ditto .	5000	0	.	.	7	0	0
.	5000	0	ditto .	10000	0	.	.	9	0	0
.	10000	0	ditto .	15000	0	.	.	12	0	0
.	15000	0	ditto .	20000	0	.	.	15	0	0
.	20000					.	.	20	0	0

Sundries.

Agreements	each 6s.	Debentures each . 4s.
Almanacks	1s.	Deeds & Indentures 1l. 10s. & up.
Awards	1l. 10s.	Inventories . 5s.
Bills of Lading	3s.	Protests and Notarial Acts 4s.

the *fiftieth* Year of the Reign of our Sovereign Lord George the Third, by the Grace of God of the United Kingdom of Great Britain and Ireland, King, Defender of the Faith, and so forth, and in the Year of our Lord One Thousand Eight Hundred and Ten.

The Condition of this Obligation is such, That if the above bounden Abraham Darnel, his Heirs, Executors or Administrators, do well and truly pay, or cause to be paid to the above-named John Melvil, his Executors, Administrators, or Assigns, the full Sum of twenty-five Pounds of good and lawful Money of Great Britain, on the twentieth Day of August next ensuing the Date hereof, with the lawful Interest thereof, then this Obligation to be void, or else to remain, continue, and be in full force and virtue.

Sealed and Delivered
(being first duly stamped)
in the Presence of   Abraham Darnel.   O
    George Needy,
    Thomas Trusty.

A Bill with a Penalty.

KNOW all men by these presents, that I, *John Jenkins*, of the city of *Chichester*, in the county of *Sussex*, Victualler, do acknowledge myself indebted to *Martin Moneyman* of *East Grinstead*, in the county aforesaid, Grazier, in the sum of twenty Pounds of good and lawful Money of *Great Britain*, to be paid unto the said *Martin Moneyman*, his Heirs, Executors, Administrators or Assigns, in or upon the 20th Day of *September* next ensuing the date hereof, without fraud or further delay : for and in consideration of which payment well and truly to be made and done, I bind myself, my Heirs, Executors, and Administrators, in the penal sum of forty Pounds, of the like lawful money, firmly by these Presents : In witness whereof I have hereunto set

Note. The Mark O in this and the Form following, represents the Seal, which in this and all those in which it appears, ought to be affixed: the person who executes any of them (a Will excepted, concerning which directions will be given in its place) is in the Presence of the Witnesses to take off the Seal (that is, the Instrument with which the impression was made) and then taking the paper or parchment in his or her right hand, is to pronounce these words, I deliver this as my Act and Deed for the Purposes within mentioned.

M 3   my

my Hand and Seal, this twenty-fifth day of *March*, in the fiftieth year of the Reign of our Sovereign Lord King *George* the Third, and in the year of our Lord God, 1810.

Signed, Sealed and Deli-
    vered in the Presence of   *John Jenkins.* O.
        Titus Testimony,
        Andrew Affidavit.

A short Bill, or Note of Hand.

KNOW all Men by these Presents, that I *Peter Penny-less*, of the Parish of *St. Saviour, Southwark*, in the county of *Surrey*, Blacksmith, do owe, and own myself to stand indebted to *Robert Rich*, of the Parish of *St. Andrew, Holborn*, in the county of *Middlesex*, Gent. in the just and due sum of five Pounds of lawful money of *Great Britain*, which by these Presents I promise to pay unto him the said *Robert Rich*, at or upon the sixth day of *October* next ensuing the date hereof: for the true performance of which payment well and truly to be made, and in witness hereof I have set my Hand to these Presents, the 4th day of *July*, 1810.
                    Peter Pennyless.

Among men of business the following form is commonly used, and is equally effectual in law :

£5 0 0   London, *May* 10, 1810.
Five Months after date, I promise to pay to Mr. *Robert Rich*, or order, the sum of five Pounds, for value received.
                    Peter Pennyless.

This Note is transferable to another, if *Robert Rich* writes his name on the back of it; but then if *Peter Pennyless* does not pay it, *Robert Rich* is liable to be called on for the money.

A penal Bill from Two to One.

KNOW all Men by these Presents, that we Lawrence Luckless and Peter Pauper, both of the Parish of Saint Dunstan, Stepney, in the county of *Middlesex*, Weavers, do acknowledge and own ourselves to stand indebted to Gabriel Greedy, of the Parish of St. Olave, Southwark, in the county of *Surrey*, Feltmaker, in the just and due sum of ten Pounds of good and lawful money of *Great Britain*, to be paid unto

unto him the said Gabriel Greedy, his Heirs, Executors, Administrators, or Assigns, at or upon the thirteenth day of October next ensuing the date hereof, without fraud or further delay; for and in consideration of which payment well and truly to be made, we do bind our Heirs, Executors, and Administrators, in the penal sum of twenty Pounds of the like lawful Money, firmly by these Presents. In witness whereof, we have hereunto set our Hands and Seals, this sixteenth day of *May*, in the fiftieth Year of the Reign of our Sovereign Lord King *George* the Third, &c. and in the Year of our Lord One Thousand Eight Hundred and Ten.

Signed, Sealed and Deli-
vered in the presence of   *Laur. Luckless.* ⊙
Winbledon Witness,   *Peter Pauper.*
Timothy Testis.

A Letter of Attorney.

KNOW all Men by these Presents, that I Charles Careful, of Lewes in the County of Sussex, Apothecary, (for divers considerations and good causes me hereunto moving) have made, ordained, constituted and appointed, and by these Presents do make, ordain, constitute, and appoint my trusty friend William Wagstaff, of Pemsey, in the County aforesaid, Gentleman, my true and lawful Attorney, for me, in my name, and to my use, to ask, demand, recover or receive of or from *A. B.* of Rye, in the said County, the sum of forty Pounds; giving, and by these Presents granting to my said Attorney, sole and full Power and Authority, to take, pursue, and follow such legal courses for the recovery, receiving, and obtaining the same, as I myself might or could do, were I personally present; and upon the Receipt of the same Acquittances, and other sufficient discharges, for me, and in my name to make, sign, seal, and deliver, as also, one or more Attorney or Attorneys under him to substitute or appoint, and again at his pleasure to revoke; and further to do, perform, and execute for me, and in my name, all and singular thing or things, which are or may be necessary touching and concerning the premises, as fully, thoroughly, and entirely, as I the said Charles Care-

·Note. *All Obligations must be in* English, *and the words in full length; also Bonds, Notes of Hand, Bills, Letters of Attorney, Indentures, &c. must be on stamped paper (See the Table, p.* 268) *to render them valid.*

M 4

ful

ful in my own person, ought, or could do in and about the same; ratifying, allowing, and confirming whatsoever my said Attorney shall lawfully do, or cause to be done in and about the execution of the Premises, by virtue of these Presents. In witness whereof I have hereunto set my Hand and Seal the sixth day of July, in the fiftieth year of Reign of our Sovereign Lord *George* the Third, by the Grace of God of the United Kingdom of *Great Britain* and *Ireland*, King, &c. and in the Year of our Lord One Thousand Eight Hundred and Ten.

A Letter of Attorney by a Seaman.

KNOW all Men by these Presents, that I *Timothy Tarpaulin*, Mariner, now belonging to his Majesty's ship the *Rye*, for divers good Causes and Considerations me thereunto moving, have and by these Presents do make my trusty Friend *Henry Hearty*, Citizen and Baker of London, (or my beloved Wife *Penelope Tarpaulin*) my true and lawful Attorney, for me, and in my name, and for my Use, to ask, demand, and receive of and from the Right Honourable the Treasurer, or Paymaster of his Majesty's Navy, and the Commissioners of Prize-money, and whom else it may concern, as well all such Wages and Pay, Bounty-money, Prize-money, and all other sum or sums of money whatsoever, as now are, and which hereafter shall and may be due, or payable unto me; also all such Pensions, Salaries, Smart-money, or other money and things whatsoever, which now are, or at any time hereafter shall or may be due to me, for my service, or otherwise, in any one of his Majesty's Ship or Ships, Frigates or Vessels: Giving and hereby granting, unto the said Attorney, full and whole Power, to take, pursue, and follow such legal ways and courses, for the recovery, receiving, and obtaining and discharging the said sum or sums of money, or any of them, as I myself might or could do were I personally present; and I do hereby ratify, allow, and confirm all and whatever my Attorney shall lawfully do or cause to be done in and about the execution of the Premises, by virtue of these Presents. In witness whereof I have hereunto set my Hand and Seal, this twenty-second day of March, One Thousand Eight Hundred and Ten, &c.

Timothy Tarpaulin. O

A

A short Will in legal Form.

IN the Name of God, Amen. I, *William Weakly*, of the City of London, Haderdasher, being very sick and weak in [or, in perfect health of] Body, but [or, and] of perfect Mind and Memory of my Body, and knowing that it is appointed for all Men once to die, do make and ordain this my last Will and Testament : That is to say principally, and first of all, I give and recommend my Soul into the Hand of Almighty God that gave it, and my Body I commend to the Earth, to be buried in decent Christian Burial, at the discretion of my Executors; nothing doubting but at the general Resurrection I shall receive the same again by the mighty power of God. And as touching such worldly Estate wherewith it hath pleased God to bless me in this life, I give, devise, and dispose of the same in the following Manner and Form :

First. I give and bequeath to *Elizabeth*, my dearly beloved Wife, the sum of Five Hundred Pounds of lawful Money of *Great Britain*, to be raised and levied out of my Estate, together with all my Household Goods, Debts, and moveable Effects.

Also. I give to my well-beloved Daughter *Elizabeth Weakly*, whom I likewise constitute, make, and ordain the sole Executrix of this my last Will and Testament, all and singular my Lands, Messuages, and Tenements, by her freely to be possessed and enjoyed. And I do hereby utterly disallow, revoke, and disannul all and every other former Testaments, Wills, Legacies, Bequests, and Executors by me in any wise before named, willed, and bequeathed, ratifying and confirming this, and no other, to be my last Will and Testament. In Witness whereof I have hereunto set my Hand and Seal, this 12th day of May, in the year of our Lord one thousand eight hundred and ten.

Signed, sealed, published, pronounced, and declared by the said *William Weakly* as his last Will and Testament, in the Presence of us, who, in his Presence, and in the Presence of each other, have hereunto subscribed our Names.

   Henry Hardy,
   Samuel Short,
   William Wortle.

Will. Weakly. ☉

The

The Testator, after taking off the Seal, must, in the presence of the Witnesses, pronounce these words, I publish and declare this to be my last Will and Testament.

Note. If a Will be already made, and the Person hath no mind to alter it, but to add something more, there may be affixed the following Codicil or Schedule to it, and it will stand good in Law, as part of the Will.

A Codicil to a Will.

BE it known unto all Men by these Presents, that I *William Weakly*, of the City of London, Haberdasher, have made and declared my last Will and Testament in writing, bearing date the 12th day of May, One Thousand Eight Hundred and Ten. I the said *William Weakly* by this present Codicil do ratify and confirm my said last Will and Testament; and do further give and bequeath unto my loving Cousin and Godson *William Weakly*, junior, the sum of fifty Pounds of good and lawful Money of *Great Britain*, to be paid unto him the said *William Weakly*, by my Executrix, out of my Estate. And my will and meaning is, that this Codicil be adjudged to be a part and parcel of my last Will and Testament; and that all things therein mentioned and contained be faithfully and truly performed, and as fully and amply in every respect, as if the same were so declared and set down in my said last Will and Testament. Witness my Hand this 20th Day of May, One Thousand Eight Hundred and Ten.

Signed in the Presence of us,   *William Weakly.* O
       A. B.
       C. D.

A Deed of Gift.

TO all People to whom these Presents shall come: I *George Generous* do send Greeting. Know ye, that I the said *George Generous*, of the Parish of Pancras, in the County of Middlesex, Brick-maker, for and in consideration of the Love, Good-will, and Affection, which I have and do bear towards my loving Sister *Sarah Sorrowful*, of the same Parish and County, Widow, have given and granted, and by these Presents do freely give and grant unto the said *Sarah Sorrowful*, her Heirs, Executors, or Administrators, all and singular my Goods and Chattels now being in my present Dwelling-house in the Parish aforesaid, known by the Name of *Fishers Piggery*, of which (before the signing
of

of these Presents) I have delivered her, the said *Sarah Sor-rowful*, an Inventory signed with my own Hand, and bearing even Date, to have and to hold all the said Goods and Chattels in the said Premises or Dwelling-house, to her the said Sarah Sorrowful, her Heirs, Executors, or Administrator, from henceforth, as her and their proper Goods and Chattels absolutely, without any manner of condition. In witness whereof, I have hereunto set my Hand and Seal, this 10th Day of May, One Thousand Eight Hundred and Ten.

Signed, Sealed, and Delivered, in the presence of   George Generous. Q
Daniel Drayton.
Aaron Atkins.

Note. This Precedent may be extended to the giving away of Cattle, Corn, House or Land, if not entailed, &c. but the Particulars must be named, &c.

An Indenture of Apprenticeship.

This Indenture witnesseth, that *Richard Reynolds*, Son of *Robert Reynolds*, late of Pomsey, in the County of Sussex, hath put himself, and by these Presents doth voluntarily put himself Apprentice to Charles Carpenter, Citizen and linen-draper of London, to learn his Art, Trade, or Mystery, and after the Manner of an Apprentice, to serve him from the Day of the Date hereof for and during the full term of seven Years next ensuing: During all which time he the said Apprentice his said Master shall faithfully serve, his Secrets keep, his lawful Commands every where gladly obey. He shall do no Damage to his said Master, nor see it to be done by others, without letting or giving Notice thereof to his said Master. He shall not waste his said Master's Goods, nor lend them unlawfully to others. He shall not commit Fornication, nor contract Matrimony within the said Term. At Cards, Dice, or any unlawful Game he shall not play, whereby his said Master may be damaged. With his own, or the Goods of others, during the said term, without licence of his Master, he shall neither buy nor sell. He shall not absent himself day or night from his said Master's Service without his leave. Nor haunt Alehouses, Taverns, or Playhouses: but in all things behave himself as a faithful Apprentice ought to do during the said term. And the said Master shall use the utmost of his endeavours to teach, or cause to be taught and instructed the said Apprentice

prentice in the Trade and Mystery he now professeth, occupieth, or followeth : and procure for him the said Apprentice sufficient Meat, Drink, Apparel, Washing and Lodging, fitting for an Apprentice, during the said Term : and for the true performance of all and every the Covenants and Agreements, either of the said Parties bind themselves unto the other by these Presents.

In witness whereof they have interchangeably put their Hands and Seals, this 16th day of *April,* in the forty-ninth Year of the Reign of our Sovereign Lord *George* the Third, by the Grace of God of the United Kingdom of *Great Britain* and *Ireland,* King, &c. and in the Year of our Lord God, One Thousand Eight Hundred and Nine.

Note. If an Apprentice be inrolled before a Justice of the Peace or other proper Officer, (the Chamberlain being such in *London)* he cannot sue out his Indenture, but upon proof of unmerciful Usage, want of Victuals, or other necessaries, or his Master's being incapable of teaching him his Trade, or not choosing it so to be done at his proper charge by others. And the same holds good in relation to a Mistress ; but there being no Inrolment, an Indenture may be sued out without showing cause, in Cities and Corporations, &c.

A General Release.

KNOW all Men by these Presents, that I, *Peter Peaceable,* of *Hastings,* in the County of Sussex, Tobacconist, have demised, released, and for ever quit Claim, to *William Winter,* of *Rye* in the County aforesaid, Fish-Chapman, his Heirs, Executors and Administrators, of all and all manner of Action or Actions, Suits, Bills, Bonds, Writings, Debts, Dues, Duties, Accompts, Sum and Sums of Money, Leases, Mortgages, Judgments by Confession, or otherwise obtained, Executions, Extents, Quarrels, Controversies, Trespasses, Damages and Demands whatsoever, which by Law or Equity, or otherwise soever, I the said *Peter Peaceable* against the said *William Winter* ever had, and which I, my Heirs, Executors, or Administrators, shall or may claim, challenge or demand, for or by reason, or means, colour of any Matter, Cause or Thing whatsoever, to the day of the date of these Presents. In witness whereof I have hereunto set my Hand and Seal, this 15th day of *April,* &c.

Peter Peaceable. O.
The

*The Practice of Gardening in all its Branches
for the twelve Months in the Year.*

JANUARY.—*Pleasure-Garden.*

FROST is to be expected now, and nothing is so hurtful
to tender Flower-roots, and their Shoots for Spring.

Ranunculuses, Anemonies and Tulips will be in danger;
cover the Beds to guard them; lay on Pea-straw, where
they are not come up, but where the Shoot appears, place
Hoops with Mats and Cloth upon them. This is the common Practice; but in that excellent Work, The *Complete
Body of Gardening,* there is a Method proposed, much
easier and better. This is to place behind them a Reed-
hedge, sloping three Feet forward. A Mat is to be let
down from the Top in severe Weather, and taken up in
mild. This preserves them, and yet does not draw them
weak, or make them tender. Cover the Beds and Boxes
of Seedling Flowers, and take off the Defence when the
Weather is milder. Cover Carnation Plants from Wet, and
defend them from Mice and Sparrows.

Clean the Auricula Plants, pick off dead Leaves, and
scrape away the Surface of the Mould; put fresh Mould in
the place of it, and set the Pots up to the brim in the Mould
of a dry Bed, and place behind them a Reed-hedge.

For the Kitchen Garden. Throw up some new Dung in
a heap to heat, that it may be ready to make Hot-beds both
for the early Cucumbers and Melons in this part of the
ground, and for raising seeds of Annuals in the Flower
garden. Dig up the ground that is to be sown with the
Spring Crops, that it may lie and mellow.

Nurse the Cauliflower Plants kept under glasses, carefully: shut out the Frost, but in the middle of milder days
let in a little air; pick up the dead leaves, and gather up
the mould about the stalks.

Make a slight Hot-bed in the open ground, for young
Salading, and place hoops over it, that it may be covered
in hard weather. Plant out Endive for Seed into warm
borders; earth and blanch Celery. Sow a few Beans and
Peas, and seek and destroy Snails and other Vermin.

Fruit-Trees, whether in Orchards, or Espaliers, or against
Walls, demand the same general management.

Cut off dead Wood and irregula Branches; clean the
Stumps and Boughs from Moss with a hollow Iron, and
repair
aloof

repair Espaliers, fastening the Stakes and Poles with Nails, &c. and tie the Shoots down with the twigs of Osier.

Place Stakes by all new-planted Trees; and cut Grafts to be ready; lay them in the Earth under a warm Wall.

FEBRUARY.—*Pleasure-Garden.*

Make Hot-beds for annual flowers with the Dung laid up for that purpose, and sow them upon a good bed of Mould, laid regularly over the dung.

Transplant perennial Flowers and hardy Shrubs, Canterbury Bells, Lilacs, and the like. Break up and new lay the Gravel-walks. Weed, rake, and clean, the box borders.

Sow Auricula and Polyanthus seeds in boxes; these should be made of rough boards six inches deep, with holes at the bottom for carrying off of water; they must be filled with light mould, and the seeds scattered thinly over the surface, then some more mould must be sifted over them a quarter of an inch thick, and be set where they can have the morning Sun.

Plant out Carnations into pots for flowering.

Dig and level Beds for sowing Radishes and Onions, Carrots and Parsnips, and Dutch Lettuce: Leeks and Spinach should also be sown now, also Beets, Celery, Sorrel and Marygolds, with any other of the hardy kinds.

Make up the Hot-beds for early Cucumbers, and sow Cauliflower-seeds and some others.

Plant Beans and sow Peas; the best way is to sow a Crop every Fortnight, that if one succeeds and another fails, as will often be the case, there may still be a constant supply, at the due season, for table. Plant Kidney Beans upon a Hot-bed for an early crop. The Dwarf, White, and Battersea Bean, are the best sorts. They must have air in the middle of mild days when they are up, and once in two days they must be gently watered. Transplant Cabbages, plant out Silesia and Cos Lettuce from the beds where they grew in Winter, and plant Potatoes and Jerusalem Artichokes.

Most kinds of Trees may now be pruned, but it will be better to do it in Autumn; whatever has been omitted must be done now, the hardiest kinds being pruned first, and such as are more tender at the latter end of the month, when there will be less danger of their suffering from frost.

Transplant Fruit-trees to places where they are wanted, opening a large hole, settling the earth carefully about their
                                                             Roots,

Roots, and nailing them at once to the wall, or fastening them to strong stakes. Nail up the tender Trees with care. Sow the kernels of Apples and Pears, and stones of Plums for stocks, and keep off the birds.

MARCH.—*Pleasure-Garden.*

Watch the Beds of tender Flowers, and throw Mats over them supported by hoops in hard weather.

Transplant all the hardy perennial fibrous-rooted Flowers, Sweet-Williams, and Golden-rods. Dig up the Earth about those which were planted in Autumn, and clean the ground between.

All the pots of flowering plants must now be dressed. Pick off dead leaves, remove the Earth at the top, and put fresh in the place, give them a gentle watering, and set them in their places for flowering. Taking care the Roots are not wounded, repeat this once in three days.

The third week in *March* is the time to sow sweet Peas, Poppies, Catchflies, and all the hardy annual plants.

The last week is proper for transplanting Evergreens; but for this purpose a showery day should be chosen. New Hot-beds must be made to receive the Seedlings of annual flowers raised in the former.

Sow in the Beds of the Kitchen-garden some Carrots and also the large Peas, Rouncevals and Grey.

In better Ground sow Cabbages and Savoys, also Carrots and Parsnips for a second crop, and towards the end of the month put in a large parcel of Beans and Pease.

Sow Parsley and plant Mint; also Cos and Imperial Lettuce; and transplant the finer kinds.

In the first week sow *Dutch* Parsley for the roots.

In the last week if dry days, make Asparagus-beds.

Clear up the Artichoke-roots, slip off the weakest and plant them out for a new crop, leaving four from each good root to bear; and from such as are weaker, two. Dig up a warm border, and sow *French* Beans. Let them have a dry soil; and give them no water till they appear.

The grafts which were cut off early and laid in the ground to be ready for use, are now to be brought into service, those of the earlier kinds are to be used first, and the Apple last of all. Look to the Stocks inoculated last year, and take off their heads. A hand-breadth should be left on the place: This holds the bud secure by tying to it, and the sap rises more freely for its nourishment.

The

The Fruit-trees planted last *October* must be handed, and should be cut down to almost four Eves; the sap then rises more freely.

APRIL.—*Pleasure-Garden.*

Tie up the Stalks of all Flowers to sticks two feet long, thrusting eight inches into the ground, and let them be hid among the leaves, rake the ground between them,

Take off the slips of Auriculas, and plant them out carefully for an increase. Transplant perennial Flowers and Evergreens, and take up the roots of Colchicams, and other bulbous plants.

Sow *French* Honeysuckles, Wall-flowers, and other hardy plants, upon the natural ground; and the tenderer kinds on Hot-beds. Transplant those sown last month into the second Hot-bed. Plant some Tuberoses in a moderate Hot-bed, and sow Carnations and Pinks on the natural ground on open borders.

Plant a large crop of *French* Beans, choosing a dry warm border. Plant cuttings of Sage and other aromatic plants. Sow Marrowfat Peas and plant some Beans for a late crop; also Thyme, Sweet-marjoram, and Savory.

Prepare dung for making ridges to receive Cucumber or Melon-plants designed for bell or hand-glasses.

Sow young Salading once in ten days; also Cos and *Silesia* Lettuces.

The seeds of all kinds being in the ground, look to the growing crops, clear away the weeds among them, and dig up the earth between the rows of Beans, Peas, and all other kinds that are planted at distances. This will give them a strong growth, and bring them soon to perfection.

Draw up the mould to the stalks of the Cabbages and Cauliflower-plants; and in cold nights cover with glasses early Cucumbers and Melons.

Look to the Fruit-trees against the walls and espaliers. Take off all foreright shoots, and train such as rise kindly.

Thin Apricots, as there are usually more than can ripen, the sooner this is done the better the other succeed.

Water new-planted trees.

Plant cuttings of Vines, and look over the grown ones. Nip off improper shoots. When two rise from the same eye, always take off the weakest.

Weed Strawberry-beds; cut off the strings; stir the earth between them; and once in three days water them.

MAY.

MAY.—*Pleasure-Garden.*

When the leaves of sow-breads are decayed take up the roots, and lay them carefully by till the time of planting.

Take up the Hyacinth-roots which have done flowering, and lay them sideways in a bed of rich dry mould, leaving the stems and leaves out to die away; this practice greatly strengthens the roots. Clean all borders from weeds; take off all straggling branches from the large flowering plants, and trim them up in a handsome shape.

Plant out *French* and *African* Marygolds, with other Autumnals, from the Hot-beds the last week of this month, choosing a cloudy warm day.

Tie up the stalks of Carnations. Plant cuttings of the Lychinis, and Lychinideas, and sow the small annuals. Candytuft, and *Venus*' Looking-glass, in the open ground.

Pot the tender annuals, as Balsams, Amaranths, and the like, and set them in a Hot-bed frame till Summer is more advanced for planting them in the open ground.

Water once in two days those plants that require it. Destroy weeds in all parts of the ground, and dig up the earth between the rows, and about the large kinds.

Sow small Salading once in ten days, as in the former month : choosing a warm border, and sow some Purslain; also Endive, and plant Beans and Peas for a large crop, and *French* Beans to succeed the others. With care these kinds may be had fresh and young throughout the season.

On a moist day, an hour before Sun-set, plant some Savoys, Cabbages, and red Cabbages, draw the earth carefully up the stems, and give them a few careful waterings.

If any fresh shoots have sprouted up on the Fruit-trees, nip them off, and train the proper ones to the wall or poles, at due distances, and in a regular manner.

Look over Vines, and stop every shoot that has fruit upon it, to three eyes beyond the fruit. Train the branches regularly to the wall, and let such as are designed for next year's fruiting, grow some time longer, as their leaves will give a proper shade to the fruit.

Water new-planted trees, and keep the borders clean; and pick off snails and other vermin.

JUNE.—*Pleasure-Garden.*

In the evening of a mild showery day plant out into the open ground the tender annuals hitherto kept in pots in the

Hot-

Hot-bed frame; they must be carefully loosened from the sides of the pot, and shaken out with all the mould about them : a large hole must be opened for each ; they must be placed upright in it, and when settled by a gentle watering, tied to sticks.

Let Pinks, Carnations, and Sweet-Williams, be laid this month for an increase. Let the layers be covered lightly, and watered every day a little at a time.

The Spring Flowers being now over, and their leaves faded, the roots must be taken up and laid by for planting again at a proper season. Snow-drops, Winter-aconite, and the like, are to be thus managed.

The Hyacinth roots, laid flat in the ground, must now be laid up, the dead leaves nipped off, and the mould ; and, when clean, laid upon a mat in an airy room to harden, and then laid by. Tulip roots must now be taken up also as the leaves decay ; the like method must be followed with Ane-monies and Ranunculuses.

Cut the cups or pods of Carnations that are now blowing, in three or four places, that they may blow regularly.

Inoculate some of the fine kinds of Roses.

In the Kitchen Garden, transplant the Cauliflower plants sown in *May* ; give them a rich bed and frequent waterings.

Plant out Thyme and other savory plants sown before, and in the same manner shade and water them. Take the advantage of cloudy weather to sow turnips ; and if there be no showers, water the ground once in two days.

Sow Brocoli upon a rich border, and plant out Celery for blanching. This must be done in trenches a foot and a half deep, and the plants must be set half a foot asunder in the rows. Endive should also be planted out for blanching ; but in this the plants should be set fifteen inches asunder, and at the same time some Endive-seed must be sown for a second crop. Pick up snails ; and in the damp evening kill the naked slugs.

Fruit-Garden. Continue the taking off fore-right shoots upon Wall and Espalier-trees, directed as in last month. Train proper branches to their situation, where they are wanted ; once more thin the Wall-fruit ; leave Nectarines at four inches distance, and Peaches at five, but not nearer ; the fruit will be finer, and the tree stronger for next year. Inoculate the Apricots, and choose for this operation a cloudy evening. Water new planted trees, and pick off snails and vermin.

JULY.

JULY.—*Pleasure-Garden.*

Roll the gravel frequently, and mow grass.

Clip Box-edgings; cut and trim hedges; look over all the borders, clearing them from weeds; stirring up the mould between the plants.

Inoculate Roses and Jessamines of all kinds that require this propagation; and any other flowering shrubs.

Take up the roots of Frittallarias and Maragons, and others of this sort that are past flowering time.

Gather the seeds of flowers you design to propagate, and lay them upon a shelf in an airy room in the pods. When they are well hardened tie them up in paper bags, and do not take them out of the pods till they are to be used.

Lay Pinks and Sweet-Williams, as the former, in earth.

Cut down the stalks of those plants which have done flowering, and which you do not keep for seed; and tie up those now coming into flower to sticks, as directed for the earlier kinds.

Sow Lupines, Larkspurs, and the like, on dry warm borders, to stand the winter, and flower next year.

Sow a crop of *French Beans* to come in late, when they will be very acceptable. Clear all the ground from weeds.

Dig between the rows of Beans and Peas, mow the ground about the Artichokes.

Water the crops in dry weather.

Spinach seed will be now ready for gathering, as also that of the Welch Onion, and some others; take them carefully off, and dry them in the shade.

Take up large Onions, and spread them upon mats to dry for the Winter. Clear away the stalks of Beans and Peas that have done bearing.

Watch the Melons as they ripen, and give them but little water. Water Cucumbers more freely.

Inoculate Peaches and Nectarines. Take off all foreright shoots in the Espalier and Wall-fruit trees.

Hang phials of honey and water upon the fruit-trees, and look carefully for snails. Keep the borders where the fruit-trees stand clear from weeds, and stir the earth about them. This will greatly assist the fruit in ripening.

Look to the fruit-trees that have been grafted and budded the last season. See that there are no shoots from the stocks. Whenever they rise, take them off, for they will rob the intended growth of its nourishment.

Look

Look carefully to the new planted trees, water them often; and whatever shoots they properly make, fasten to the wall or espalier.

Repeat the care of the Vines, take off improper shoots, and nail any that are loose to the wall. Let no weeds rise in the ground about them, for they will exhaust the nourishment, and impoverish the fruit.

AUGUST.—*Pleasure-Garden.*

See whether the Layers of Sweet-Williams, Carnations, and the like, be rooted; transplant such as are, and give frequent gentle waterings to the others to promote it.

Dig up a mellow border, and draw lines at five inches distance, lengthwise and across; in the centre of these squares, plant the seedling Polyanthuses, one in each.

In the same manner plant out the seedling Auriculas. Shade them till they have taken root, and water them once in twenty-four hours.

Cut down the stalks of plants that have done flowering. Save the seeds as they ripen.

Water the tender annuals every evening.

Sow Anemonies and Ranunculuses, as also Fritillary, Tulip and Narcissus seed.

Dig up a border for early Tulip roots, and others for Hyacinths, Anemonies, and Ranunculuses. Sow annuals to stand the winter, and shift Auriculas into fresh pots.

Sow Spinach upon a rich border, and upon such another sow Onions. These crops will live through the winter, unless very severe, and be valuable in the Spring. The second week in August sow Cabbage-seed of the early kinds; and a week after sow Cauliflower-seed. Some of these may be also ventured in a very well defended open situation. The last week of this month sow another crop to supply the place of these in case of accidents; for if the season be severe they may be lost; and if very mild, they will run to seed in Spring. These last crops must be defended by a Hot-bed frame. Sow Lettuces, the Cabbage, and brown Dutch kinds, in a warm and well-sheltered piece of ground. Transplant Lettuces, sown earlier in warm and well-sheltered borders. Take up Garlic, and spread it on a mat to harden; also Onions and Rocombole; and, at the latter end of the month, Shalots.

Watch the fruit on your Wall-trees, and keep off vermin swarming about them. Pick up snails, and hang bottles of sweet

sweet water for flies and wasps. Fasten loose branches, and gather the fruit carefully as it ripens.

Go round the Vines, and pull off trailing branches so very luxuriantly produced at this time. See that the fruit is not shaded by loose branches; keep the borders clear of weeds. This tends greatly to the ripening of the fruit.

SEPTEMBER.—*Pleasure-Garden.*

A new kind of work begins this month, which is, preparing for the next season. Tear up the annuals that have done flowering; and cut down such Perennials as are past beauty; bring in other Perennials from the nursery beds, and plant them with care at regular distances.

Take up the Box-edgings where they have outgrown their proper size, and part and plant them afresh.

Plant Tulip and other flower roots.

Slip Polyanthuses, and place them in rich shady borders. Sow the seeds of Flower-de-luces and Crown Imperial, as also of Auriculas and Polyanthuses.

Also part off the roots of Flower-de-luce, Piony, and others of these kinds. In the last week transplant hardy flowering shrubs.

Sow Lettuces of various kinds, Silesia, Cos, and Dutch, and when they come up shelter them carefully.

Make up fresh warm beds with the dung that has laid a month in the heap. Plant the spawn in these beds upon pasture mould, the same they were found in, and raise the top of the bed to a ridge, to throw off wet.

Look to the Turnip-beds and thin them, leave the turnips at six inches distance.

Weed the Spinach, Onions, and other new-sown plants.

Transplant Sage, Lavender, and sweet plants. Earth up Celery as it grows in height.

Sow Salading upon warm and well-sheltered borders.

Clean Asparagus beds in this manner: cut down the stalks, and pare the earth off the surface of the alleys, throw this upon the beds half an inch thick, and sprinkle over it a little dung from an old Melon-bed.

Dig up the ground where Summer crops have ripened; and lay it in ridges for the Winter. These should be disposed East and West, and turned once in two months, they have thus the advantage of a fallow.

Plant some Beans and sow some Peas, on warm and well-sheltered borders, to stand out the Winter.

The

The fruit must now be gathered with care every day, and the best time is an hour after Sun-rise. Then it should be laid in a cool place till used.

Keep birds from the grapes, for as they now begin to ripen they will be in continual danger.

Transplant Gooseberries and Currants, and plant Strawberries and Rasberries; they will be rooted before Winter and flourish the succeeding season.

OCTOBER.—*Pleasure-Garden.*

Let all the bulbous roots for Spring flowering be put into the ground. Narcissus Maragon, Tulips, and such Ranunculuses and Anemonies, as were not planted sooner.

Transplant Columbines, Monks-hood, and all kinds of fibrous-rooted perennials. Place the Auriculas and Carnations, that are in pots, under shelter. The best way is by sloping reed-hedge. Dig up a dry border, and if not dry enough naturally, dig in some sand. In this set pots up to the brim. Place the reed-hedge sloping behind them, and fasten a mat to its top that may be let down in bad weather. Take off the dead leaves of the Auriculas before they are thus planted.

Plant out the Cauliflower plants where they are to be sheltered; and it will be proper to plant two for each glass, where that method is used, for fear of one failing.

Sow another crop of Peas, and plant Beans; choose a dry spot well sheltered from the cold wind of Winter.

Transplant the Lettuces sowed last month, where they can be defended by a reed-hedge, or under walls

Transplant Cabbage-plants and Coleworts where they are to remain.

Take great care of the Cauliflower-plants sown early in Summer; they now begin to show their heads, so break in the leaves upon them to keep off the Sun and rain; it will both harden and whiten them.

Prune the Peach and Nectarine trees, and the Vines. This is a very useful practice, for it strengthens the buds for Spring. Cut Grapes for preserving, with a joint of the vine to each bunch.

Gather fruits for Winter-keeping as they ripen. Transplant all Garden trees for flowering; prune Currant-bushes, and preserve seeds for sowing.

NOVEMBER.—*Pleasure-Garden.*

Throw together a good heap of Pasture Ground, with the turf among it, to rot for mould on the borders.

Transplant Honey-suckles and Spireas, with other hardy flowering shrubs.

Rake over the beds of seedling flowers, and strew some Pea-straw over them to keep out the frost.

Cut down the stems of Perennials which have done flow-ering; pull up annuals that are spent, and rake and clear the ground. Place hoops over the beds of Ranunculuses and Anemonies, and lay mats or cloths in readiness to draw over them, in case of hard rain or frost.

Clean up the borders in all parts of the Garden, and take care to destroy the weeds, and look over the seeds of those flowers which were gathered in Summer. See they keep dry and sweet, and in a condition of growth, and dig a bor-der or two for the hardier kinds. Weed the crops of Spi-nach, and such other kinds as were sown late, for the wild growth will else smother and starve the crop.

Dig up a border under a warm wall, and sow some Car-rots for Spring; sow Radishes in such another place, and see the ground be well and deep dug for both. Turn the mould that was trenched and laid up for fallowing.

Prepare Hot-beds for Salading; cover them five inches with mould, and sow upon them Lettuces, and common small Salading, Mustard, Rape, Cresses, and Radish. Plant another crop of Beans, and sow more Peas for a succession,

Trench the ground between the Artichokes, and throw a thick ridge of earth over the roots.

Take up Carrots and Parsnips, and lay them in sand to be ready for use. Give air at times to the plants under hand-glasses and in Hot-beds, or they will suffer as much by want of that, as they would have done by the frost.

Stake up all trees planted for standards, or the winds will rock them at the bottom, and the frost, if it set in, will destroy them.

Throw a good quantity of Pea-straw about them, and lay on it some brickbats or pebbles to keep it fast; this will mellow the ground, and keep out frost.

Prune the Wall-fruit trees, and at this time also the Apple and Pear kinds.

DECEMBER.—*Pleasure-Garden.*

Draw the mats and cloths over the Ranunculus and Ane-mone beds in severe weather, whether frost or cold rain; but give them air in the middle of every tolerable day, and as soon as possible uncover them all day, but draw on the mats against night.

Throw up the earth where flowering shrubs are to be planted in the Spring; and once in a fortnight turn it.

Dig up the borders that are to have flower-roots planted in them in the Spring, and give them the advantage of a fallow, by throwing up the ground in a ridge.

Scatter over it a very little rotten dung from a Melon-bed, and after this turn it twice during the Winter.

Look over the flowering shrubs and prime them. Cut away all the dead wood, shorten luxuriant branches, and if any cross each other, take away one. Leave them so that the air can have free passage between them.

Strew good fresh mould over the roots of Perennial flowers whose stalks have been cut down, and rake over the borders. This will give the whole an air of culture and management.

In the Kitchen-Garden.

Plant Cabbages and Savoys for seed. This is to be with great care; dig up a dry border, and break the mould well; then take up some of the stoutest Cabbage and Savoy plants, hang them up by the stalks five days, and then plant them half way of the stalk into the ground; draw up a good quantity of the mould about the part of the stalk that is out of the ground, and make it into a kind of hill round each, then leave them to Nature.

Sow another crop of Peas, and plant another parcel of Beans to take their chance for succeeding the others.

Make another Hot-bed for Asparagus, to yield a supply, when the former is exhausted. Continue to earth up Celery, and cover some Endive with a good quantity of Pea-straw, as it is growing, that you may take up when wanted, which otherwise the frost will prevent.

Prepare for planting trees where they will be wanted in Spring, by digging the ground deep, and turning it well in the places where they are to stand.

Scatter over the borders, where the Fruit-trees are planted, some fresh mould, and some old dung, and in a mild day dig it with a strong three-pronged fork.

Look over the Orchard-trees, and cut away superfluous and dead wood. Let the branches stand clear of one another that the air may get between, and the fruit will be better flavoured.

FS.

J. BAILEY, Printer, 116, Chancery-Lane, London.